Table of Contents

Table of Contents

GRADE 6

McGraw Hill

Math

Third Edition

New York Chicago San Francisco Athens London Madrid
Mexico City Milan New Delhi Singapore Sydney Toronto

1 2 3 4 5 6 7 8 9 LWI 27 26 25 24 22

ISBN 978-1-264-28567-9
MHID 1-264-28567-1

e-ISBN 978-1-264-28568-6
e-MHID 1-264-28568-X

McGraw Hill thanks Wendy Hanks for her invaluable contributions to this new edition.

Letter to Parents and Students

Welcome to McGraw Hill's Math!

Parents, this book will help your child succeed in sixth grade mathematics. It will give your sixth grader:

- **A head start** in the summer before sixth grade
- **Extra practice** during the school year
- **Helpful preparation** for standardized mathematics exams

The book is aligned to **National and State Standards**. A chart beginning on the next page summarizes those standards and shows how each state that does not follow the national standards differs from those standards. The chart also includes comparisons to Canadian standards.

If you live in a state that has adopted the national Common Core standards, you won't need the information in this table, although you may find its summary of standards helpful. Parents who live in Canada or states that have not adopted Common Core standards will find the table a useful tool and can be reassured that most of these regions have standards that are very similar to national standards. This book contains ample instruction and practice for students in **any state** or in **Canada**.

Students, this book will help you do well in mathematics. Its lessons explain math concepts and provide lots of interesting practice activities.

Open your book and look at the **Table of Contents**. It tells what topics are covered in each lesson. Work through the book at your own pace.

Begin with the **Pretest**, which will help you discover the math skills you need to work on.

Each group of lessons ends with a **Unit Test**. The results will show you what skills you have learned and what skills you may need to practice more. A **Posttest** completes your work in this book and will show how you have done overall.

Take time to practice your math. Practicing will help you use and improve your math skills.

Good luck!

Sixth Grade National and State Standards

Sixth Grade U.S. Common Core Standards	Texas*	Virginia	Indiana	South Carolina
Understand ratio concepts and use ratio reasoning to solve problems.				
Apply and extend previous understandings of multiplication and division to divide fractions by fractions.				
Compute fluently with multi-digit numbers and find common factors and multiples.			Also: prime vs. composite	
Apply and extend previous understandings of numbers to the system of rational numbers.	Also: convert between fraction, decimal, and percent	Also: convert between fraction, decimal, and percent	Also: know common equivalents of fraction, decimal, percent	Also: translate between fraction, decimal, percent
Apply and extend previous understandings of arithmetic to algebraic expressions.				
Reason about and solve one-variable equations and inequalities.				Also: graph inequalities
Represent and analyze quantitative relationships between dependent and independent variables.				
Solve real-world and mathematical problems involving area, surface area, and volume.	Also: measurement conversions; angles of triangles	Also: derive π; properties of circles; congruence. No volume or surface area standards.	Also: measurement conversions; angles of triangles and polygons	
Develop understanding of statistical variability.				
Summarize and describe distributions.		Also: circle graphs	Specifies using technology to organize data	

*Texas also has a section on personal financial literacy.

Minnesota	Oklahoma	Nebraska	Alaska	Canadian Provinces
Includes percents		Fewer standards about rate and ratios		
More work on factoring				ON and WNCP omit factoring out a common multiple to simplify. WNCP doesn't require use of standard algorithm.
	No standards for absolute value	Also: convert between fraction, decimal, and percent		All omit absolute value notation to describe distances from 0. None require measuring lengths on coordinate grid.
				All omit writing an inequality as a problem condition
Also: relationships between angles; choosing measurement system; estimating	Also: angles, congruence, symmetry, and measurement systems. No volume or surface area standards.	Includes basics of coordinate plane; omits volume of prisms with fractional edge lengths	Does not include volume of prisms with fractional edge lengths; also includes properties of circles	All omit finding volume of prisms with fractional edge lengths
Omitted		Fewer standards		
Focus is on probability		Only focuses on mean, median, mode, and range	Also: analyze fairness; solve combination problems	All omit dot plots. WNCP and QC also omit box plots. ON and WNCP omit calculation of mean absolute deviation and interquartile range

Pretest

Name ________________________________

Complete the following test items.

1. The Mayor of Tampa told Angela that there are three hundred thousand, six hundred, thirty five people living in their city. When she writes this number in standard form, Angela will write ____________

2. Yousef is collecting signatures to build a park in his town. He needs 8000 signatures to submit his petition. So far he has collected 2875. Rounding to the nearest thousand, how many signatures can we estimate Yousef still needs to collect? ____________

Calculate.

3. $\begin{array}{r} 48 \\ \times\ 19 \\ \hline \end{array}$

4. $\begin{array}{r} 15 \\ \times\ 55 \\ \hline \end{array}$

5. $\left|-\frac{5}{6}\right|$

6. $|0.02|$

7. Miguel bought 11 cheese pizzas for his math club at school, but the club members only ate half of each pizza. How would Miguel express the amount of remaining pizza as an improper fraction? How would Miguel express the amount of remaining pizza as a mixed number? ____________

Calculate.

8. $\begin{array}{r} \$33.25 \\ \$27.50 \\ +\ \$16.15 \\ \hline \end{array}$

9. $\begin{array}{r} \$99.45 \\ -\ \$22.47 \\ \hline \end{array}$

10. What is the least common multiple of 6 and 9?

11. What is the greatest common factor of 6 and 18?

12. George has been measuring the amount of rainfall for the last three months. He measured 3.562 inches in April, 2.765 inches in May, and 3.015 inches in June. Rounding to the nearest tenth of an inch, what was the total amount of rainfall during these three months? ____________

Calculate.

13. $78\overline{)1951}$

14. $34\overline{)625}$

15. $16\overline{)77}$

16. $11\overline{)145}$

17. Kaleigh is mixing green paint for art class. The directions call for her to mix 17.25 milliliters of blue paint and 13.45 milliliters of yellow paint to achieve the right amount of green paint for her assignment. How much blue paint and how much yellow paint will she need in order to mix the right amount of green paint for herself and two other classmates? ____________

    About how much green paint will she be making, altogether, for the three of them? ____________

18 What is 60% of 120? ____________

19 What is 40% of $\frac{3}{4}$? Express the number in both decimal and fraction form.

____

20 Terrence has a length of rope that is $14\frac{3}{4}$ meters long. Forty percent of the rope's length is covered by a plastic film that makes it waterproof. What length of the rope is not waterproof? Express your answer as a mixed fraction. ____________

21 If $x + 4 \geq 12$, could the value of x be 10? ________ Could x be 8? ________

22 Maynard bought a scale that records weight digitally. His math book weighs 2 kilograms, his science workbook weighs $\frac{3}{4}$ of a kilogram, his social studies book weighs $1\frac{1}{3}$ kilograms, and his language arts book weighs $3\frac{1}{2}$ kilograms. What is the total weight of the four books, in kilograms? ____________

If a student is only allowed to carry 12.25 kilograms of books, will Maynard's four books exceed the limit? ____________

What if Maynard removes the science workbook and adds a 3.75-kilogram dictionary? ____________

Average Monthly Temperature

Temperature (°F)

80
60
40
20
0

Dayton, Ohio
Sydney, Australia

Jun Jul Aug Sep

Month

23 The chart shows how much time Nick and Laura spent last week listening to their favorite music. On which day did Laura listen to 90 minutes of music?

____

On which day did Nick listen to music 85 minutes longer than Laura?

____

24 Which city is colder in June?

During which month is the difference in temperature the greatest?

____

25 Travis is looking at a solid figure that has a circular base, with curved sides that meet at a single point. What shape is he looking at?

____

Pretest

Name ____________________

26 Fiona puts three small oranges, two apples, five pears, and ten carrots into a basket. What is the probability that if she reaches into the basket that she will pick a fruit? ____________________

27 Which of the following triangles is

obtuse? ____________

right? ____________

acute? ____________

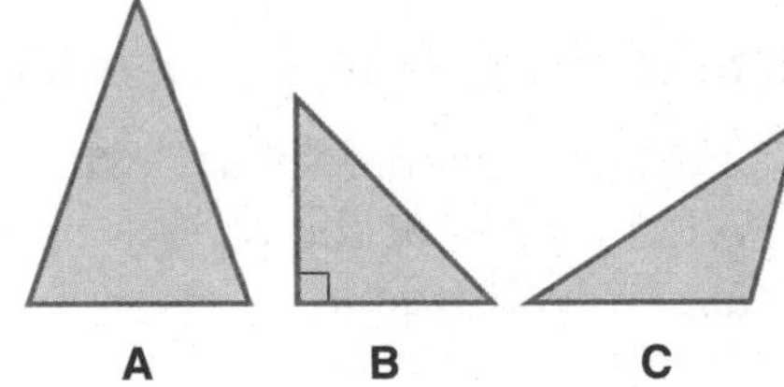

28 Calculate the following expression: $5 + (7 - 4)^2 + 4(3 + 2) - 6(2) =$ ____________

29 Write the following number using scientific notation: 1,678,483.0043.

____

30 Leslie collects teacups and saucers. Her collection consists of 3 teacups and 2 saucers from England, 2 teacups and 4 saucers from France, and 3 teacups from Japan. If each teacup costs \$9 and each saucer costs \$7, how much did Leslie spend for her collection? ____________

31 Which of the following angles is

acute? ____________

right? ____________

obtuse? ____________

123° C 90° D 55° E

32 $32 \div 0.25 =$ ____________

33 $0.2505 \div 0.05 =$ ____________

34 What is $\frac{24}{35} \div 6$?

____

35 What is $16 \div \frac{8}{17}$?

____

36 What is $\frac{32}{57} \div \frac{16}{19}$?

____

37 Harry is distributing rations for the class hike to the nature conservancy. Each student will carry $\frac{3}{4}$ liters of water and $\frac{1}{3}$ pound of trail mix for consumption during the trip. If there are 24 students on the trip, how much water and trail mix should Harry bring to distribute?

____

Name ______________________________

Pretest

38 Last week Jonas spent $9\frac{1}{6}$ hours working on his homework over a period of $4\frac{2}{3}$ days. Approximately how many hours a day, on average, did Jonas spend on his homework? ______________________

39 What is the decimal form of $7\frac{7}{8}$?

____

40 What is the fraction form of 1.2?

____

41 Freda is making a batch of multi-grain bread for the school picnic. Each loaf requires $1\frac{1}{2}$ cups of flour and $\frac{3}{4}$ cups of water. Create a ratio table to show the amounts Freda will need to make 2, 3, or 4 loaves of bread.

42 What is $\frac{1}{3}$ of 60%? ______________

43 What is 40% of $\frac{3}{4}$

in decimal form? ______________

in fraction form? ______________

44 What are the perimeter and area of the figure?

Perimeter ______________

Area ______________

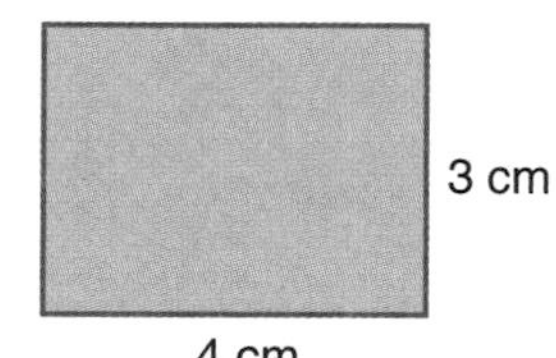

45 One inch is equivalent to 2.54 centimeters.

How many inches is 2.54 meters?

How many centimeters are in 100 inches?

__________ inches = 2.54 meters

100 inches = __________ centimeters

46 What figure is formed by connecting vertices at points A: (2, 5), B: (2, 2), C: (5, 2), and D: (5, 5)? ______________

What is the distance between points A and B? ______________________

47 What are the volume and surface area of the figure?

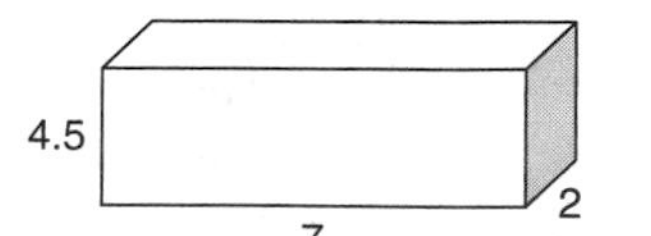

Volume ______________

Surface area ______________

48 Write an inequality to show that a number is greater than or equal to 10. ______________

Answers to the Pretest are on page 8

Pretest

Name ______________________

Answers and Explanations for Pretest

1. 300,635 is the standard form.

2. 5000 Round the number he has collected to the nearest thousand: 2875 rounds up to 3000 since the number after the rounding place is an 8. Now subtract 3000 from the 8000 needed to get 5000 remaining.

3. 912

$$\begin{array}{r} {}^{7}48 \\ \times 19 \\ \hline {}^{1}432 \\ 480 \\ \hline 912 \end{array}$$

4. 825

$$\begin{array}{r} {}^{2}15 \\ \times 55 \\ \hline 75 \\ {}^{1}750 \\ \hline 825 \end{array}$$

5. $\frac{5}{6}$

6. 0.02

7. $\frac{11}{2}; 5\frac{1}{2}$ Since they ate $\frac{1}{2}$ of the 11 pizzas, we can divide 11 by 2 to get the fraction $\frac{11}{2}$. As a mixed number, this is $5\frac{1}{2}$.

8. $76.90

$$\begin{array}{r} \$33.22 \\ \$27.50 \\ +\$16.15 \\ \hline \$76.90 \end{array}$$

9. $76.98

$$\begin{array}{r} \$99.45 \\ -\$22.47 \\ \hline \$76.98 \end{array}$$

10. 18 The multiples of 6 are {6, 12, 18, 24 …} and the multiples of 9 are {9, 18, 27 …}. The smallest multiple they have in common is 18.

11. 6 The factors of 6 are {1, 2, 3, 6} and the factors of 18 are {1, 2, 3, 6, 9, 18}. The largest number they have in common is 6.

12. 9.3 in.

$$\begin{array}{r} 3.562 \\ 2.765 \\ +\ 3.015 \\ \hline 9.342 \end{array}$$

9.342 rounded to the nearest tenth is 9.3.

13. 25 R1

$$\begin{array}{r} 25 \\ 78\overline{)1951} \\ 156\downarrow \\ \hline 391 \\ 390 \\ \hline 1 \end{array}$$

14. 18 R13

$$\begin{array}{r} 18 \\ 34\overline{)625} \\ 34\downarrow \\ \hline 285 \\ 272 \\ \hline 13 \end{array}$$

15. 4 R13

$$\begin{array}{r} 4 \\ 16\overline{)77} \\ 64 \\ \hline 13 \end{array}$$

16. 13 R2

$$\begin{array}{r} 13 \\ 11\overline{)145} \\ 11\downarrow \\ \hline 35 \\ 33 \\ \hline 2 \end{array}$$

17. 51.75 mL of blue, 40.35 mL of yellow, and about 90 mL total

$$\begin{array}{r} {}^{2}17.{}^{1}25 \\ \times\quad 3 \\ \hline 51.75 \end{array} \qquad \begin{array}{r} {}^{1}13.45 \\ \times\quad 3 \\ \hline 40.35 \end{array}$$

blue yellow

Approximately 50 + 40 = 90 mL total

18. 72

$$\frac{60}{100} \times 120 = \frac{6}{10} \times 120 = \frac{3}{5} \times 120$$

$$= \frac{360}{5} = 72$$

19. 0.3 and $\frac{3}{10}$

$$\frac{40}{100} \times \frac{3}{4} = \frac{120}{400} = \frac{12}{40} = \frac{3}{10}$$

and $\frac{3}{10} = 0.3$

20. $8\frac{17}{20}$

This one may be easier as a decimal. If 40% is waterproof, then 60% is NOT waterproof.

$$\begin{array}{r} 14.75 \\ \times\ 0.60 \\ \hline 8.8500 \end{array}$$

4 decimal places

80

= 8.85

$$= 8\frac{85}{100} = 8\frac{17}{20}$$

21. Yes; yes

$$\begin{array}{r} x + 4 \geq 12 \\ -4 \quad -4 \\ \hline x \geq 8 \end{array}$$

22. 7.58 kg; no; no

$$\begin{array}{r} 2.00 \\ 0.75 \\ 1.33 \\ +3.50 \\ \hline 7.58 \end{array}$$

$$\begin{array}{rr} \text{dictionary} = & 3.75 \\ \text{Science} = & -0.75 \\ \hline & 3.00 \end{array}$$

New total: 10.58

23. Tuesday, Thursday

24. Sydney, August

25. Cone

26. $\frac{1}{2}$

There are 20 items in the basket and 10 of them are fruits, so the probability of picking a fruit is $\frac{10}{20} = \frac{1}{2}$.

27. C, B, A

Name ____

Pretest

28. 22 Use PEMDAS.

$5+(3)^2+4(5)-6(2)$
$5+9+20-12=22$

29. 1.6784830043 × 10^6 since the decimal is moved to the left 6 places.

30. $114 She has 8 teacups and 6 saucers, so $8 \times \$9 = \$72$ for the teacups and $6 \times \$7 = \$42$ for the saucers. 72 + 42 = 114.

31. E is acute; D is a right angle; C is obtuse

32. 128

$0.25\overline{)32.00}$ so

$$\begin{array}{r} 128 \\ 25\overline{)3200} \\ \underline{25} \\ 70 \\ \underline{50} \\ 200 \end{array}$$

33. 5.01

$0.05\overline{)0.2505}$

so $$\begin{array}{r} 5.01 \\ 5\overline{)25.05} \\ \underline{25} \\ 05 \end{array}$$

34. $\frac{4}{35}$

$\frac{24}{35} \div \frac{6}{1} = \frac{\cancel{24}^{4}}{35} \times \frac{1}{\cancel{6}_1} = \frac{4}{35}$

35. 34

$\frac{16}{1} \div \frac{8}{17} = \frac{\cancel{16}^{2}}{1} \times \frac{17}{\cancel{8}_1} = \frac{34}{1} = 34$

36. $\frac{2}{3}$

$\frac{32}{57} \div \frac{16}{19} = \frac{\cancel{32}^{2}}{\cancel{57}_{3}} \times \frac{\cancel{19}^{1}}{\cancel{16}_{1}} = \frac{2}{3}$

37. 18 L of water, 8 lb trail mix

$24 \times ¾ = 18$, $24 \times 1/3 = 8$

38. About 2 hours. Since the question says "approximately," we can estimate the average number of hours. $10 \div 5 = 2$.

$9\frac{1}{6} = \frac{55}{6}$ hours

$4\frac{2}{3} = \frac{14}{3}$ days

$\frac{55}{6} \div \frac{14}{3} = \frac{55}{\cancel{6}_2} \times \frac{\cancel{3}^1}{14} = \frac{55}{28} = 1\frac{27}{28}$

39. 7.875

$7\frac{7}{8} = \frac{63}{8}$

$$\begin{array}{r} 7.875 \\ 8\overline{)63} \\ \underline{56} \\ 70 \\ \underline{64} \\ 60 \\ \underline{56} \\ 40 \end{array}$$

40. $\frac{6}{5}$ or $1\frac{1}{5}$

$1.2 = 1\frac{2}{10} = \frac{12}{10} = \frac{6}{5}$ or $1\frac{1}{5}$

41.

# Loaves	Flour	Water
1	$1\frac{1}{2}$	$\frac{3}{4}$
2	3	$1\frac{1}{2}$
3	$4\frac{1}{2}$	$2\frac{1}{4}$
4	6	3

To increase from 1 loaf, multiply the amounts of flour and water in 1 loaf by the number of loaves.

42. $\frac{1}{5}$

$\frac{1}{\cancel{3}_1} \times \frac{\cancel{60}^{20}}{100} = \frac{20}{100} = \frac{1}{5}$

43. 0.3; $\frac{3}{10}$

$\frac{\cancel{40}^{10}}{100} \times \frac{3}{\cancel{4}_1} = \frac{30}{100} = \frac{3}{10} = 0.3$

44. 14 cm; 12 cm^2

P = 3 + 3 + 4 + 4 = 14

$A = 3 \times 4 = 12.$

45. 100 in.; 254 cm because 1 meter is 100 centimeters.

46. Square; 3

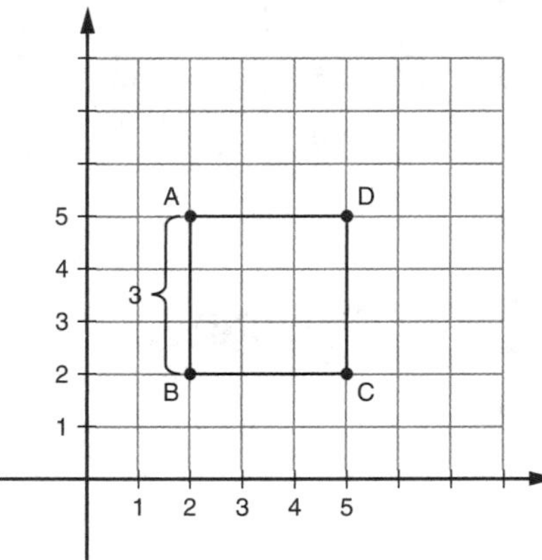

47. 63; 109

$V = 4.5 \times 7 \times 2 = 63.$

$SA = 2(4.5 \times 7) + 2(4.5 \times 2) + 2(7 \times 2)$
$= 2(31.5) + 2(9) + 2(14)$
$= 63 + 18 + 28 = 109$

48. $x \geq 10$

1.1

Name ______________________

Place Value

Place value tells you what each digit in a number means. The value of the digit depends on the place it occupies.

Example: In the number 238, the 2 is in the hundreds place, the 3 is in the tens place and the 8 is in the ones place. So 238 means 2 hundreds + 3 tens + 8 ones.

USE A PLACE-VALUE CHART This place-value chart shows the places occupied by all the digits in the number 574,232,951.

Millions Period			Thousands Period			Ones Period		
Hundreds	Tens	Ones	Hundreds	Tens	Ones	Hundreds	Tens	Ones
5	7	4,	2	3	2,	9	5	1

In this number, the digit 5 is in the hundred millions place, the digit 7 is in the ten millions place, and so on.

NUMBER FORMS You can write a number in three different forms:

- **Standard form:** 4,368,129
- **Expanded form:** $(4 \times 1{,}000{,}000) + (3 \times 100{,}000) + (6 \times 10{,}000) + (8 \times 1000) + (1 \times 100) + (2 \times 10) + (9 \times 1)$
- **Word form:** four million, three hundred sixty-eight thousand, one hundred twenty-nine

Exercises **SOLVE**

1. In 57,761, the underlined digit is in which place? ______________________

2. The number 6 is in which place in 467,901,324? ______________________

3. In 8,730,562, which digit is in the hundreds place? ______________________

4. The standard form of the number 458,905 has the number 9 in which place? __________

5. Standard Form: 303,201

   Expanded Form: ______________________

   ____

   ____

   ____

Name ____________________

6 Standard Form: ____________________

Expanded Form: $(7 \times 100{,}000) + (3 \times 10{,}000) + (2 \times 1000) + (9 \times 100) + (9 \times 10) + (8 \times 1)$

____

____

7 Standard Form: ____________________

Expanded Form: ____________________

____

Word Form: Twelve million, four hundred fifty-four thousand, seven hundred twenty-one

8 Nadine was watching her mom fill out a check to pay the electric bill. On the check she is required to write the amount of the check in standard form and in word form. Nadine's mother wrote a check for $1396. What is that in word form? ____________________

____

1.2

Name ____________________

Rounding

To estimate, we round a number to a certain place value. **Rounding** tells you *approximately* what the number is. To round, look at the place value that you want to round to in the number. That's called the rounding place. Then look at the second highest place value. If that is less than 5, keep the original digit in the rounding place. If the second highest place value is 5 or more, add 1 to the digit in the rounding place. When you have decided what digit should go in the rounding place, substitute 0 for *all* the other digits after the rounding place in the original number.

Example: What is 13,637 to the nearest hundred?

rounding place → 6; 2nd highest place value → 3

13,637
=13,600

Remember...

When you estimate, your answer will not be exact. But it will probably be much better than a guess.

Exercises

Round to the nearest hundred.

1. 71,235
2. 25,854
3. 68,396

Round to the nearest ten.

4. 71,235
5. 25,854
6. 68,396

Round to the nearest thousand.

7. 71,235
8. 25,854
9. 68,396

10. If the distance from the Earth to the moon is rounded to the ten thousands place as 240,000 miles, which of the following could be the actual distance?

A. 234,761 miles

B. 238,855 miles

C. 246,017 miles

Name ______________________________

1.3

Adding and Subtracting Whole Numbers

A **whole number** is a number that does not include any fractions or decimals. To add or subtract whole numbers, follow the steps shown below.

ADDING To add a group of whole numbers, line them up by place value. Add each place value separately, starting on the right. If the numbers in a column add up to a 2-digit number, "**carry**" the first digit over to the next column on the left. Look at the following example.

Example:

```
     21 ← The small numbers in
    254   the top row represent
     70   numbers that are carried.
 + 1389
 ------
   1713
```

Remember...

When you are adding, don't worry about how many numbers you start with—or how large they are. Line up the numbers by place value. Then work on one place-value column at a time. Use "carrying" whenever a column adds up to a number greater than 9.

SUBTRACTING To subtract one whole number from another, line the numbers up by place value. Subtract each number separately beginning from the right. In the example below, how do you subtract 9 ones from 8 ones? The answer is by "**regrouping**." You reach into the tens column of 458 and take 1 ten. You regroup that 1 ten with the 8 in the ones column to make 18. Then subtract 9. But remember that there are now only 4 tens in the tens column of 458, not 5. Now subtract the number in the tens column. Finally, subtract the number in the hundreds column. In this example, the answer is 209.

Example:

```
  418 ← The small numbers in
  458   the top row represent
- 249   "regrouping."
-----
  209
```

Exercises ADD

1.
```
    389
 28,456
     21
 +    2
 ------
```

2.
```
    10
    11
    12
    13
    15
 + 111
 -----
```

Exercises SUBTRACT

3.
```
  5888
 - 790
 -----
```

4.
```
  12,112
  - 9325
  ------
```

5.
```
  1001
 - 988
 -----
```

Name ____________________

6 Mei likes to jog 3 times per week. This week she jogged for 62 minutes on Tuesday. On Thursday she only jogged half of that time. On Friday, she jogged for 87 minutes. How many total minutes did she jog this week? ____________________

____

7 Cameron has a collection of 73 toy dinosaurs. His aunt gave him a set of 25 more for his birthday, so he gave his little sister 6 from his original collection. How many dinosaurs did Cameron have after that?

____

8 Miguel makes 100 sandwiches for the sixth grade school picnic. One class eats 34 sandwiches. The other two classes each eat 31 sandwiches. How many sandwiches are left over?

____

To **estimate sums and differences**, round each number to the highest place value. Then look at the second highest place value to see if you need to round up. For example, in the number 482, 4 hundreds is the highest place value, so we look at the 8 to see that we need to round the 4 up to a 5 to get 500. Do this for each number you want to add or subtract. Then add or subtract the rounded numbers as indicated.

rounding place → 5 ; second highest place value → 4

Example:

$$\begin{array}{r} 5481 \\ +\ 2733 \\ \hline \end{array} \qquad \begin{array}{r} 5000 \\ +\ 3000 \\ \hline 8000 \end{array}$$

Exercises SOLVE

1 1333 + 56,750

2 21,111 – 14,750

3 1110 + 250

4 Candidate A received 28,459 votes and Candidate B received 42,671 votes. Approximately how many more votes did Candidate B receive? ____________________

____

5 There are 317 fifth graders and 384 sixth graders at Furse Middle School. About how many total students are there? ____________________

____

Name ______________________________

Multiplying Whole Numbers

When you multiply whole numbers, start by lining up the numbers correctly. It is easy to line the numbers up if you're multiplying by a 1-digit number.

Example: Line up 593 × 7 this way

$$\begin{array}{r} {}^{6\,2} \\ 593 \\ \times\ \ 7 \\ \hline 4151 \end{array}$$

Multiply the 3 in the first line by the 7 in the second line. 3 × 7 = 21. You cannot write 21 in the ones place, so you do just what you did when adding. You write the 1 and save the 2 for the tens place. Keep that 2 in mind. Go back to the first line, and move one digit *to the left* to multiply 9 × 7 = 63. Then you are ready to add that 2. You get 63 + 2 = 65. Write the 5 and set the 6 aside. Now go back to the first line again, and move one more digit to the left. Multiply 5 × 7 = 35. But remember the 6 you set aside. So 35 + 6 = 41. The **product**, or answer to this multiplication problem, is 4151.

When you are multiplying a number by a 2-digit or 3-digit number, you have to be careful to line up the place values correctly.

Remember...

Always multiply the entire top number by just one bottom digit at a time. Use a different line for the product of each bottom digit.

Exercises MULTIPLY

1. $\begin{array}{r} 854 \\ \times\ 23 \\ \hline \end{array}$

2. $\begin{array}{r} 987 \\ \times\ 638 \\ \hline \end{array}$

3. $\begin{array}{r} 286 \\ \times\ 354 \\ \hline \end{array}$

4. $\begin{array}{r} 7895 \\ \times\ \ 26 \\ \hline \end{array}$

5. $\begin{array}{r} 12 \\ \times\ 677 \\ \hline \end{array}$

6. $\begin{array}{r} 65 \\ \times\ 781 \\ \hline \end{array}$

7. A grocery store received an order for 50 bags of apples. 15 apples can fit into each bag. How many apples will the grocery store need to fill the bags?

____

8. Kerry is organizing his baseball cards into large envelopes. He can place 100 cards in each envelope. Kerry can fill 16 envelopes. How many baseball cards are in his collection?

____

Name ______________________________

9. A school bus holds 72 children. If a school has 43 buses, how many children do they hold all together?

____

10. Alina, Li, and Caleb each have 7 dozen trading cards. How many cards do they have all together?

____

11. At the start of a bake sale, there were 14 cakes cut into 24 slices each. At the end of the sale, only 3 slices were left. How many slices were sold?

____

12. Martin works 5 hours per day, 5 days a week. He makes $6 per hour. How much has he earned at the end of a year (52 weeks)?

____

13. If Lorenzo does 16 math problems every day for a year (365 days), how many math problems has he done?

____

14. A new theater has 560 seats. If every seat is sold every night for a week, what is the total number of tickets the theater sold that week?

____

15. One crate at a warehouse holds 120 boxes. The workers pack 342 of the crates. How many total boxes are packed?

____

Estimating Products

To estimate products, begin by rounding. Then multiply the two rounded numbers.

> **Example:** Estimate 73 × 49
>
> **Step 1:** Round 73 *downward* to 70 and round 49 *upward* to 50.
>
> **Step 2:** Multiply 70 × 50

When multiplying two numbers that both end in zero, start by ignoring the final zeros. To multiply 70 × 50, just multiply 7 × 5 = 35.

After you have done that, restore all the zeros that you ignored to the right side of the product. 70 × 50 = 35**00**.

Remember...

When you round both numbers *downward*, you know your estimate is *less* than the actual product. If you round both numbers *upward*, your estimate will be *more* than the actual product.

Name ______________________

Exercises **ESTIMATE**

1. 545 × 737
2. 234 × 901
3. 454 × 3111
4. 792 × 44
5. Will the estimated answer from question 4 be larger or smaller than the actual number?

____

6. 55 × 57

____

7. Will the estimated answer from question 6 be larger or smaller than the actual number?

____

8. 457 × 949

____

9. 1111 × 5555

____

10. What is the actual product for question 9?

____

11. If Ms. Azah's homeroom class wants to purchase a computer for each of the 28 students and each computer costs $389, approximately what will be the total cost?

____

12. Will the estimated total for question 11 be larger or smaller than the actual amount?

____

1.5

Name ______________________________

Dividing Whole Numbers

When you divide, you have to know which number is the **dividend** and which number is the **divisor**. The **dividend** is the number to be divided. The **divisor** is the number that goes into the dividend. The answer, called the **quotient**, is the number of times the divisor can go into the dividend. If there is something left over when you are finished, you call that the **remainder**.

Example: Set up 653 ÷ 3 this way.

$$\begin{array}{rl} \text{quotient} \longrightarrow & 217 \text{ R2} \longleftarrow \text{remainder} \\ \text{divisor} \longrightarrow 3\overline{)653} & \longleftarrow \text{dividend} \\ & \underline{6} \\ & 5 \\ & \underline{3} \\ & 23 \\ & \underline{21} \\ & 2 \end{array}$$

Begin by looking at the *highest* place value in the dividend, the digit on the *left* side. Can that number be divided by the divisor? In this case, the answer is yes. 6 ÷ 3 = 2. Put the 2 above the line as the beginning of the quotient. Since 2 × 3 = 6, place this 6 under the 6 in dividend.

Next, subtract: 6 − 6 = 0. Now carry down from the dividend the digit in the next place value, 5. Can 5 be evenly divided by 3? This time the answer is no, but there is one 3 in 5. So write 1 in the quotient, and subtract again. Keep repeating these steps until you get to the last digit in the dividend. How many times can 23 be divided by 3? 23 ÷ 3 = 7, with 2 left over. The 2 is the remainder.

Remember...

When dividing, always begin on the *left* side of the dividend.

Exercises DIVIDE

1. $89\overline{)627}$
2. $14\overline{)341}$
3. $15\overline{)346}$
4. $36\overline{)2814}$
5. $12\overline{)182}$
6. $9\overline{)84}$
7. $96\overline{)7499}$
8. $18\overline{)22220}$
9. $38\overline{)17330}$
10. $55\overline{)23270}$
11. $5\overline{)3647}$
12. $82\overline{)1399}$

Name ______________________________

13 $45\overline{)6621}$

14 Post office workers are placing envelopes in boxes. Each worker can place 625 envelopes per day. How many days will it take one worker to place 2500 envelopes?

____

15 Mr. Romanski is making information packets for all his new students. Each packet is 19 pages long. If he uses 342 sheets of paper, how many new students are in his class?

____

Estimating Quotients

When you estimate the quotient of a division problem, you *do not* round the numbers. Instead, you try to find **compatible numbers**. These are numbers that you can work with easily in your head.

Example: Estimate 5831 ÷ 8

Step 1: Look at the first two digits in the dividend, 58. Can you divide that evenly by the divisor, 8? No.

Step 2: Think about multiplying by 8.
$8 \times 6 = 48$ $8 \times 7 = 56$ $8 \times 8 = 64$
Select the one that is closest to 58.
That is 56.

Step 3: Add zeros to the dividend as placeholders. In this example, the dividend has four place values, so you need to add 2 zeros. 56**00**

Step 4: Divide by 8.
$5600 \div 8 = 700$

Exercises ESTIMATE

1 146 ÷ 12

2 244 ÷ 8

3 91 ÷ 9

4 399 ÷ 13

5 412 ÷ 25

6 1321 ÷ 13

7 447 ÷ 9

8 672 ÷ 33

Name ______________________________

9. $441 \div 91$

10. $252 \div 23$

11. $49 \div 4$

12. $3211 \div 80$

13. $1247 \div 50$

14. If a pair of jeans costs $32 including tax and you have $300, about how many pairs of jeans can you buy?

____

15. Sandy has calculated that she needs 352 tiles to replace her kitchen flooring. The tiles are sold in boxes of 12. Approximately how many boxes of tiles will she need?

____

Name ______________________________

2.1

Commutative and Associative Properties

Numbers behave in specific ways. Each kind of number behavior is called a **property**.

The Commutative Property of Addition: Addends may be added in any order without changing the sum. An **addend** is any number in an addition problem. It does not matter the order in which you add those numbers. The sum will always be the same.

The Commutative Property of Multiplication: Numbers may be multiplied in any order without changing the product.

The Associative Property of Addition: Addends may be grouped in any way without changing the sum.

The Associative Property of Multiplication: Numbers may be grouped in any way without changing the product.

Examples:

Find the answers to the following problems and tell which property they represent.

$26 + 41 + 10 = ?$ $10 + 26 + 41 = ?$

(Answers are 77 and 77, examples of the commutative property.)

$25 \times 2 \times 3 = ?$ $3 \times 25 \times 2 = ?$

(Answers are 150 and 150, examples of the commutative property.)

$(13 + 17) + 10 = ?$ $13 + (17 + 10) = ?$

(Answers are 40 and 40, examples of the associative property.)

$(5 \times 6) \times 3 = ?$ $5 \times (6 \times 3) = ?$

(Answers are 90 and 90, examples of the associative property.)

Exercises

Use the commutative property to rewrite each of the following.

1. $3 \times 4 \times 2 = 24$

 ____

2. $12 + 16 = 28$

 ____

3. $84 \times 63 = 5{,}292$

 ____

4. $17 + 19 + 5 = 41$

 ____

5. $(4 \times 2) + (2 \times 3) = 14$

 ____

Use the associative property to rewrite each of the following.

6. $(2 + 3) + 4 = 9$

 ____

7. $7 \times (2 \times 1) = 14$

 ____

8. $(3 \times 4) \times 6 = 72$

 ____

9. The desks in a classroom are arranged in 3 rows of 6 desks each. They could also be arranged in 6 rows of _____ desks each.

 ____

Name ____________________

10 Which is the same as 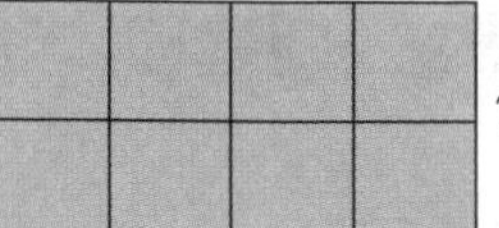 ?

A. 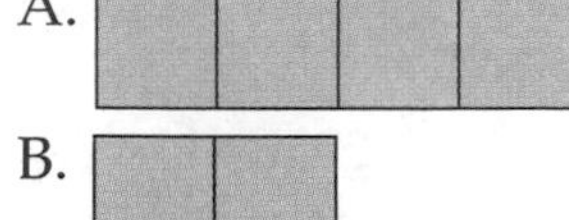

B.

C.

Fill in the missing number.

11 $42 + 16 + 5 = 16 + 5 + \_\_\_\_$

12 $(36 + 12) + 10 = \_\_\_\_ + (12 + 10)$

13 $4 \times (1 \times 5) \times 8 = (4 \times 1) \times (5 \times \_\_\_\_)$

14 $7 \times 5 \times 10 \times 10 = 5 \times 10 \times \_\_\_\_ \times 10$

15 $(3 \times 6) + (8 \times 9) = (8 \times 9) + (6 \times \_\_\_\_)$

Name ______________________________

Distributive Property and Identity

The Distributive Property of Multiplication: When you multiply numbers, you may multiply by each separately, and then add their products.

Example:

$7 \times (3 + 1) = (7 \times 3) + (7 \times 1)$

$28 = 21 + 7$

Multiplication and division are closely related. When you learned how to divide fractions, you were shown that division is the same thing as multiplication by a reciprocal. You can use the Distributive Property of Multiplication when you are dividing. But you may use the Distributive Property only when the addends are in the dividend.

Identity elements are numbers in a problem that do not affect the answer.

When adding, the identity element is 0. Any addend or addend + 0 will not change the total. In multiplication, the identity element is 1. Any factor or factors × 1 will not change the product. Subtraction and division do *not* have identity elements.

Remember...

You cannot use the Distributive Property when addends are in the divisor.

$90 \div (2 + 3)$ *does not* $= (90 \div 2) + (90 \div 3)$ *because . . .*

$(90 \times \frac{1}{5})$ *does not* $= (90 \times \frac{1}{2}) + (90 \times \frac{1}{3})$

18 *does not* $= 45 + 30$

Exercises

Fill in the missing number.

1. $6(4+5) = 24 + \_\_\_\_$

2. $3(8 \times 6) = \_\_\_\_ \times 18$

3. $12 + 14 = 2(\_\_\_\_ + \_\_\_\_)$

4. $9 + 15 = 3(\_\_\_\_ + \_\_\_\_)$

5. $15 + 25 = 5(\_\_\_\_ + \_\_\_\_)$

6. $18 + 9 = 9(\_\_\_\_ + \_\_\_\_)$

7. $3(9+4) = \_\_\_\_ + \_\_\_\_$

8. $6(2+1) = \_\_\_\_ + \_\_\_\_$

9. The 12 boys and 13 girls in Mr. Ali's class each have 6 pencils. Which shows a way to express this?

   A. 12 + 13 + 6

   B. 6(12 + 13)

   C. 6(12 × 13)

10. Jake bought 4 packs of pencils for $0.89 each and 4 packs of pens for $1.29 each. Which shows a way to express this?

   A. $1.29 + $0.89(4)

   B. 4($1.29) + $0.89

   C. 4($0.89 + $1.29)

2.3 Name ____________________

Zero Property, Equality Properties

Learning these properties will make your mathematics work easier.

Did you ever try to multiply by 0? The answer is 0.

Zero Property of Multiplication: Any number $\times 0 = 0$.

Remember that an equation is a mathematical statement that two things are equal.
$5 + 3 = 2 + 6$

Equality Property of Addition: If you add a number on one side of an equation, you must add *the same number* on the other side of the equation. Both sides will then still be equal.
$(5 + 3) + \mathbf{7} = (2 + 6) + \mathbf{7}$

Equality Property of Subtraction: If you subtract a number on one side of an equation, you must subtract *the same number* on the other side of the equation. Both sides will then still be equal.
$(5 + 3) - \mathbf{1} = (2 + 6) - \mathbf{1}$

Equality Property of Multiplication: If you multiply one side of an equation by a number, you must multiply the other side of the equation by *the same number*. Both sides will then still be equal.
$(5 + 3) \times \mathbf{9} = (2 + 6) \times \mathbf{9}$

Equality Property of Division: If you divide one side of an equation by a number, you must divide the other side of the equation by *the same number*. Both sides will then still be equal. **But you may never divide by 0.**
$(5 + 3) \div \mathbf{4} = (2 + 6) \div \mathbf{4}$

Exercises

Answer yes or no.

1. If $6 + 2 = 4 + 4$, then does $4\,(6 + 2) = 4\,(4 + 4)$? __________

2. If $5 \times 8 = 4 \times 10$, then does $\frac{(5 \times 8)}{4} = \frac{(4 \times 10)}{4}$? __________

3. If $2 \times 12 = 3 \times 8$, then does $4 - 2 \times 12 = 3 \times 8 - 4$? __________

4. If $10 \times 8 = 4 \times 20$, then does $10 \times 8 - 2.53 = 4 \times 20 - 2.53$? __________

5. If $\frac{3}{4} = \frac{12}{16}$, then does $\frac{3}{4} - 5 = \frac{12}{16} - 5$? __________

Name ____________________

Factors and Multiples

Multiples of a number are that number multiplied by an integer. For example, the first few multiples of 3 are 3, 6, 9, 12, and 15. A **common multiple** is a number that is a multiple of two or more numbers. For example, 8 is a multiple of both 2 and 4, so 8 is a common multiple of 2 and 4. The **least common multiple (LCM)** of two numbers is the smallest non-zero number that is a multiple of both numbers. To find the least common multiple, list a few multiples for each number and then choose the smallest number they have in common.

Example:

The least common multiple of 3 and 4

Multiples of 3: 3, 6, 9, 12, 15, 18 …

Multiples of 4: 4, 8, 12, 16, 20 …

The smallest number 3 and 4 have in common is 12, so 12 is the LCM of 3 and 4.

Factors are numbers you can multiply together to get another number. For example, 2 and 4 are factors of 8 because $2 \times 4 = 8$. The **greatest common factor (GCF)** is the greatest factor that divides two numbers. To find the greatest common factor, list the factors of each number. Find the largest factor that both numbers have in common.

Example:

The greatest common factor of 8 and 12

Factors of 8: 1, 2, 4, 8

Factors of 12: 1, 2, 3, 4, 6, 12

The largest number 8 and 12 have in common is 4, so the GCF of 8 and 12 is 4.

Exercises FIND THE LEAST COMMON MULTIPLE

1. 8 and 12 __________

2. 6 and 10 __________

3. 2 and 7 __________

4. 3 and 5 __________

5. 18 and 36 __________

6. 9 and 6 __________

7. Ginger is planning a party. Plates are sold in packs of 16 and cups are sold in packs of 12. If she wants to have the same number of plates and cups with none left over, how many of each pack will she need to purchase?

   ____

8. Britt does the dishes every other day and laundry every 4 days. If he did both on Monday, what is the next day when he will do both?

   ____

2.4

Name ______________________

Exercises **FIND THE GREATEST COMMON FACTOR**

9. 8 and 24 __________

10. 12 and 24 __________

11. 12 and 30 __________

12. 9 and 12 __________

13. 4 and 10 __________

14. 16 and 80 __________

15. Ahmed is making picnic lunch bags for his class. He has assembled 9 sandwiches, 27 pickles, and 36 cookies. What is the greatest number of lunch bags he can make with no food left over?

____

Name ______________________

3.1

Understanding Negative Numbers

Negative numbers are numbers that are less than zero. You identify them by adding a minus sign to the front of a number. So −1 is 1 less than 0. −53.5 is 53.5 less than 0.

Remember...

Zero (0) is neither positive, nor negative.

Example:

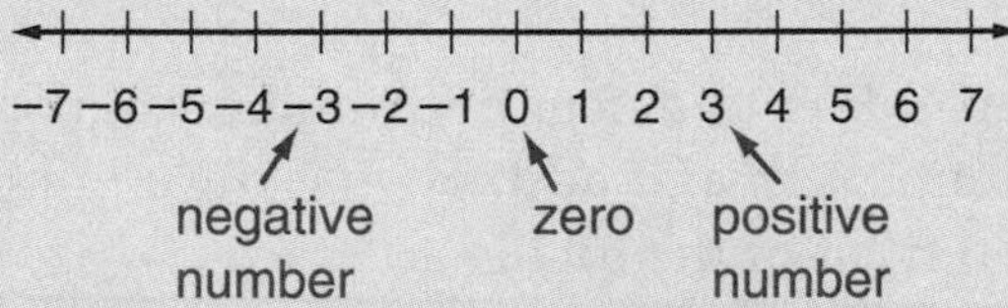

Look at the number line. Notice that −3 is three spaces to the left of 0 on the negative side. Also note that 3 is three spaces to the right of 0 on the positive side.

The Property of Additive Inverses: When you add a negative number to its **inverse** (its exact opposite on the other side of the number line), the total is 0. For example, $-7 + 7 = 0$.

Exercises SOLVE

1. $(-8) + 8 =$ ______

2. $(-134) + 134 =$ ______

3. $(-12) + 13 + 11 + (-13)$ ______

4. $A + (-A) =$ ______

5. $20 + (-17) =$ ______

6. $(-65) + 65 + 61 + (-58) =$ ______

7. $\frac{1}{2} + \left(-\frac{1}{2}\right) =$ ______

8. $212 + 200 + (-212) + (-212) =$ ______

9. $31 + (-34) + 0 =$ ______

10. $76 + \frac{1}{4} + \left(-\frac{1}{4}\right) + (-76) =$ ______

11. Is −6 to the left or the right of −6.2 on the number line? ______

12. Is −4.5 greater or less than −4.0? ______

3.2

Name ______________________________

Adding with Negative Numbers

When you add a positive number and a negative number, compare the numbers as if they do not have positive or negative signs. If the positive number is larger, just subtract.

Example:

$6 + (-4) = ?$

Step 1: Remove the + sign and the parentheses.

Step 2: Do the math. $6 - 4 = 2$

If the negative number is greater, ignore the minus sign for the time being. Subtract the smaller number from the greater. Then put a minus sign in front of the difference.

Example:

$1 + (-3) = ?$

Step 1: Subtract: $3 - 1 = 2$

Step 2: Write a minus sign in front of the difference. So $1 + (-3) = -2$

When adding two negative numbers, ignore the minus sign and **add**. Then write a minus sign in front of the total.

Example:

$(-1) + (-6) = ?$

Step 1: Ignore the negative signs and add. $1 + 6 = 7$

Step 2: Write a minus sign in front of the total. $(-1) + (-6) = -7$

Exercises **SOLVE**

1. $12 + (-4)$
2. $(-14) + 8$
3. $3 + (-13)$
4. $45 + (-23)$
5. $123 + (-43) + 22$
6. $90 + (-45) + (-3)$
7. $(-10) + (-10) + 3$
8. $45 + (-32) + 2$
9. $15 + (-14)$
10. $16 + 14 + (-13)$
11. $(-15) + 14$
12. $67 + 12 + 13 + (-14)$
13. $43 + (-32) + 5$
14. $(-43) + 32 + (-5)$
15. $2 + 2 + (-3) + (-2)$
16. If it is 5°C on Friday and on Saturday it is 7 degrees colder, what is the temperature on Saturday? ______________________________
17. Allan owes his sister \$20. He pays her back \$12 on Monday, but then borrows \$5 on Thursday. How much does he owe her now? ______________________________
18. In a trivia game, you get 5 points for each correct answer and lose 3 points for each incorrect answer. If you got 4 questions correct and missed 7 questions, how many points do you have? ______________________________

Name ______________________________

Absolute Value

The absolute value of a number is that number's distance from zero on a number line. It does not matter whether the number is positive or negative. Absolute value is simply how far the number is from zero in either direction. For example, −3 and +3 have the same absolute value because they are both a distance of 3 away from zero on the number line. Absolute value is written as $|-3| = 3$ or $|+3| = 3$. An absolute value of 3 does not tell you whether the number is positive or negative; it just means that the number is 3 away from zero.

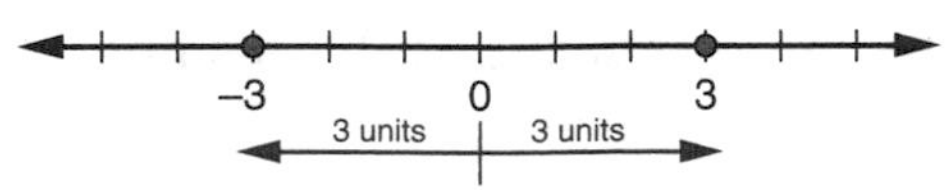

Examples:

$|-5| = 5$

$|+3| = 3$

$|-4| = 4$

Exercises SOLVE

1. $|-3| =$ ________
2. $|-26| =$ ________
3. $|423| =$ ________
4. $|-.7| =$ ________
5. $\left|-\frac{5}{6}\right| =$ ________
6. $\left|\frac{2}{3}\right| =$ ________

Compare using <, >, or =.

7. $|-6|$ ________ $|-7|$
8. $|21|$ ________ $|-21|$
9. $|-8|$ ________ $|-4|$
10. $|-5|$ ________ $|7|$
11. $|10|$ ________ $|-12|$
12. $|423|$ ________ $|425|$
13. If Elena's bank account balance is −$53.86, how much would she need to deposit in order to bring her balance to $10.00? ____________________
14. If the temperature was 4 degrees lower than normal on Tuesday and 6 degrees higher than normal on Wednesday, which day's temperature was more different than normal?

    ____
15. Vivian's bank account balance is −$3.46. Evelyn's bank account balance is −$2.98. Who has the greater debt? ____________________

Name ______________________________

Improper Fractions and Mixed Numbers

In a fraction, the number on the bottom is the **denominator**. The denominator tells what kind of units the whole is divided into. The number on the top is the **numerator**. It tells how many of those units there are.

When the numerator is the same as the denominator, a fraction is equal to 1. When the numerator is *greater* than the denominator, a fraction is equal to more than 1. This is called an **improper fraction**. Sometimes, it is easier to perform a calculation when you change an improper fraction into a **mixed number**, part whole number and part fraction. These are mixed numbers:

$$8\frac{3}{4},\ 21\frac{1}{2},\ 147\frac{5}{9}$$

To change an improper fraction to a mixed number, divide the numerator by the denominator. The quotient is the whole number part. If there is a remainder, that becomes the fraction part. Simply use the remainder as the numerator and keep the original denominator.

Example: Change $\frac{17}{5}$ to a mixed number.

Step 1: Divide the numerator by the denominator. $17 \div 5 = 3\text{ R}2$

Step 2: The quotient becomes the whole number and the remainder becomes the fraction. So $\frac{17}{5} = 3\frac{2}{5}$

To change mixed numbers into improper fractions, find the fraction part of the mixed number. Multiply the whole number by the denominator of the fraction. Then, add the numerator to that product and place the total over the denominator.

Example: Change $9\frac{7}{8}$ into an improper fraction.

Step 1: Multiply $9 \times 8 = 72$

Step 2: $72 + 7 = 79$

Step 3: $\frac{79}{8}$ So $9\frac{7}{8} = \frac{79}{8}$

Exercises CHANGE TO MIXED NUMBERS

1. $\frac{22}{7}$
2. $\frac{35}{4}$
3. $\frac{73}{10}$
4. $\frac{47}{3}$
5. $\frac{87}{11}$

Exercises CHANGE TO IMPROPER FRACTIONS

6. $2\frac{2}{3}$
7. $5\frac{4}{7}$
8. $21\frac{3}{5}$
9. $5\frac{3}{8}$
10. $22\frac{6}{7}$

Name ______________________________

Adding and Subtracting Fractions with Like Denominators

Like denominators are exactly the same. For example, $\frac{1}{4}$ and $\frac{3}{4}$ have like denominators. But $\frac{1}{4}$ and $\frac{1}{2}$ do *not* have like denominators.

Remember...

Like denominators are the same and are sometimes called common denominators.

To add fractions with like denominators, just add the numerators. Place the total over the denominator.

Example: Add: $\frac{3}{7} + \frac{4}{7} + \frac{6}{7}$

Step 1: Add $3 + 4 + 6 = 13$

Step 2: Place the total over the like denominator. $\frac{13}{7}$

You may notice that your total is an improper fraction. But you learned how to change that into a mixed number if you need to.

To subtract fractions with like denominators, look at the numerators. Place the difference over the like denominator.

Example: Subtract: $\frac{13}{25} - \frac{9}{25}$

Step 1: Subtract $13 - 9 = 4$

Step 2: Place the difference over the like denominator. $\frac{4}{25}$

Remember...

When adding or subtracting fractions with like denominators, just work with the numerators. You can *ignore* the like denominators while adding or subtracting. However, do not forget to put your total or difference over the like denominator when you have finished your calculations.

Exercises ADD FRACTIONS

1. $\frac{3}{7} + \frac{6}{7}$
2. $\frac{4}{3} + \frac{2}{3}$
3. $\frac{1}{5} + \frac{4}{5}$
4. $\frac{9}{33} + \frac{17}{33}$

Exercises SUBTRACT FRACTIONS

5. $\frac{2}{3} - \frac{1}{3}$
6. $\frac{10}{47} - \frac{10}{47}$
7. $\frac{43}{96} - \frac{18}{96}$
8. $\frac{12}{13} - \frac{11}{13}$

9. A cookie recipe calls for $\frac{2}{3}$ cup of brown sugar and $\frac{2}{3}$ cup of white sugar. How much sugar does the recipe call for in total?______________________________

10. Kathy has one piece of lace that is $6\frac{3}{4}$ inches long and another that is $5\frac{1}{4}$ inches long. She needs 12 inches of lace for a project. Does she have enough if she combines the two pieces?

____

4.3

Name ______________________

Adding and Subtracting Fractions with Unlike Denominators

To add or subtract fractions with unlike, or different, denominators, you have to change them into fractions with common or like denominators. This process is called finding the **common denominator**.

Example: Add $\frac{3}{4} + \frac{2}{6} = \frac{9}{12} + \frac{4}{12} = \frac{13}{12} = 1\frac{1}{12}$

Subtract $\frac{3}{4} - \frac{2}{6} = \frac{9}{12} - \frac{4}{12} = \frac{5}{12}$

To find a common denominator in these fractions, first, look at the denominators, 4 and 6. What number is a multiple of both 4 and 6? A simple way to find the **common multiple** is to multiply the two numbers. $4 \times 6 = 24$. In some cases, there is a smaller number that is a common multiple that would be easier to work with. In these examples, 12 is a lower common multiple than 24, so it will work as your common denominator. In each fraction, multiply the original denominator to make it become the common denominator. Then multiply the original numerator by that same number.

Exercises ADD OR SUBTRACT

1. $\frac{2}{7} + \frac{3}{5}$
2. $\frac{4}{13} + \frac{2}{3}$
3. $\frac{3}{4} + \frac{1}{8}$
4. $\frac{3}{11} + \frac{2}{7}$
5. $\frac{2}{3} - \frac{1}{4}$
6. $\frac{5}{6} - \frac{1}{8}$
7. $\frac{12}{13} - \frac{2}{3}$
8. $\frac{3}{4} - \frac{2}{5}$
9. Bruce uses $\frac{1}{3}$ cup of almonds, $\frac{3}{4}$ cup of peanuts, and $\frac{1}{2}$ cup of walnuts in his trail mix. How many cups of nuts are in the trail mix? ______________________
10. Preston normally walks $\frac{5}{7}$ of a mile to work each day. On Thursday, he found a shortcut that took only $\frac{1}{3}$ of a mile. How much shorter is the new route he found?

____

Name ______________________________

Adding and Subtracting Mixed Numbers with Unlike Denominators

There are two ways to do this. You could change each mixed number to an improper fraction and then add them. But an easier way to add mixed numbers is to add the whole number parts first and then add the fractions.

Example: Add $2\frac{3}{5} + 5\frac{2}{3}$

Step 1: Add the whole numbers. $2 + 5 = 7$

Now add the fractions $\frac{3}{5} + \frac{2}{3}$

Step 2: Change the fractions with unlike denominators to fractions with a common denominator.

$\frac{3 \times 3}{5 \times 3} = \frac{9}{15}$ $\frac{2 \times 5}{3 \times 5} = \frac{10}{15}$

Step 3: Add the fractions. $\frac{9}{15} + \frac{10}{15} = \frac{19}{15}$

Step 4: If the numerator in the total is greater than the common denominator, you have an improper fraction. Change it to a mixed number. $\frac{19}{15} = 1\frac{4}{15}$

Step 5: Add your two totals.

$7 + 1\frac{4}{15} = 8\frac{4}{15}$

To subtract mixed numbers, first subtract the whole numbers, then subtract the fractions.

Example: Subtract $7\frac{3}{8} - 3\frac{1}{4}$

Step 1: $7 - 3 = 4$

Step 2: Change the fractions with unlike denominators to fractions with a common denominator. The lowest common multiple of 8 and 4, is 8. In this case $4 \times 2 = 8$. The best common multiple is the *higher* number.

Step 3: Subtract the fractions. $\frac{3}{8} - \frac{2}{8} = \frac{1}{8}$

Step 4: Add your two differences.

$4 + \frac{1}{8} = 4\frac{1}{8}$

Exercises ADD OR SUBTRACT AS INDICATED

1. $11\frac{2}{7} + 12\frac{3}{8}$
2. $12\frac{5}{6} + 1\frac{1}{15}$
3. $13\frac{2}{7} + 3\frac{2}{9}$
4. $21\frac{1}{9} + 3\frac{5}{6}$
5. $7\frac{7}{9} - 2\frac{1}{4}$
6. $5\frac{3}{7} - 2\frac{1}{6}$
7. $5\frac{1}{4} - 2\frac{2}{13}$
8. $19\frac{6}{7} - 3\frac{3}{10}$

Name ______________________________

9 Marisa wants to walk $8\frac{1}{2}$ miles this week and she walked $3\frac{1}{8}$ miles today. How far does she have left to walk?

____

____

10 Randy needs $1\frac{3}{5}$ pounds of gravel to finish a walkway. He carried one bag that weighed $1\frac{7}{8}$ pounds but spilled $\frac{1}{4}$ pound. Will he still have enough to finish the walkway?

____

____

Name ______________________________

Estimating Sums and Differences of Fractions and Mixed Numbers

FRACTIONS When you add or subtract fractions, ask: Is each fraction closest to 0, to $\frac{1}{2}$, or to 1?

Example: Estimate $\frac{2}{5} + \frac{8}{9} + \frac{1}{8}$

Step 1: $\frac{2}{5}$ is a little bit less than $\frac{1}{2}$.

$\frac{8}{9}$ is very close to 1.

$\frac{1}{8}$ is not much more than 0.

Step 2: Add: $\frac{1}{2} + 1 + 0 = 1\frac{1}{2}$

MIXED NUMBERS To estimate mixed numbers when you are adding, start by estimating the total of the whole numbers. Then estimate the total of the fractions. Add your two estimates together. See the subtraction example.

Example: Estimate $51\frac{15}{16} - 39\frac{4}{7}$

Step 1: Estimate the difference of the whole numbers.
51 − 39 can be rounded to
50 − 40 = 10.

Step 2: Then estimate the difference of the fractions. $\frac{15}{16}$ is almost 1.
$\frac{4}{7}$ is slightly more than $\frac{1}{2}$. $1 - \frac{1}{2} = \frac{1}{2}$

Step 3: Add the two differences. A good estimate would be $10 + \frac{1}{2} = 10\frac{1}{2}$

Exercises ESTIMATE

1. $\frac{3}{4} + \frac{5}{6}$

2. $\frac{4}{5} + \frac{1}{7}$

3. $\frac{1}{3} + \frac{4}{7}$

4. $\frac{5}{6} + \frac{4}{8}$

5. $1\frac{1}{5} + 2\frac{5}{6}$

6. $7\frac{4}{5} + 4\frac{1}{3}$

7. $5\frac{1}{5} - 2\frac{3}{5}$

8. $7\frac{1}{2} - \frac{3}{4}$

9. $12\frac{1}{8} + \frac{2}{3}$

10. $4\frac{4}{7} + 4\frac{4}{7}$

11. $13\frac{5}{8} - 12\frac{1}{4}$

12. $17\frac{1}{7} - 13\frac{3}{4}$

13. Leslie had $25\frac{4}{9}$ ounces of cat food left in a bag. If she feeds each of her two cats $1\frac{7}{8}$ ounces of food, about how much cat food will she have left?

____

14. James was gathering wood for the fireplace. He already had $1\frac{4}{5}$ cords of wood and he gathered another $2\frac{1}{3}$ cords today. About how many cords of wood does James have now?

____

4.6 Name ______________________

Multiplying Fractions and Whole Numbers

To multiply a fraction and a whole number, you need to multiply the *numerator* by the whole number. Then place the product over the denominator.

Example: Multiply $13 \times \frac{7}{8}$

Step 1: Multiply the whole number by the numerator of the fraction.
$13 \times 7 = 91$

Step 2: Place the product over the denominator of the original fraction. $\frac{91}{8}$

Step 3: The product will often be an improper fraction. You may need to change it to a mixed number.
$\frac{91}{8} = 11\frac{3}{8}$

Exercises MULTIPLY

1. $5 \times \frac{3}{4}$
2. $4 \times \frac{2}{7}$
3. $21 \times \frac{5}{8}$
4. $11 \times \frac{2}{9}$
5. $4 \times \frac{3}{11}$
6. $13 \times \frac{13}{14}$
7. $21 \times \frac{10}{23}$
8. $7 \times \frac{2}{3}$
9. $12 \times \frac{7}{19}$
10. $14 \times \frac{3}{5}$
11. $14 \times \frac{11}{3}$
12. $13 \times \frac{4}{17}$
13. $10 \times \frac{9}{23}$
14. $13 \times \frac{21}{22}$
15. $5 \times \frac{14}{27}$
16. Chet found a pair of sunglasses that he would like to buy. They normally cost $43.00, but this week they are on sale for only $\frac{7}{8}$ of the usual price. How much money will Chet need to buy the sunglasses?

    ____

17. Ashlee is riding her bike to the beach. If the beach is 17 miles from her home, and she has already traveled $\frac{3}{5}$ of the way, how much farther does she have to cycle?

    ____

Name ______________________________

4.7

Multiplying Fractions and Fractions

To multiply fractions, two treat the numerators and the denominators as two different multiplication exercises. Multiply the numerators to find the numerator of the product. Then multiply the denominators to find the denominator of the product.

Example: $\frac{4}{5} \times \frac{3}{7}$

Step 1: Multiply the numerators.
$4 \times 3 = 12$

Step 2: Multiply the denominators.
$5 \times 7 = 35$

Step 3: Write the product. $\frac{12}{35}$

Remember...

To multiply fractions, multiply the numerators first, then the denominators.

You may need to multiply **reciprocals**. Reciprocals are two fractions that look like upside-down reflections of one another. The numerator of the first is the denominator of the second, and the numerator of the second is the denominator of the first.

Example: $\frac{2}{3} \times \frac{3}{2}$

You *could* go through the steps of multiplying the numerators ($2 \times 3 = 6$), and then multiplying the denominators ($3 \times 2 = 6$). Notice that the products are the same. When multiplying reciprocals, the product of the numerators and the product of the denominators will *always* be the same. A fraction with the same numerator and denominator equals 1, so multiplying reciprocal fractions will always give you a result of 1!

Exercises MULTIPLY

1. $\frac{1}{2} \times \frac{1}{2}$
2. $\frac{2}{3} \times \frac{6}{7}$
3. $\frac{5}{9} \times \frac{3}{11}$
4. $\frac{10}{13} \times \frac{1}{3}$
5. $\frac{3}{11} \times \frac{11}{3}$
6. $\frac{7}{3} \times \frac{3}{11}$
7. $\frac{4}{5} \times \frac{7}{8}$
8. $\frac{3}{4} \times \frac{4}{3}$
9. $\frac{17}{27} \times \frac{5}{3}$
10. $\frac{6}{10} \times \frac{6}{11}$
11. $\frac{13}{14} \times \frac{2}{3}$
12. $\frac{4}{5} \times \frac{4}{5}$
13. $\frac{133}{145} \times \frac{145}{133}$
14. $\frac{8}{19} \times \frac{5}{7}$
15. $\frac{11}{13} \times \frac{9}{14}$

16. Monday night John ate $\frac{1}{3}$ of a pizza. The next morning, he ate $\frac{1}{2}$ of what was left. How much did he eat that morning?

____

17. Molly had $\frac{3}{4}$ of a bag of leftover popcorn. She ate $\frac{3}{4}$ of that. How much did she eat?

____

4.8

Name ______________________________

Multiplying Fractions and Mixed Numbers

MULTIPLY FRACTIONS AND MIXED NUMBERS The easiest way to multiply fractions and mixed numbers is to change the mixed number into an improper fraction. Then multiply the fractions just as you normally would.

> **Example:** Multiply: $3\frac{1}{2} \times \frac{4}{9}$
>
> **Step 1:** Change the mixed number to an improper fraction. $3\frac{1}{2} = \frac{7}{2}$
>
> **Step 2:** Restate the problem. $\frac{7}{2} \times \frac{4}{9}$
>
> **Step 3:** Multiply the numerators. $7 \times 4 = 28$
>
> **Step 4:** Multiply the denominators. $2 \times 9 = 18$
>
> **Step 5:** Write the product. $\frac{28}{18}$

REDUCING You may already know about reducing a fraction. Reducing changes a fraction into its simplest form. For example: $\frac{3}{15} = \frac{1}{5}$. To reduce, see if you can divide *both* the numerator and the denominator by the *same* number. In this case, you were able to divide both 3 and 15 by 3.

When you have an improper fraction, you can reduce it. $\frac{28}{18} = \frac{14}{9}$ because you were able to divide both 28 and 18 by 2. You can also reduce the fraction part of a mixed number. $1\frac{10}{18} = 1\frac{5}{9}$ because both 10 and 18 are divisible by 2.

Remember...

When you reduce a mixed number, the whole number will *always* stay the same.

Exercises MULTIPLY, REDUCE

1. $1\frac{1}{2} \times \frac{4}{5}$
2. $\frac{2}{9} \times 4\frac{1}{4}$
3. $\frac{3}{4} \times 2\frac{1}{7}$
4. $5\frac{1}{3} \times \frac{1}{2}$
5. $\frac{8}{9} \times 3\frac{1}{5}$
6. $1\frac{2}{3} \times \frac{2}{7}$
7. $5\frac{1}{4} \times \frac{2}{3}$
8. $7\frac{1}{8} \times \frac{1}{4}$
9. $1\frac{1}{2} \times \frac{8}{9}$
10. $\frac{3}{7} \times 5\frac{1}{7}$
11. Zane spent $1\frac{3}{4}$ hours exercising. He spent $\frac{1}{3}$ of that time lifting weights. How much time did he spend lifting weights?

    ____

12. Jenna used $3\frac{1}{3}$ containers of white paint to paint her house. She used $\frac{1}{4}$ of that amount to paint the bathroom. How much paint did she use to paint the bathroom?

    ____

Name ____________________

4.8

Multiplying Fractions and Mixed Numbers (cont.)

MULTIPLY MIXED NUMBERS You can probably figure out the easiest way to multiply mixed numbers. Change them to improper fractions.

> **Example:** Multiply: $4\frac{2}{3} \times 3\frac{3}{8}$
>
> **Step 1:** Change the first mixed number to an improper fraction. $4\frac{2}{3} = \frac{14}{3}$
>
> **Step 2:** Change the next mixed number to an improper fraction. $3\frac{3}{8} = \frac{27}{8}$
>
> **Step 3:** Restate the problem. $\frac{14}{3} \times \frac{27}{8}$
>
> **Step 4:** Multiply the numerators. $14 \times 27 = 378$
>
> **Step 5:** Multiply the denominators. $3 \times 8 = 24$
>
> **Step 6:** Write the product. $\frac{378}{24}$
>
> Reduce the fraction, if you can. In this example, both 378 and 24 can be divided by 6. $\frac{378}{24} = \frac{63}{4}$

MORE ABOUT REDUCING Here is a good trick for reducing when you multiply two fractions. Look at both numerators and then at both denominators. If you can divide *either* of those numerators by the same number as *either* of the denominators, you can reduce!

> **Example:** Multiply $\frac{14}{3} \times \frac{27}{8}$
>
> The numerator 14 and the denominator 8 can both be divided by 2.
>
> So $\frac{14}{3} \times \frac{27}{8} = \frac{7}{3} \times \frac{27}{4}$
>
> Now, look again. The numerator 27 and the denominator 3 can both be divided by 3.
>
> So $\frac{7}{3} \times \frac{27}{4} = \frac{7}{1} \times \frac{9}{4}$. Since $\frac{7}{1} = 7$, now you have a much simpler exercise to solve.
>
> $7 \times \frac{9}{4} = \frac{63}{4}$

Exercises MULTIPLY, REDUCE

13 $1\frac{1}{4} \times 2\frac{2}{3}$

14 $5\frac{1}{8} \times 2\frac{2}{3}$

15 $2\frac{1}{7} \times 1\frac{1}{3}$

16 $3\frac{1}{2} \times 2\frac{1}{7}$

17 $4\frac{1}{2} \times 3\frac{1}{3}$

18 Ryan finds the area of a rectangle by multiplying its length times its width. If the rectangle is $3\frac{3}{5}$ inches long and $2\frac{2}{3}$ inches wide, what is its area? ____________________

____

____

4.9

Name ______________________________

Dividing Fractions by Whole Numbers and Whole Numbers by Fractions

To divide a fraction by a whole number, multiply the denominator of the fraction by the whole number.

Example: Divide: $\frac{5}{8} \div 2$

Step 1: Keep the original numerator.

Step 2: Multiply the denominator of the fraction by the whole number. $8 \times 2 = 16$. This is the new denominator.

So $\frac{5}{8} \div 2 = \frac{5}{16}$

To divide a whole number by a fraction, you have to remember that a reciprocal is a fraction turned upside-down. For example, $\frac{2}{5}$ is the reciprocal of $\frac{5}{2}$, and $\frac{5}{2}$ is the reciprocal of $\frac{2}{5}$. To divide a whole number by a fraction, multiply the whole number by the reciprocal of the fraction.

Example: Divide: $4 \div \frac{3}{4}$

Step 1: Find the reciprocal of the fraction. The reciprocal of $\frac{3}{4}$ is $\frac{4}{3}$

Step 2: Multiply the whole number by the fraction's reciprocal. $4 \times \frac{4}{3} = \frac{16}{3}$

Remember...

A whole number can always be expressed as a fraction, with 1 as the denominator. So $2 = \frac{2}{1}$. When you divide a fraction by a whole number, you are *really* multiplying the fraction by the whole number's reciprocal. So $\frac{5}{8} \div 2 = \frac{5}{8} \div \frac{2}{1} = \frac{5}{8} \times \frac{1}{2} = \frac{5}{16}$.

Exercises DIVIDE

1. $\frac{10}{13} \div 3$
2. $\frac{4}{5} \div 4$
3. $\frac{12}{13} \div 5$
4. $\frac{2}{11} \div 4$
5. $\frac{3}{4} \div 7$
6. $16 \div \frac{4}{17}$
7. $4 \div \frac{1}{19}$
8. $21 \div \frac{7}{3}$
9. $55 \div \frac{11}{10}$
10. $23 \div \frac{46}{51}$

11. Mrs. Spinosa brought $\frac{15}{19}$ pounds of chocolate for her fourth grade class to enjoy. If all 15 students want an equal portion of chocolate, how much will each student receive?

____

12. Mr. Lewis bought $\frac{10}{13}$ liters of apple cider to divide equally among his three children. How much apple cider will each child receive?

____

Name ______________________________

Dividing Fractions by Fractions

To divide a fraction by another fraction, multiply the first fraction by the reciprocal of the second fraction.

Example: Divide: $\frac{2}{3} \div \frac{6}{7}$

Step 1: Find the reciprocal of the second fraction.
The reciprocal of $\frac{6}{7}$ is $\frac{7}{6}$

Step 2: Multiply the first fraction by the reciprocal of the second fraction.
$\frac{2}{3} \times \frac{7}{6}$

Step 3: Multiply the numerators.
$2 \times 7 = 14$

Step 4: Multiply the denominators:
$3 \times 6 = 18$

Step 5: Write the product: $\frac{14}{18}$. The product of that multiplication is *also* the quotient of the original division problem.

Step 6: Reduce the fraction if possible.
$\frac{14}{18} = \frac{7}{9}$

Remember...

When you divide fractions, you will *multiply* by the reciprocal!

Exercises DIVIDE

1. $\frac{5}{7} \div \frac{3}{4}$
2. $\frac{2}{3} \div \frac{2}{7}$
3. $\frac{1}{9} \div \frac{3}{7}$
4. $\frac{3}{4} \div \frac{1}{9}$
5. $\frac{3}{13} \div \frac{2}{9}$
6. $\frac{1}{9} \div \frac{1}{3}$
7. $\frac{2}{13} \div \frac{1}{5}$
8. $\frac{3}{13} \div \frac{2}{13}$
9. $\frac{4}{3} \div \frac{1}{4}$
10. $\frac{15}{4} \div \frac{4}{3}$
11. $\frac{6}{7} \div \frac{1}{7}$
12. $\frac{3}{17} \div \frac{4}{17}$
13. $\frac{1}{11} \div \frac{22}{3}$
14. $\frac{3}{7} \div \frac{1}{21}$
15. $\frac{5}{14} \div \frac{1}{7}$

16. Nicholle has a piece of yarn that is $\frac{7}{8}$ of a yard long. She needs pieces that are $\frac{1}{4}$ of a yard long. How many pieces can she cut?

____

17. Emma Lee has $\frac{9}{10}$ of a gallon of gas left in the tank of her car. If driving a round trip to work uses $\frac{1}{6}$ of a gallon of gas, how many trips can she make before she runs out of gas?

____

4.11

Name ____________________

Dividing Mixed Numbers

To divide mixed numbers, change each mixed number into an improper fraction. If only one number in your division problem is a mixed number, change *it* to an improper fraction.

If *both* numbers in your division problem are mixed numbers, change *both* to improper fractions.

Example: Divide: $5\frac{1}{2} \div 2\frac{2}{3}$

Step 1: Change the first mixed number to an improper fraction. $5\frac{1}{2} = \frac{11}{2}$

Step 2: Change the second mixed number to an improper fraction. $2\frac{2}{3} = \frac{8}{3}$

Step 3: Restate the problem. $5\frac{1}{2} \div 2\frac{2}{3}$ is the same as $\frac{11}{2} \div \frac{8}{3}$

Step 4: Find the reciprocal of the second fraction. The reciprocal of $\frac{8}{3}$ is $\frac{3}{8}$

Step 5: Multiply the first fraction by the reciprocal of the second fraction. $\frac{11}{2} \times \frac{3}{8}$

Step 6: Multiply the numerators: $11 \times 3 = 33$

Step 7: Multiply the denominators: $2 \times 8 = 16$

Step 8: Write the product $\frac{33}{16}$. The product of that multiplication is *also* the quotient of the original division problem.

Step 9: Change the quotient to a mixed number.

$\frac{33}{16} = 2\frac{1}{16}$

$5\frac{1}{2} \div 2\frac{2}{3} = 2\frac{1}{16}$

Exercises **DIVIDE**

1. $1\frac{1}{2} \div 2\frac{1}{2}$
2. $3\frac{3}{5} \div 1\frac{1}{8}$
3. $7\frac{1}{7} \div 3\frac{1}{3}$
4. $3\frac{4}{7} \div 2\frac{2}{5}$
5. $6\frac{4}{5} \div 3\frac{2}{5}$
6. $5\frac{1}{2} \div 3\frac{3}{4}$
7. $4\frac{2}{9} \div 2\frac{4}{9}$
8. $9\frac{2}{7} \div 2\frac{1}{2}$
9. Frankie was making batches of cookies to bring to the school activities meeting. The recipe called for $1\frac{3}{4}$ cups of flour per batch. He had $5\frac{1}{4}$ cups of flour left in a bag. How many batches of cookies can Frankie bake?

   ____

10. Jonas was making balloon decorations for the school dance. Each balloon needs $3\frac{2}{3}$ feet of ribbon to tie it down to the refreshment table. He has $51\frac{1}{3}$ feet of ribbon. How many balloons can he secure to the table?

    ____

Name ______________________________

Understanding Decimals

Decimal Place Value and Rounding

Sometimes you will be asked to round a number with a decimal to the nearest whole number. You need to look at the number on the right side of the decimal point. If that number is less than five, keep the whole number as it is. If that number is 5 or greater, add 1 to the whole number.

Tens	Ones		Tenths	Hundredths	Thousandths
6	3	.	5	1	2

Example: Round 63.512 to a whole number.

Step 1: Look only at the number to the immediate right of the decimal point. 5

Step 2: Ask yourself: Is that number 5 or greater? Yes.

Step 3: Add 1 to the whole number. $63 + 1 = 64$

In other exercises, you might need to round a decimal to the nearest tenth, the nearest hundredth, or the nearest thousandth. Always look at the number to the *right* of the place you are rounding to. For example, if you are rounding to tenths, look at the hundredths place. If the number you look at is less than 5, keep the original number, *but only to the place you need.* If that number is 5 or greater, add 1 to *that* place.

Example: Round 5.18499 to the nearest hundredth.

Step 1: Look at the place to the right of the hundredths place. (It will be the number in the thousandths place.)

Step 2: Ask yourself: Is that number 5 or greater? No.

Step 3: Keep the original decimal *up to the place you need.* 5.18

Exercises ROUND

Round to the nearest whole number.

1. 68.1 ________
2. 17.7 ________
3. 22.2 ________
4. 47.5 ________
5. 76.4 ________

Round to the nearest tenth.

6. 18.47 ________
7. 21.23 ________
8. 44.44 ________
9. 11.14 ________
10. 59.49 ________

Round to the nearest hundredth.

11. 429.345 ________
12. 39.746 ________
13. 313.313 ________
14. 528.456 ________
15. 832.832 ________

Round to the nearest thousandth.

16. 32.3456 ________
17. 1.4141 ________
18. 12.1728 ________
19. 592.4219 ________
20. 837.8198 ________

5.1

Name ______________________________

Comparing and Ordering Decimals

When you compare whole numbers, you look at place value. To compare decimals, you will look at place value. Line up your decimals so that the decimal points are in a column. Then begin by looking at the column to the immediate *right* of the decimal point, the tenths place. As you arrange your numbers, work toward the *right*.

Example: Place these decimals in order from least to greatest.
0.31 0.186 0.7 0.09 0.34 0.091

Step 1: Line up the decimal points.
0.31
0.186
0.7
0.09
0.34
0.091

Step 2: Find the greatest number in the tenths place. 0.7

Step 3: Find the next greatest number in the tenths place. 0.31 and 0.34

Step 4: If two decimals have the same number in the tenths place, you must look at the next place value, the hundredths place. With 0.31 and 0.34, 4 is greater than 1.

Step 5: Continue to put all decimals in the correct order.
0.7
0.34
0.31
0.186

What do you do with 0.09 and 0.091?

Add a zero to 0.09 as a placeholder for the thousandths place. That gives you 0.090. Now, when you look at the thousandths place, you can see that 0.091 is slightly greater!

Remember...

When comparing numbers with decimals, always look at the whole numbers first. If two whole numbers are the same, *then* compare *to the right* from the decimal point.

Exercises COMPARE AND ORDER

Put the numbers in order from least to greatest.

21. 0.33 0.333 0.3333

____

22. 0.39 1.39 0.388 0.393

____

23. 4.44 4.441 0.44 4.439

____

24. 7.78 7.7778 7.778 7.7777

____

25. 4.45 44.5 0.445 445

____

26. 22.2323 22.2332 22.3 22.23222

____

27. 1.765 1.7655 1.766 1.76559

____

28. In a science experiment, Dr. Denton timed the length of a sneeze for 4 people and wrote the results in a table.

Person A	0.09 seconds
Person B	1.09 seconds
Person C	0.0888 seconds
Person D	0.090001 seconds

If the people were put in order from shortest time to greatest, what would the order be?

____

____

____

____

Name ______________________________

5.2

Changing Between Fractions and Decimals

A decimal is really a fraction expressed in another way. So $\frac{3}{10} = 0.3$, and $3\frac{17}{100} = 3.17$. Decimals are expressed in tenths, hundredths, thousandths, and so on. However, you can convert a fraction into a decimal. Just divide the fraction's numerator by its denominator.

Example: What decimal equals $\frac{1}{4}$?

Step 1: $\frac{1}{4} = 1 \div 4$ Set this up as a regular division problem: $4\overline{)1}$. However, 4 does not go into 1. You need to add a decimal point to the 1 and as many placeholder zeros as necessary for you to divide. You must also use a decimal point in the quotient. Be sure to line it up with the decimal point in the dividend.

Step 2: Add a decimal point and one placeholder zero. Then add a decimal point to the quotient.

$$\begin{array}{r} . \\ 4\overline{)1.0} \end{array}$$

Step 3: Begin dividing.

$$\begin{array}{r} 0.2 \\ 4\overline{)1.0} \\ \underline{8} \\ 2 \end{array}$$

Step 4: If you have a remainder, add another placeholder zero.

$$\begin{array}{r} .25 \\ 4\overline{)1.0} \\ \underline{8} \\ 20 \\ \underline{20} \\ 0 \end{array}$$

Step 5: Keep adding placeholder zeros until you have no remainder. If you have already added four placeholder zeros, think about rounding your decimal to the nearest thousandths place.

Changing decimals to fractions is easier than changing fractions to decimals. Look at the place value farthest to the right, and use that as your denominator. Use the actual decimal as your numerator.

Example: Change 0.36 to a fraction.

Step 1: Look at the place value. Use it as your denominator. The place value farthest to the right in 0.36 is the hundredths place. So the denominator will be 100.

Step 2: Use the decimal as the numerator. $\frac{36}{100}$

Step 3: Simplify the fraction if you can. Divide the numerator and the denominator by the same number. $\frac{36 \div 4}{100 \div 4} = \frac{9}{25}$

Remember...

A rounded decimal will not *exactly* equal the fraction you started with.

Name ______________________________

Exercises CHANGE FRACTIONS TO DECIMALS

Round to the nearest ten thousandth, if necessary.

1. $\frac{5}{4}$ __________
2. $\frac{7}{8}$ __________
3. $\frac{1}{9}$ __________
4. $\frac{5}{7}$ __________
5. $\frac{5}{11}$ __________

Exercises CHANGE DECIMALS TO FRACTIONS

6. 0.8 __________
7. 0.125 __________
8. 0.65 __________
9. 0.53 __________
10. 0.44 __________

11. A recipe calls for 1.375 cups of flour to be mixed together with 0.125 cups of cornstarch. If Stefano has only an 1/8 cup measuring cup to measure the flour and cornstarch, how many measuring cups full of flour and how many measuring cups of cornstarch will he need to fill to complete the recipe?

    __________ measuring cups of flour

    __________ measuring cups of cornstarch

12. Alphonse uses a pedometer to record how far he walks during his morning workout. After walking a while, he rests and notices that the pedometer shows he has walked 0.9 mile. If he walks $1\frac{4}{5}$ miles every day as part of his workout, how much farther does Alphonse need to walk to finish his workout? __________

Name ______________________________

5.3

Adding Decimals

Adding decimals is *just like* adding whole numbers, except that you must be careful to line up the decimals correctly. Once you do that, you can add as if the decimal is not there.

Example: Add 85.38 + 6.99

Step 1: Line up the numbers. Make sure that the decimal points line up in a column.

$$\begin{array}{r} 85.38 \\ +\ 6.99 \\ \hline \end{array}$$

Step 2: Place a decimal point in the answer line under the other decimal points.

$$\begin{array}{r} 85.38 \\ +\ 6.99 \\ \hline . \end{array}$$

Step 3: Add:

$$\begin{array}{r} 85.38 \\ +\ 6.99 \\ \hline 92.37 \end{array}$$

What if a number has no decimal point?
For example: Add 17 + 34.972
Just put a decimal point at the end of the whole number and write placeholder zeros.

$$\begin{array}{r} 17\mathbf{.000} \\ +\ 34.972 \\ \hline 51.972 \end{array}$$

Exercises **ADD**

1. $\begin{array}{r} 1.345 \\ +\ 2.34 \\ \hline \end{array}$

2. $\begin{array}{r} 7.772 \\ +\ 3.333 \\ \hline \end{array}$

3. $\begin{array}{r} 1.23 \\ +\ 0.123 \\ \hline \end{array}$

4. $\begin{array}{r} 12.35 \\ +\ 125.43 \\ \hline \end{array}$

5. $\begin{array}{r} 4.4224 \\ +\ 44.2442 \\ \hline \end{array}$

6. $\begin{array}{r} 53.111 \\ +\ 0.3341 \\ \hline \end{array}$

7. $\begin{array}{r} 0.251 \\ +\ 2.51 \\ \hline \end{array}$

8. $\begin{array}{r} 10.101 \\ +\ 0.990 \\ \hline \end{array}$

9. $\begin{array}{r} 11.1 \\ +\ 11.111 \\ \hline \end{array}$

10. $\begin{array}{r} 113.31 \\ +\ 31.113 \\ \hline \end{array}$

11. $\begin{array}{r} 345 \\ +\ 0.345 \\ \hline \end{array}$

12. $\begin{array}{r} 239.54 \\ +\ 23.454 \\ \hline \end{array}$

13. $\begin{array}{r} 525.525 \\ +\ 52.5525 \\ \hline \end{array}$

14. $\begin{array}{r} 101.55 \\ +\ 0.101 \\ \hline \end{array}$

15. Hailey is on the school track team. Her event is the triple jump. In her last meet the "hop" portion of her jump was 12.256 feet, the "skip" 11.114 feet, and the "jump" portion was 13.4455 feet. How far did she jump in total?

____

16. During a flight to the International Space Station, the space shuttle pilot had to conduct a mid-course correction by firing the shuttle's rockets three times lasting 12.354 seconds, 11.4538 seconds, and 9.7392 seconds. What is the total time the rockets were fired?

____

5.4

Name ____________________

Subtracting Decimals

Subtracting decimals is *just like* subtracting whole numbers. However, you must correctly line up the decimals. Write placeholder zeros if you need to.

Example: Subtract 173.29 − 97.6

Step 1: Line up the numbers. Make sure that the decimal points line up. Write placeholder zeros if you need to. Place a decimal point in the answer line under the other decimal points.

$$\begin{array}{r} 173.29 \\ -\ 97.6\mathbf{0} \\ \hline . \end{array}$$

Step 2: Subtract.

$$\begin{array}{r} 173.29 \\ -\ 97.6\mathbf{0} \\ \hline 75.69 \end{array}$$

See if you can figure out how to provide an answer for this exercise. Perform this subtraction: 62 − 11.73 If you added a decimal point and placeholder zeros to the whole number, you were correct!

$$\begin{array}{r} 62.\mathbf{00} \\ -\ 11.73 \\ \hline 50.27 \end{array}$$

Remember...

The value of a number does not change if you add a decimal point and placeholder zeros. Add as many placeholder zeros as you need in order to solve the problem.

Exercises **SUBTRACT**

1. $\begin{array}{r} 23.01 \\ -\ 22.99 \\ \hline \end{array}$

2. $\begin{array}{r} 113.525 \\ -\ 45.67 \\ \hline \end{array}$

3. $\begin{array}{r} 32.11 \\ -\ 11.99 \\ \hline \end{array}$

4. $\begin{array}{r} 10.25 \\ -\ 0.75 \\ \hline \end{array}$

5. $\begin{array}{r} 45.54 \\ -\ 33.522 \\ \hline \end{array}$

6. $\begin{array}{r} 14.6 \\ -\ 14.444 \\ \hline \end{array}$

7. $\begin{array}{r} 32.004 \\ -\ 11.01 \\ \hline \end{array}$

8. $\begin{array}{r} 222.3 \\ -\ 41.22 \\ \hline \end{array}$

9. $\begin{array}{r} 6.19 \\ -\ 4.334 \\ \hline \end{array}$

10. $\begin{array}{r} 8.565 \\ -\ 0.006 \\ \hline \end{array}$

11. $\begin{array}{r} 345.34 \\ -\ 53.678 \\ \hline \end{array}$

12. $\begin{array}{r} 53.7 \\ -\ 4.88 \\ \hline \end{array}$

13. Sergio's standing long jump measured 249.24 cm and Lori's measured 243.967 cm. How much farther did Sergio jump?

____

14. Landon has a piece of wooden trim that is 32.3 inches long and he needs 21.28 inches for a project. How much will he have left over?

____

Name ________________________________

Adding and Subtracting Money

You may not realize it, but you work with a great many decimals in your life.

Look at this problem: \$98.42 + \$11.79

American money is written in decimals. A dollar is divided into 100 hundredths, each of which is called "a cent." If something costs 11 dollars and 79 cents, it really costs 11 dollars + 79 hundredths of a dollar.

Adding and subtracting money is done *exactly* the same way as adding and subtracting decimals.

Example: Add \$98.42 + \$11.79

Step 1: Line up the decimals.

$$\begin{array}{r} \$\,98.42 \\ +\ \$\,11.79 \\ \hline \end{array}$$

Step 2: Add, just as you would any other decimals.

$$\begin{array}{r} \$\,98.42 \\ +\ \$\,11.79 \\ \hline \$\,110.21 \end{array}$$

Remember...

You can add placeholder zeros to money, too. Doing this does not change its value! For example, \$35 = \$35.**00**

Exercises ADD OR SUBTRACT

1. $\begin{array}{r} \$5 \\ +\ \$5.67 \\ \hline \end{array}$

2. $\begin{array}{r} \$3.45 \\ +\ \$133.56 \\ \hline \end{array}$

3. $\begin{array}{r} \$10.87 \\ +\ \$21.65 \\ \hline \end{array}$

4. $\begin{array}{r} \$11 \\ -\ \$4.55 \\ \hline \end{array}$

5. $\begin{array}{r} \$6.77 \\ -\ \$3.88 \\ \hline \end{array}$

6. $\begin{array}{r} \$12.30 \\ -\ \$\ 5.45 \\ \hline \end{array}$

7. $\begin{array}{r} \$20.50 \\ -\ \$15.39 \\ \hline \end{array}$

8. $\begin{array}{r} \$62.32 \\ -\ \$\ 7.54 \\ \hline \end{array}$

9. $\begin{array}{r} \$22.22 \\ +\ \$11.33 \\ \hline \end{array}$

10. $\begin{array}{r} \$65 \\ +\ \$33 \\ \hline \end{array}$

11. $\begin{array}{r} \$5.12 \\ +\ \$3.50 \\ \hline \end{array}$

12. $\begin{array}{r} \$71.42 \\ +\ \$36.54 \\ \hline \end{array}$

13. $\begin{array}{r} \$1000 \\ -\ \$312.80 \\ \hline \end{array}$

14. $\begin{array}{r} \$21.10 \\ -\ \$11.33 \\ \hline \end{array}$

15. $\begin{array}{r} \$2.25 \\ -\ \$0.30 \\ \hline \end{array}$

16. $\begin{array}{r} \$45.53 \\ -\ \$32.55 \\ \hline \end{array}$

17. $\begin{array}{r} \$12.30 \\ -\ \$11.98 \\ \hline \end{array}$

18. $\begin{array}{r} \$56 \\ -\ \$37.98 \\ \hline \end{array}$

19. $\begin{array}{r} \$33 \\ -\ \$12 \\ \hline \end{array}$

20. $\begin{array}{r} \$41.65 \\ -\ \$38.78 \\ \hline \end{array}$

5.6

Name ______________________

Estimating Decimal Sums and Differences

You can use rounding to estimate sums and differences of decimal numbers. However, you have to decide what rounding place to use. Sometimes, a problem will tell you. If it does not, round to the nearest whole number.

Example: Estimate 5.87 + 7.061

Step 1: Round 5.87 to the nearest whole number. 6

Step 2: Round 7.061 to the nearest whole number. 7

Step 3: Add: 6 + 7 = 13

The sum of 5.87 + 7.061 is *about* 13.

Example: 17.365 – 14.229 to the nearest tenth

Step 1: Round 17.365 to the nearest tenth. 17.4

Step 2: Round 14.229 to the nearest tenth. 14.2

Step 3: Subtract: 17.4 – 14.2 = 3.2

When estimating money, ask yourself: Is the cents part of each number closest to 0 dollars, to a $\frac{1}{2}$ dollar, or to a dollar?

Example: Estimate \$7.37 + \$9.89

Step 1: Ask yourself: Is \$7.37 closer to \$7.00, \$7.50, or \$8.00? \$7.50

Step 2: Ask yourself: Is \$9.89 closer to \$9.00, \$9.50, or \$10.00? \$10.00

Step 3: Add: \$7.50 + \$10.00 = \$17.50

Since you rounded *both* dollar amounts up, you know that your estimated total is *higher* than the actual total.

Exercises ESTIMATE

1. 44.55 + 5.67

2. 34.57 + 24.57

3. 75.55 − 9.45

4. 4.55 + 4.9

5. 9.6 − 3.5

6. \$7.82 + \$11.54

7. 12.78 − 11.6

8. \$34.89 − \$24.7

9. 54.55 − 7.65

10. \$15.4 − \$9.6

11. 12.78 + 77.34

12. 49.78 − 41.22

Name ______________________

5.7

Multiplying Decimals

Multiplying decimals and whole numbers is *exactly like* multiplying whole numbers—except for one important thing. You have to count the *total* decimal places in the numbers you multiply. When you multiply decimals, you do *not* have to line up the decimal points.

Example: Multiply 22.6 × 3.21
Then multiply 0.226 × 0.321

Step 1: Set up your multiplication exercise as you would any other multiplication exercise. Do *not* line up the decimal points.

$$\begin{array}{r} 22.6 \\ \times\ 3.21 \\ \hline \end{array} \qquad \begin{array}{r} 0.226 \\ \times\ 0.321 \\ \hline \end{array}$$

Step 2: Multiply. At this time, pay no attention to the decimal points.

$$\begin{array}{r} 22.6 \\ \times\ 3.21 \\ \hline 226 \\ 452\mathbf{0} \\ 678\mathbf{00} \\ \hline 72546 \end{array} \qquad \begin{array}{r} 0.226 \\ \times\ 0.321 \\ \hline 226 \\ 452\mathbf{0} \\ 678\mathbf{00} \\ \hline 72546 \end{array}$$

Step 3: Count the *total* number of decimal places in the **factors**. Factors are the numbers you multiplied. 22.6 has 1 decimal place. 3.21 has 2 decimal places. 1 + 2 = 3

Step 4: Starting at the right of the product and moving *left*, count off the same number of places. Then place your decimal point. The product of
22.6 × 3.21 = 72.546
(three decimal places)

Step 5: But what about 0.226 × 0.321? There are six decimal places in those factors, but only five places in the product. The answer is: You have to add enough zeros to make the *total* number of places in the product equal the total number of decimal places in the numbers you multiplied. Add the needed zeros *after* the decimal point.
So the product of
0.226 × 0.321 = 0.**0**72546
(six decimal places)

Remember...

A power of ten is the number of times you multiply by 10. Each column is 10 times the column to its right. For example:

1 × 10 = 10; 1 × 10 × 10 = 100;

1 × 10 × 10 × 10 = 1000

0.1 × 10 = 1; 0.01 × 10 = 0.1; 0.001 × 10 = 0.01

Here is a trick: If you multiply a whole number or a decimal by a power of ten that is greater than 1, move the decimal point 1 place to the right for each power of 10. If you need more places, add placeholder zeros at the end of the whole number. If you multiply by a power of 10 that is less than 1, move the decimal point one place to the left for each decimal place in the power of 10.

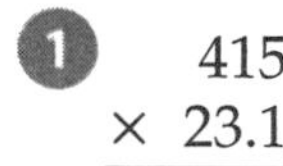

MULTIPLY

1. $\begin{array}{r} 415 \\ \times\ 23.1 \\ \hline \end{array}$

2. $\begin{array}{r} 7 \\ \times\ 7.77 \\ \hline \end{array}$

3. $\begin{array}{r} 324.56 \\ \times\ 54 \\ \hline \end{array}$

4. $\begin{array}{r} 10.01 \\ \times\ 11 \\ \hline \end{array}$

5. $\begin{array}{r} 3232 \\ \times\ 42.42 \\ \hline \end{array}$

Name ______________________

Multiplying Decimals (cont.)

6. $\begin{array}{r} 87.3 \\ \times\ 233 \\ \hline \end{array}$

7. $\begin{array}{r} 65.8 \\ \times\ 68 \\ \hline \end{array}$

8. $\begin{array}{r} 120 \\ \times\ 14.56 \\ \hline \end{array}$

9. $\begin{array}{r} 438 \\ \times\ 1.1 \\ \hline \end{array}$

10. $\begin{array}{r} 14.7 \\ \times\ 101 \\ \hline \end{array}$

11. $\begin{array}{r} 10.1 \\ \times\ 1.01 \\ \hline \end{array}$

12. $\begin{array}{r} 55.5 \\ \times\ 5.55 \\ \hline \end{array}$

13. $\begin{array}{r} 41.0 \\ \times\ 4.41 \\ \hline \end{array}$

14. $\begin{array}{r} 13.82 \\ \times\ 10.51 \\ \hline \end{array}$

15. $\begin{array}{r} 21.12 \\ \times\ 81.93 \\ \hline \end{array}$

16. $\begin{array}{r} 2.7 \\ \times\ 3.1 \\ \hline \end{array}$

17. $\begin{array}{r} 17.89 \\ \times\ 41.1 \\ \hline \end{array}$

18. $\begin{array}{r} 1.414 \\ \times\ 2.71 \\ \hline \end{array}$

19. $\begin{array}{r} 73.75 \\ \times\ 7.5 \\ \hline \end{array}$

20. $\begin{array}{r} 20.01 \\ \times\ 30.02 \\ \hline \end{array}$

21. $\begin{array}{r} 19.9 \\ \times\ 100 \\ \hline \end{array}$

22. $\begin{array}{r} 2.4 \\ \times\ 10 \\ \hline \end{array}$

23. $\begin{array}{r} 0.001 \\ \times\ 112.34 \\ \hline \end{array}$

24. $\begin{array}{r} 1.56 \\ \times\ 0.01 \\ \hline \end{array}$

25. $\begin{array}{r} 71.782 \\ \times\ 1000 \\ \hline \end{array}$

26. $\begin{array}{r} 76.76 \\ \times\ 1000 \\ \hline \end{array}$

27. $\begin{array}{r} 10 \\ \times\ 1.32 \\ \hline \end{array}$

28. $\begin{array}{r} 63.45 \\ \times\ 1000 \\ \hline \end{array}$

29. $\begin{array}{r} 13.45 \\ \times\ 0.0001 \\ \hline \end{array}$

30. $\begin{array}{r} 1111.111 \\ \times\ 0.01 \\ \hline \end{array}$

Name ______________________________

Multiplying Money

Since American money is expressed as a decimal, you multiply money exactly as you would multiply decimals. However, there are two important things to remember about multiplying money.

First, you *cannot* multiply money times money. You can only multiply money by a number. However, that number *can* be a decimal.

Second, the product will *always* be money. Therefore, you *always* have to round the product to the nearest hundredth.

Example: Multiply $1.35 × 2.75

Step 1: Set up your multiplication.

```
 $1.35
× 2.75
```

Step 2: Multiply.

```
 $1.35
× 2.75
   675
  9450
 27000
 37125
```

Step 3: Count the decimal places in your two numbers and add the decimal point to the product. 2 decimal places in $1.35 + 2 decimal places in 2.75 = 4 decimal places. So the product is 3.7125.

Step 4: Round the product to the nearest hundredth and add the dollar sign. $3.71

Exercises MULTIPLY

1. $10.45 × 2.50
2. $101.91 × 1.1
3. $5.76 × 3.75
4. $78.90 × 9.92
5. $7.29 × 5.5
6. $89.21 × 3
7. $67.50 × 6.75
8. $10.00 × 2.3
9. $5.50 × 11
10. $4.75 × 9.5
11. $85.30 × 5
12. $33.00 × 2.2
13. Petra needs to buy gasoline for her car. Gasoline costs $3.66 for a gallon, and she needs 6.75 gallons to fill her tank. How much money will Petra need to spend, in order to fill her tank?

    ____

14. Jerry is going to start a collection of marbles with the $5 he received for his weekly allowance. He wants at least 120 marbles to begin his collection. If each individual marble costs 4 cents, will he have enough money to buy 120?

    ____

5.9

Name ______________________________

Estimating Decimal Products

To estimate decimal products, round each number to its highest place value.

Examples: Estimate 121.9 × 0.352

Step 1: Round the first number to its highest place value: 121.9 rounds to 100

Step 2: Round the second number to its highest place value: 0.352 rounds to 0.4

Step 3: Multiply the rounded amounts: 100 × 0.4 = 40 (Did you notice that you could use the trick you learned in Lesson 10.1?)

So a fairly good estimate of 121.9 × 0.352 is 40.

Estimate $4.99 × 1.75

Step 1: Round the first number to its highest place. $4.99 rounds to 5

Step 2: Round the second number to its highest place value. 1.75 rounds to 2

Step 3: Multiply the rounded amounts. $5 × 2 = $10

Did you notice that you rounded both numbers upward? That means your estimate is *higher* than the actual product.

Exercises **ESTIMATE**

1. 23.01 × 8.1
2. $6.75 × 4.73
3. 101.51 × 4.5
4. 32.25 × 21.1
5. $2.25 × 49.999
6. 0.230 × 4.657
7. 10.501 × $5.43
8. 45.45 × 21.21
9. 57.35 × 0.499
10. 0.867 × $19.30
11. 0.75 × 25.43
12. 1.95 × 36.36
13. 23.986 × 11.111
14. 22.989 × $13.89
15. 1.8 × 1.982
16. 27.63 × $3.54
17. 10.1010 × 7.3
18. 7.75 × 4.1
19. 17.11 × 1.499
20. $19.45 × 1.73

Name ______________________________

5.10

Dividing Decimals by Whole Numbers

Dividing a decimal by a whole number is *exactly like* dividing whole numbers except that you have to know where to put the decimal point in your quotient.

If *only* the dividend has a decimal point, put the decimal point in exactly the same column in the quotient.

Example: Divide 25.8 ÷ 3

Step 1: Set up your division problem and put the decimal point in its proper place in the quotient.

$3\overline{)25.8}$ (decimal point placed in the quotient above the decimal point of the dividend)

Step 2: Divide.

$$\begin{array}{r} 8.6 \\ 3\overline{)25.8} \\ \underline{24} \\ 1\,8 \\ \underline{1\,8} \\ 0 \end{array}$$

Exercises **DIVIDE**

1. $2\overline{)10.1}$
2. $4\overline{)22.45}$
3. $10\overline{)78.25}$
4. $11\overline{)22.22}$
5. $8\overline{)7.75}$
6. $5\overline{)14.5}$
7. $20\overline{)77.8}$
8. $30\overline{)45.45}$
9. $6\overline{)104.0}$
10. $2\overline{)55.875}$
11. $4\overline{)101.56}$
12. $7\overline{)929.6}$

13. If a candy bar that is 3.75 inches long is divided equally among 3 children, how many inches will each child get?

    ____

14. One sandbag can hold only 25 pounds of sand, and Kalee has 26.3 pounds of sand. She knows she will need to divide it between 2 bags. If she puts the same amount in each bag, what will each bag weigh?

    ____

5.11

Name ______________________________

Dividing Whole Numbers by Decimals

Dividing a whole number by a decimal is also *exactly like* dividing whole numbers, except that you need to remember to multiply the divisor by the smallest power of 10 that will move the decimal point all the way to the right. Then multiply the dividend by that same power of 10.

Example: Divide 45 ÷ 0.24

Step 1: Multiply the divisor by the smallest power of 10 that will move the decimal point all the way to the right: 0.24 × 100 = 24

Step 2: Multiply the dividend by the same power of 10: 45 × 100 = 4500

Step 3: Set up your division and divide.

```
      187 R12
24)4500.0
   24
   210
   192
    180
    168
     12
```

Instead of leaving a remainder, you can put a decimal point at the end of the dividend and add as many placeholder zeros as you need. Then continue dividing, but don't forget to put the decimal point in the quotient, too!

```
      187.5
24)4500.0
   24
   210
   192
    180
    168
     120
     120
       0
```

Exercises DIVIDE AND ROUND TO THE NEAREST TENTH

1. 0.44)33
2. 0.2)521
3. 0.45)12
4. 0.1)453
5. 0.25)44
6. 0.56)21
7. 0.65)422
8. 0.05)200
9. 0.4)7
10. If Nick has a foot-long piece of wire and needs several pieces that are 1.4 inches long each, how many pieces can he cut from the wire?

____

Name ______________________________

Dividing Decimals by Decimals

If you know how to divide a whole number by a decimal, you also know how to divide a decimal by a decimal.

Multiply the divisor by the smallest power of 10 that will move the decimal point all the way to the right. Then multiply the dividend by that same power of 10.

Example: Divide $4.29 \div 3.3$

Step 1: Multiply the divisor by the smallest power of 10 that will move the decimal point all the way to the right: $3.3 \times 10 = 33$

Step 2: Multiply the dividend by the same power of 10: $4.29 \times 10 = 42.9$

Step 3: Set up your division problem. If there is a decimal point in the dividend, line up a decimal point in the same place in the quotient.

Step 4: Divide.

$$\begin{array}{r} 1.3 \\ 33\overline{)42.9} \\ \underline{33} \\ 99 \\ \underline{99} \\ 0 \end{array}$$

Exercises DIVIDE AND ROUND TO THE NEAREST HUNDREDTH

1. $0.44\overline{)0.22}$

2. $3.12\overline{)0.2}$

3. $0.56\overline{)0.33}$

4. $0.76\overline{)0.03}$

5. $0.89\overline{)0.4}$

6. $0.784\overline{)0.08}$

7. Olga bought 3.75 pounds of candy that she will place in small boxes and give to her classmates at summer school. If each box holds 0.35 pounds of candy, how many boxes will she be able to fill?

   ____

8. Omar and his friends are getting ready to go for a hike. Omar buys 21.2 liters of water to fill 17 canteens. If each canteen holds 1.3 liters, will Omar be able to fill all 17 canteens?

   ____

5.13

Name ____________________

Dividing Money

You know that American money can be expressed as a decimal. You divide money *exactly the same way* you would divide any other kind of decimal. The only thing you need to remember is: If you're dividing with money, money *must* be in your dividend, and in your quotient. The divisor might be money, or it might not. Since your quotient is money, it should always be rounded to the nearest hundredth.

You might want to divide a restaurant check by the number of people dining to find out what each person owes.

Three people ate lunch and the total came to $37.77 including the tip. How much should each person pay?

Step 1: Set up your division exercise. If there is a decimal point in the dividend, line up a decimal point in the same place in the quotient.

$$3\overline{)37.77}$$

Step 2: Divide:

$$\begin{array}{r} 12.59 \\ 3\overline{)37.77} \\ \underline{3} \\ 7 \\ \underline{6} \\ 17 \\ \underline{15} \\ 27 \\ \underline{27} \\ 0 \end{array}$$

Exercises DIVIDE

1. $3\overline{)\$1.35}$
2. $4\overline{)\$10.00}$
3. $10.1\overline{)\$56.45}$
4. $0.8\overline{)\$27.95}$
5. $17\overline{)\$97.28}$
6. $2.5\overline{)\$21.25}$
7. $23\overline{)\$181.47}$
8. $8\overline{)\$774.35}$
9. $10.5\overline{)\$85.05}$

10. Grandma has $225.75 that she wants to divide equally between her 3 grandchildren. How much will each child receive?

____

11. Amee borrowed $2052 from her parents to buy a car. If she pays them $258 per month, how many months will it take for her to pay them back completely?

____

12. The four kids in the Espinal family cashed in their jar of pennies for a total of $312.48. If they divide the money evenly between them, how much does each kid get?

____

Name ______________________________

Estimating Decimal Quotients

How do you estimate a quotient when the dividend, the divisor, or both contain decimals? The easy answer is to forget about the decimals! There are two ways to do that. The first way is just to drop the decimals, and then round.

Example: Estimate 35.89 ÷ 6.1

Step 1: Drop the decimals: 35 ÷ 6

Step 2: Find compatible numbers: 35 cannot be divided by 6, but 36 can.

Step 3: Divide: 36 ÷ 6 = 6

So a fairly good estimate of 35.89 ÷ 6.1 is 6.

The second way is to round first, *then* drop the decimals. Estimating this way will often make your estimate better.

Example: Estimate 49.83 ÷ 4.76

Step 1: Round both numbers to the nearest whole number. 49.83 rounds to 50 and 4.76 rounds to 5.

Step 2: Divide the rounded numbers: 50 ÷ 5 = 10

Notice that if you had estimated 49.83 ÷ 4.76 using the first method, you would have dropped the decimals and started with 49 ÷ 4. Your estimated answer would have been 12. The actual quotient of 49.83 ÷ 4.76 is about 10.47. Which method of estimating was closer to the actual value?

Exercises ESTIMATE

1. 14.6 ÷ 1.2
2. 24.4 ÷ 8
3. 9.1 ÷ 9
4. 39.9 ÷ 13
5. 41.2 ÷ 25
6. 132.1 ÷ 13
7. 44.73 ÷ 9
8. 6.72 ÷ 3.3
9. 4.41 ÷ 0.91
10. 25.2 ÷ 2.3
11. 49.3 ÷ 4
12. 32.11 ÷ 8.0
13. 12.47 ÷ 5.0
14. 33.33 ÷ 1.6
15. 56.4 ÷ 11
16. 23.53 ÷ 2.0
17. 88.97 ÷ 4.5
18. 48.94 ÷ 2.4
19. 77 ÷ 5.3
20. 73.2 ÷ 9.4

6.1

Name ______________________

Understanding Percent

Notice that the word *percent* has the smaller word *cent* in it. You know cent from dealing with money. Every dollar can be divided into 100 hundredths. Therefore, it probably will not surprise you that *cent* means *hundredth*. *Per* means *by*. A **percent** is a particular kind of ratio that is used to compare numbers to hundredths.

The % sign is used to identify percents. However, a percent is really a decimal that goes to the hundredths place. A percent can also be expressed as a fraction, with 100 as the denominator.

Examples: $1\% = 0.01 = \frac{1}{100}$ $25\% = 0.25 = \frac{25}{100}$

Remember...

Every percentage can be displayed as a percentage, a decimal, or a fraction with a denominator of 100.

Exercises WRITE DECIMALS AND FRACTIONS

1. 45% = ______ (decimal) = ______ (fraction)
2. 35% = ______ (decimal) = ______ (fraction)
3. 43% = ______ (decimal) = ______ (fraction)
4. 10% = ______ (decimal) = ______ (fraction)
5. 87% = ______ (decimal) = ______ (fraction)
6. 2% = ______ (decimal) = ______ (fraction)
7. 59% = ______ (decimal) = ______ (fraction)
8. 0.1% = ______ (decimal) = ______ (fraction)
9. 0.45% = ______ (decimal) = ______ (fraction)
10. Out of 100 questions, Yoshi answered 76 questions correct on his math exam. What percentage of questions did Yoshi answer correctly?

    ____

11. Emily is dividing her birthday cake among 10 people. If each person receives an equal 10% of the cake, how could Emily use fractions to express a single piece of cake? How could she use decimals to express a single piece of cake?

    ____

Name ______________________________

Percents and Fractions

Since percents are ratios, you can change them to fractions. The denominator will be 100. The numerator will be the number in front of the percent sign.

Examples:

What is 40% of 50?

Step 1: Convert the percent to a fraction.

$40\% = \frac{40}{100}$

Step 2: Simplify the fraction if you can.

$\frac{40}{100} = \frac{2}{5}$

Step 3: Multiply $\frac{2}{5} \times 50 = \frac{100}{5}$

Step 4: Simplify the product. $\frac{100}{5} = \frac{20}{1} = 20$

You can also change fractions to percents. $\frac{3}{4} = ?\ \%$

Step 1: Divide 100 by the denominator.

$100 \div 4 = 25$

Step 2: Multiply the numerator by the product.

$3 \times 25 = 75$

Step 3: Add the percent sign. $\frac{3}{4} = 75\%$

Remember...

Some fractions *cannot* be changed easily to percents. If 100 cannot be divided evenly by the fraction's denominator, you will not be able to convert that fraction to a percent.

Exercises CONVERT

Convert the percent to a fraction and reduce where possible.

1. 35%
2. 47%
3. 25%
4. 6%
5. 91%
6. 52.3%
7. 2.05%
8. 17%
9. 49.5%
10. 0.1%

Convert the fraction to a percent. Round to two digits to the right of the decimal.

11. $\frac{7}{20}$
12. $\frac{3}{10}$
13. $\frac{3}{5}$

14. One-fourth of Mr. Castanon's biology class made an A on the final exam. What percent of the class made an A on the final exam?

____

15. Bradley got 9 questions out of 10 on the final exam correct. What percent did he miss?

____

6.3

Name ______________________

Percents and Decimals

Because percents are really hundredths, a percent can always be changed to a decimal. But be careful!

Examples:

Change 3% to a decimal.

Step 1: Think: 3% = 3 hundredths.

Step 2: Write the correct decimal: 3% = 0.03

Decimals can also be changed to percents. The easiest way to do this is to move the decimal point two places to the right and add the percent sign.

Change 0.3925 to a percent.

Step 1: Move the decimal point two places to the right. 39.25

Step 2: Add the percent sign. So 0.3925 = 39.25%

Exercises CONVERT

Convert the percent to a decimal. Round to four digits to the right of the decimal.

1. 10%
2. 67%
3. 0.02%
4. 96.4%
5. 55.32%
6. 1110.01%
7. 23.456%
8. 0.075%
9. 34%
10. 1003%

Convert the decimal to a percent. Round to two decimal places to the right of the decimal.

11. 0.03
12. 1.02
13. 0.0027
14. 0.025
15. 100.01
16. 0.145
17. 0.0101
18. 0.125
19. 0.0825
20. 0.009

Name ____________________

6.4

Multiplying Percents and Fractions

Since percents can be expressed as fractions, they can be multiplied as if they were fractions.

When finding a percent of a fraction, the answer will be a *fraction*.

Examples:

What is 24% of $\frac{5}{6}$?

Step 1: Change the percent to a fraction.

$24\% = \frac{24}{100}$

Step 2: Simplify the fraction if you can.

$\frac{24}{100} = \frac{6}{25}$

Step 3: Multiply the fractions. $\frac{6}{25} \times \frac{5}{6} = \frac{30}{150}$

Step 4: Simplify the product. $\frac{30}{150} = \frac{1}{5}$

Step 5: So 24% of $\frac{5}{6} = \frac{1}{5}$

When multiplying a fraction by a percent, the answer will be a *percent.*

Multiply: $\frac{2}{7} \times 35\%$

Step 1: Change the percent to a fraction. $\frac{35}{100}$

Step 2: Simplify the fraction if you can. $\frac{7}{20}$

Step 3: Multiply the fractions. $\frac{2}{7} \times \frac{7}{20} = \frac{14}{140}$

Step 4: Simplify the product. $\frac{14}{140} = \frac{1}{10}$

Step 5: Change the fraction to a percent. 10%

Exercises MULTIPLY

Give the answer as a fraction.

1. 35% of $\frac{1}{6}$
2. 22% of $\frac{6}{7}$
3. 25% of $\frac{1}{4}$
4. 78% of $\frac{4}{5}$
5. 4% of $\frac{2}{3}$
6. 56% of $\frac{3}{7}$
7. 37% of $\frac{3}{13}$
8. 51% of $\frac{1}{8}$
9. 44% of $\frac{4}{9}$
10. 10% of $\frac{3}{17}$

Give the answer as a percent.

11. $\frac{3}{5}$ of 20%
12. $\frac{1}{11}$ of 33%
13. $\frac{3}{4}$ of 88%
14. $\frac{2}{3}$ of 66%
15. $\frac{1}{8}$ of 80%

Name ______________________________

Understanding Exponents

An **exponent** tells how many times a number should be multiplied by itself. An exponent is usually written as a small number next to and slightly above a number that is larger in size. The larger number is called the **base of an exponent**. Each exponent represents a "power." You have already learned about the powers of 10. 10^4 is 10 to the 4th power. Any number can be a base. 2^5 is 2 to the 5th power. 3^3 is 3 to the 3rd power.

exponent exponent exponent exponent

2^5 4^2 10^4 3^3

$2^5 = 2 \times 2 \times 2 \times 2 \times 2 = 32$

$4^2 = 4 \times 4 = 16$

$10^4 = 10 \times 10 \times 10 \times 10 = 10{,}000$

$3^3 = 3 \times 3 \times 3 = 27$

Often, when the exponent is 2, people say "squared" instead of to the 2nd power. 4^2 = 4 to the 2nd power = 4 squared. Remember that squared means "to the 2nd power."

You can add or subtract numbers with exponents.

Example: $3^4 - 5^2$

Step 1: Find the value of the first **exponential expression**:
$3^4 = 3 \times 3 \times 3 \times 3 = 81$

Step 2: Find the value of the second exponential expression:
$5^2 = 5 \times 5 = 25$

Step 3: Calculate: $81 - 25 = 56$

Exercises FIND THE VALUE

1. 2^3
2. 5^2
3. 12^3
4. 4^3
5. 12^2
6. 2.5^2
7. 10^3
8. 7^4
9. 1.2^2
10. 5^4
11. 3^5
12. $(0.01)^2$
13. 2^7
14. $(0.05)^3$
15. 10^5
16. $(1.1)^2$
17. 7^3
18. 25^2
19. 30^3
20. $(0.002)^3$

21. Jasper was planning to hand out flyers to his friends to spread the word about an upcoming charity event. He wanted to give his six friends enough flyers for them to each give a flyer to six of their own friends. How many flyers will Jasper need?

____

22. Oren's dad offered him a choice of $13.00 total to buy eight newspapers, or 4 cents for the first newspaper, 8 cents for the second newspaper, 16 cents for the third newspaper, and so on up to the eighth newspaper. Which choice of payment should Oren take? Why?

____

Name ____________________

Scientific Notation

Scientific notation is a way to express any number as a decimal greater than 1, multiplied by a power of 10. For example: 3500 can be expressed as 3.5×10^3 and 4,230,000 can be expressed as 4.23×10^6.

How do you find which power of ten to use? Look at the number in standard, or regular, notation. If the number does not have a decimal, put one at the far right of the number. You want to move the decimal left or right until you create a number that is greater than 1 but less than 10. Count the number of places you had to move the decimal to do that. If you moved the decimal to the left, the power will be positive. If you moved the decimal to the right, the power will be negative.

Remember...

When dropping zeros in a decimal, you may *not* drop any zero that has a number anywhere to its *right.* For example: In 4.00010, you may drop the final zero, but you may *not* drop the zeros between the 4 and the 1.

Examples:

Express 5300 in scientific notation.

Step 1: Place a decimal at the far right, then move the decimal to the left until you have a number between 1 and 10. You should get 5.300.

Step 2: Count how many places you moved the decimal. In this case, 3 places to the left. This means the power will be positive.

Step 3: Drop the zeros at the end of the number and write the answer in scientific notation. The answer is 5.3×10^3.

Express 0.0278 in scientific notation.

Step 1: Since the number already has a decimal, move the decimal to the right until you have a number between 1 and 10. You should get 2.78.

Step 2: Count how many places you moved the decimal. In this case, 2 places to the right. This means the power will be negative.

Step 3: Write the answer in scientific notation. The answer is 2.78×10^{-2}.

Exercises CONVERT TO SCIENTIFIC NOTATION

Round to six decimal places to the right of the decimal.

1. 125
2. 7453
3. 0.0254
4. 37
5. 0.00457
6. 1,222,333
7. 898
8. 45.32
9. 190.325
10. 13,023
11. 5.567
12. 72.354
13. 4777.77
14. 0.02002
15. 233.323
16. 5672

Name ______________________________

Order of Operations

There are rules for which computations you do first, second, third, and so on. **Order of operations** is the set of rules that tells you what steps to follow when doing a computation. The order of operations is PEMDAS. These letters stand for:

Parentheses

Exponents

Multiplication and **D**ivision

Addition and **S**ubtraction

Example:

$30 - 4 \times 6 + 12 \div 2^2 - (5 - 2) = ?$

We need to solve this problem using the **order of operations.**

Step 1: Solve the parts that are inside **parentheses.** $(5 - 2) = 3$

Now you have this: $30 - 4 \times 6 + 12 \div 2^2 - 3 = 7$

Step 2: Rename the parts that have **exponents** in standard notation. $2^2 = 4$

So now you have: $30 - 4 \times 6 + 12 \div 4 - 3 = ?$

Step 3: Solve **multiplication** problems. $4 \times 6 = 24$

The string is slowly becoming shorter!

Now you have $30 - 24 + 12 \div 4 - 3 = ?$

Step 4: Work any **division** problems. $12 \div 4 = 3$

Again, this problem is starting to look even simpler. $30 - 24 + 3 - 3 = ?$

Step 5: **Add** and **subtract** as you move along from left to right.

First, $30 - 24 = 6$. Then $6 + 3 = 9$. Then $9 - 3 = 6$.

Do not group the additions separately from the subtractions, unless they are in parentheses!
Answer: $30 - (24 + 3) - 3 = 0$

Remember...

You can remember PEMDAS best if you make up a phrase. Here is one that may help: **P**eople **E**at **M**any **D**esserts **A**fter **S**chool!

Exercises SOLVE

1. $5 - (4 - 3) + 5 \times 4$
2. $(3 \times 2)^2 \times 2 - 2 + 4$
3. $(3 + 2)^2 \times 4 - 3 + \frac{4}{2}$
4. $5 - 7 + 4 \times 2 - 3$
5. $55 - 2 \times \frac{3}{2} - 10^2$
6. $(2 + 3 + 4)^{3 - 1}$
7. $(2 - 2)^2 + (4 - 2)^2$
8. $(3 - 4) + 3^2 \times 3 + 2$
9. $4 \times (11 - 7) - (44 + 28)$

Name ______________________________

8.1

Plotting Ordered Pairs

The figure on the right is a **grid**. A grid has a horizontal axis, known as the *x*-axis, and a vertical axis, known as the *y*-axis. All points on a grid can be expressed, or identified, by two numbers: the *x*-coordinate, which indicates where the point is located on the *x*-axis and the *y*-coordinate, which indicates where the point is located on the *y*-axis. Each point is identified using the *x* and *y* coordinates in an **ordered pair**.

The point where the vertical and horizontal axes meet is the **origin**. The origin is identified by the ordered pair (0, 0). The *x*-coordinate indicates how far the point is to the right (positive) or to the left (negative) of the origin. The *y*-coordinate indicates how far the point is above (positive) or below (negative) the origin.

Example:

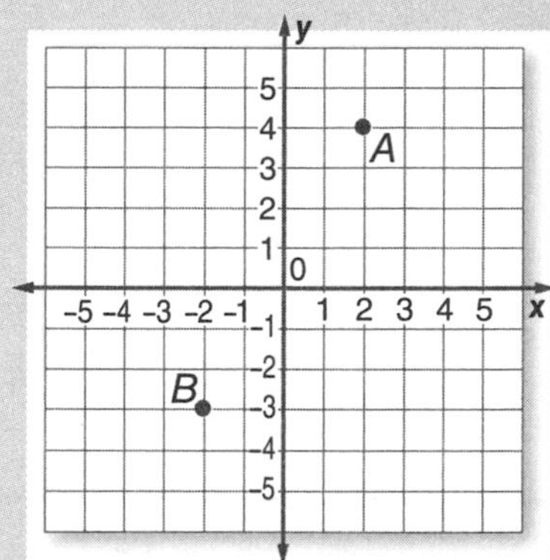

To find the *x*-coordinate, move your finger along the *x*-axis to the point. To find the *y*-coordinate, move your finger along the *y*-axis to the point. To identify the ordered pair, put the two coordinates in parentheses—the first number is the *x*-coordinate and the second number is the *y*-coordinate. In this figure, point A can be expressed as A (2, 4) and point B can be expressed as B (−2, −3).

Exercises GIVE ORDERED PAIRS

1 Give the ordered pair for each point on the graph.

A __________ B __________

C __________ D __________

E __________ F __________

G __________ H __________

I __________ J __________

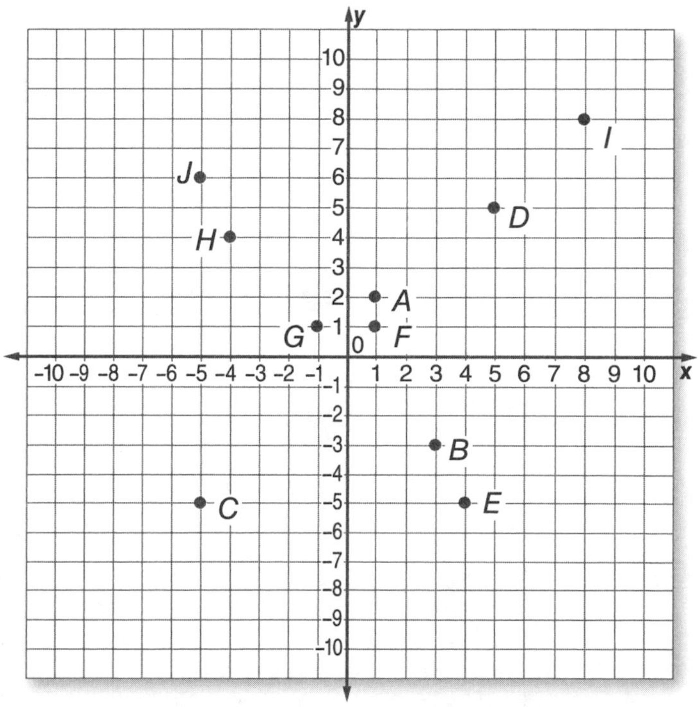

Name ______________________________

Exercises PLOT ORDERED PAIRS

Plot the ordered pairs on the graph.

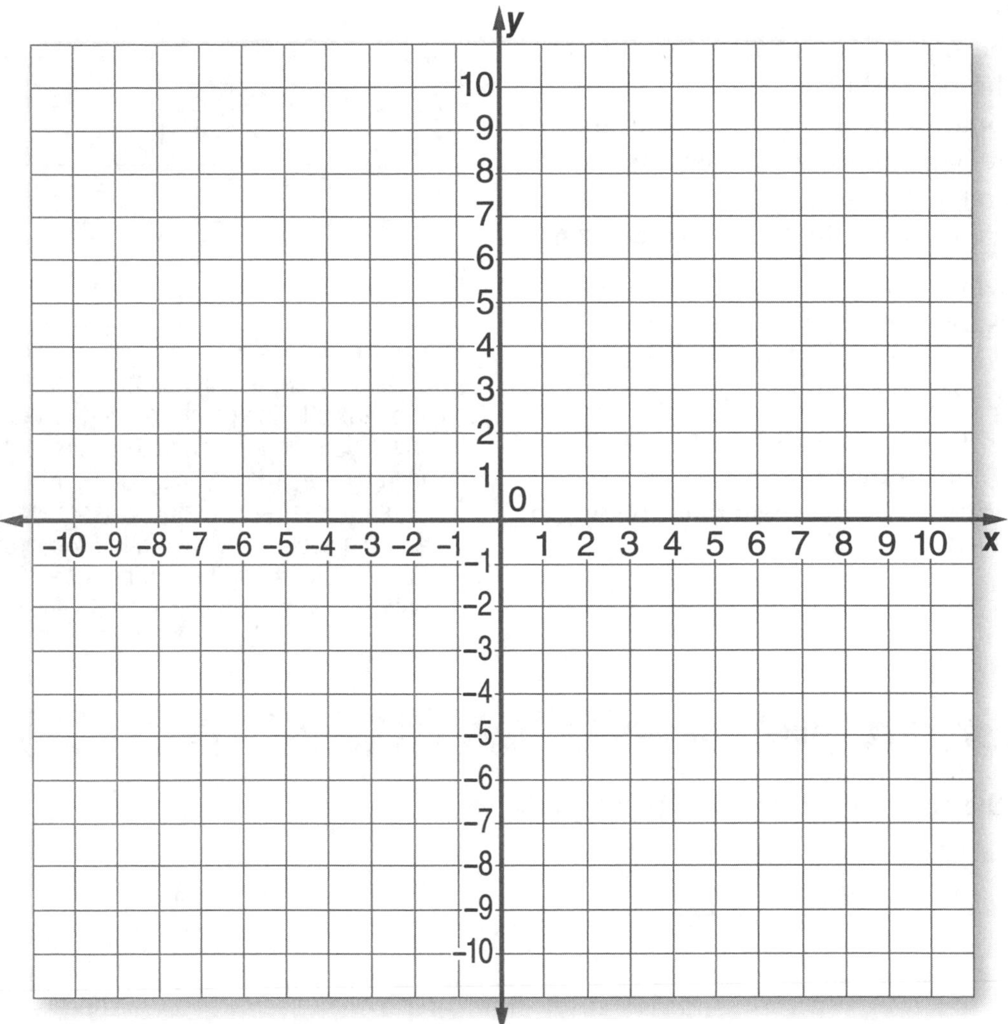

1. A (2, 3)
2. B (4, −4)
3. C (4, 4)
4. D (−4, 4)
5. E (−4, −4)
6. F (5, 2)
7. G (8, 2)
8. H (8, 6)
9. J (−5, 6)
10. K (3, −4)
11. L (−2, −2)

Name ____________________

Distance

To find the distance between two points on a graph that have the same x-coordinate, subtract the smaller y-coordinate from the larger, or count how many boxes on the grid there are in between the two points on the grid.

Example:

The distance between point A (2, 1) and point B (2, 4) is 3 because $4 - 1 = 3$.

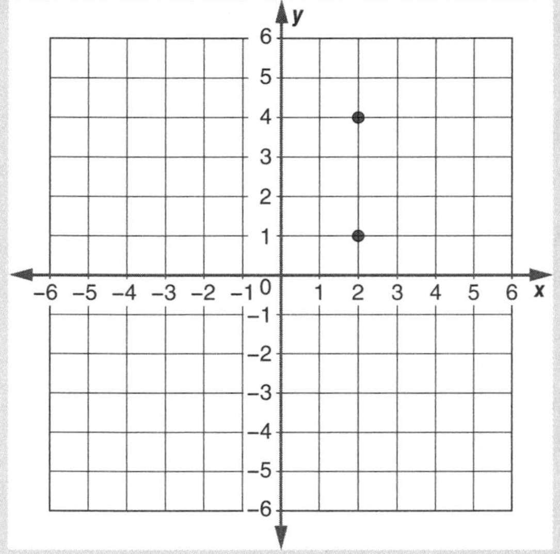

To find the distance between two points on a graph that have the same y-coordinate, subtract the smaller x-coordinate from the larger, or count how many boxes on the grid there are in between the two points on the grid.

Example:

The distance between point A (–3, 1) and point B (1, 1) is 4 because $1 - (-3) = 1 + 3 = 4$.

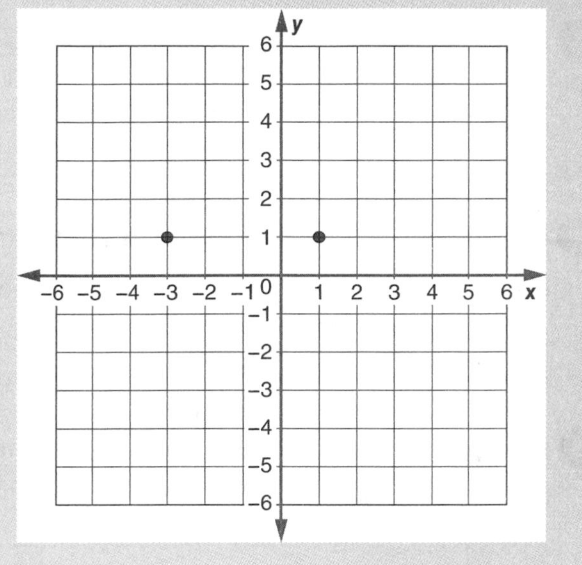

Exercises FIND THE DISTANCE BETWEEN THE POINTS

1. (2, 5) and (2, 8) ____________________
2. (–2, 1) and (–2, 3) ____________________
3. (1, –4) and (1, 1) ____________________
4. (3, 2) and (6, 2) ____________________
5. (2, 3) and (–2, 3) ____________________
6. (–4, –1) and (3, –1) ____________________

Unit 1 Test

Name ______________________________

Round.

1. Round 567,893.546 to the nearest hundredth. ______________________

2. Round 495,679.559 to the nearest ten thousand. ______________________

3. Principal Haines is planning for the school's upcoming academic year. There are 335 students in Grade 6, 407 in Grade 7, and 298 in Grade 8. How many students are in Principal Haines's middle school?

   ____

4. If Principal Haines wanted to lower the class size to 23 students in each class, how many classes will she have in Grade 6? ____________

   Grade 7? ____________ Grade 8? ____________
   (Count the remainder as another class.)

5. Last year Todd had 435 stamps in his stamp collection. This year Todd added 76 more. How many stamps does he have in his collection now?

   ____

6. Eurydice's favorite book has 47 chapters. Each chapter averages 17 pages in length. About how many pages are in the book? ____________

   How many pages exactly? ______________________

7. Matthew owes his mother $7.00. He borrows another $2.00 from her, then earns $12.00 for babysitting. After he pays his mother back everything he owes her, how much does he have left? ______________________

   ____

8. During the latest census, in 2000, the estimated population of the United States was two hundred seventy-four million, nine hundred forty-three thousand, four hundred ninety-six. What is the standard form of that number?

   ____

   The results of the 2010 Census are expected to show an increase of 30,500,950 in the population estimate. What is the new estimated population of the United States written in standard form?

   ____

   In expanded form? ______________________________

   ____

Name ______________________________

Unit 1 Test

Find all the factors.

9. 24

10. 7

11. What is the least common multiple of 6 and 32?

____

12. What is the greatest common factor of 8 and 60?

____

Absolute value.

13. $|-17.34| =$ __________

14. Which is greater: $|7|$ or $|-8|$? _______

Change to mixed numbers.

15. $\frac{85}{17}$ __________

16. $8\frac{6}{7}$ __________

17. $\frac{3}{7} + \frac{4}{5}$ __________

18. $\frac{14}{25} - \frac{12}{29}$ __________

19. $\frac{9}{4} \times 60$ __________

20. $\frac{2}{3} \times 4\frac{4}{9}$ __________

21. $\frac{3}{4} \div \frac{14}{25}$ __________

22. $15\frac{3}{5} \div 2\frac{1}{5}$ __________

Convert decimals to fractions.

23. $0.625 =$ ______

24. $\frac{4}{15} =$ ________

Put the decimals in order from greatest to least.

25. 0.22, 0.45, 0.76, 0.765, 0.43, 0.432, 0.226, 0.89

____

Unit 1 Test

Name ______________________

Add or subtract.

26
$$\begin{array}{r} 0.564 \\ 0.667 \\ +\ 0.35832 \\ \hline \end{array}$$

27
$$\begin{array}{r} 1.476 \\ -\ 0.78334 \\ \hline \end{array}$$

28 Jamie went to the store to buy lunch for his 6 friends. For each friend, he spent \$4.75 for a sandwich, \$1.25 for a cold beverage, and \$.56 for a piece of fruit. How much did he spend in total to buy lunch for his friends?

____

Calculate.

29 $0.025\overline{)0.545}$

30 Theo and his drama club raised a total of \$1563.75 for the local Boys and Girls Club. There are 15 people in the drama club. How much, per person, did the drama club raise? ______________________

31 What is $\frac{3}{4}$ of 240%? ______________________

32 What is 23% of 0.605? ______________________

Restate in exponential form, then calculate.

33 $2 \times 2 \times 2 \times 2 + 3 \times 3 \times 3$ ______________________

34 $4 \times 4 \times 4 \times 4 - 5 \times 5 \times 5$ ______________________

35 $2 \times 2 \times 2 \times 2 \times 2 \times 2 + 6 \times 6 - 5 \times 5$ ______________________

Restate using scientific notation.

36 3,456,984.01 ______________________

37 8694.1 ______________________

38 0.00945 ______________________

39 1,094,659,041 ______________________

40 63.56 ______________________

Name ______________________________

Unit 1 Test

Calculate using order of operations (PEMDAS).

41 $3 \times (6 - 4)^2 + (15 - 5) \times 5 + (5 - 3) \times 4 + 3^3$ ______________________________

42 $17 - (9 + 5) + (5 - 3) \times 2 + (9 - 4)^2$ ______________________________

43 $24 + (3 + 5) \times 5 + (6 - 3)^2$ ______________________________

44 $33 - (4 - 2)^3 + 6 \times 2 + (5)^2 - 3$ ______________________________

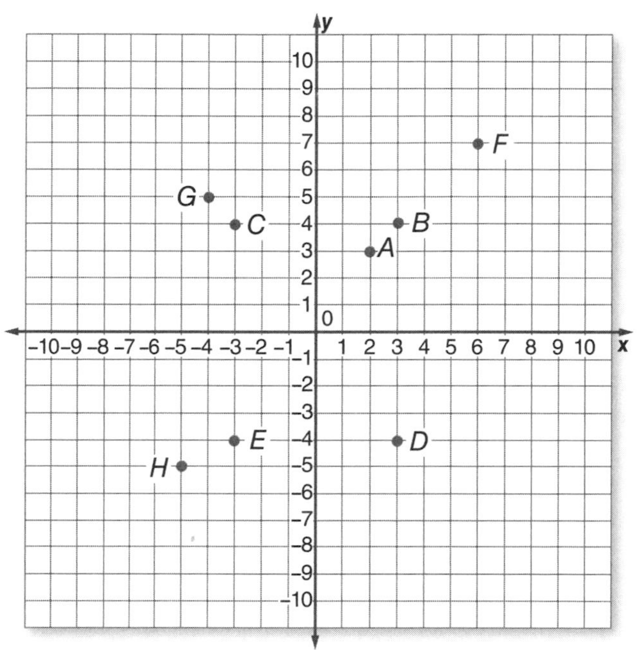

Provide the ordered pairs for the points plotted on the graph.

45 A __________ 46 D __________ 47 E __________ 48 G __________

49 Plot the following points on the grid provided.

A (4, 4)

B (8, 4)

C (8, 7)

D (−5, 5)

E (−3, −8)

F (4, −7)

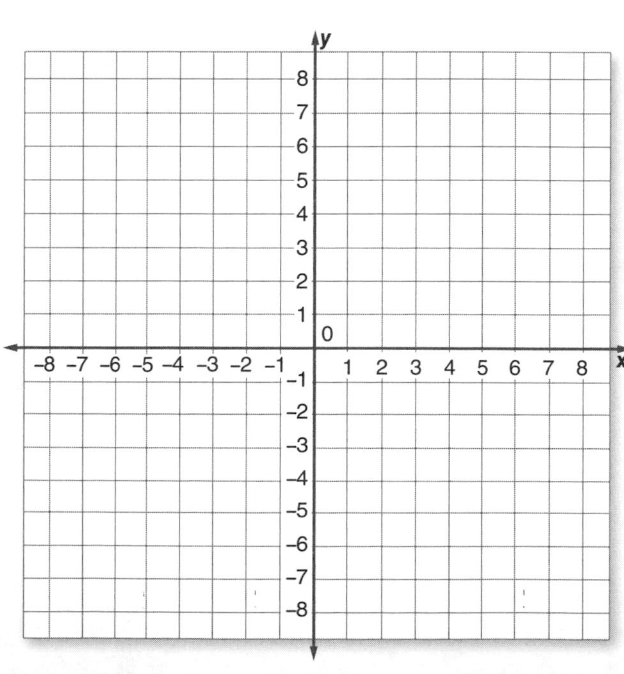

50 What is the distance between the coordinate points (3, 6) and (3, 14)?

Unit 1 Test

Name ______________________________

Answers and Explanations

1. 567,893.55
2. 500,000
3. 1040 students
4. 15; 18; 13
5. 511 stamps
6. About 1000 pages; 799
7. $3.00
8. 274,943,496; 305,444,446; $(3 \times 100{,}000{,}000) + (5 \times 1{,}000{,}000) + (4 \times 100{,}000) + (4 \times 10{,}000) + (4 \times 1000) + (4 \times 100) + (4 \times 10) + (6 \times 1)$
9. 1, 2, 3, 4, 6, 8, 12, 24
10. 1, 7
11. 96 The easiest way is to find the multiples of 32: 32, 64, 96 … and find the smallest one divisible by 6: 32 and 64 are not, but 96 is.
12. 4 factors of 8: 1, 2, 4, 8; factors of 60: 1, 2, 3, 4, 5, 6, 10, 12, 15, 20, 30, 60; GCF:4
13. 17.34 $|-17.34| = 17.34$
14. $|-8|$ $7 < 8$
15. 5 $85 \div 17 = 5$
16. $\frac{62}{7}$ $\frac{(8 \times 7) + 6}{7} = \frac{62}{7}$
17. $1\frac{8}{35}$ $\frac{3}{7} + \frac{4}{5} = \frac{15}{35} + \frac{28}{35} = \frac{43}{35} = 1\frac{8}{35}$
18. $\frac{106}{725}$ $\frac{14}{25} - \frac{12}{29} = \frac{406}{725} - \frac{300}{725} = \frac{106}{725}$
19. 135 $\frac{9}{\cancel{4}_1} \times \frac{\cancel{60}^{15}}{1} = 135$
20. $2\frac{26}{27}$ $\frac{2}{3} \times \frac{40}{9} = \frac{80}{27} = 2\frac{26}{27}$
21. $1\frac{19}{56}$ $\frac{3}{4} \div \frac{14}{25} = \frac{3}{4} \times \frac{25}{14} = \frac{75}{56} = 1\frac{19}{56}$
22. $7\frac{1}{11}$ $\frac{78}{5} \div \frac{11}{5} = \frac{78}{\cancel{5}_1} \times \frac{\cancel{5}^1}{11} = \frac{78}{11} = 7\frac{1}{11}$
23. $\frac{5}{8}$ $\frac{625}{1000} = \frac{25}{40} = \frac{5}{8}$
24. 0.2667

```
     0.266
15)4.000
   30↓
   100
    90↓
    100
     90
     10
```

25. 0.89, 0.765, 0.76, 0.45, 0.432, 0.43, 0.226, 0.22
26. 1.58932

```
   11
   0.564
   0.667
 + 0.35832
   1.58932
```

27. 0.69266

```
    3 1 5 9 1
  1.4 7 6 0 0
 -0.7 8 3 3 4
  0.6 9 2 6 6
```

28. $39.36

```
 11
 4.75      33
 1.25     6.56
+0.56    × 0.6
 6.56    39.36
```

29. 21.8 $\frac{545}{25} = 21.8$
30. $104.25

```
     104.25
15)1563.75
   15
    63
    60
     37
     30
      75
      75
       0
```

31. 180% $\frac{3}{4} \times 240 = \frac{720}{4} = 180\%$
32. 0.13915

```
   1
  0.605 } 5 decimal places
   0.23
   1815
  12100
0.13915 ←
```

33. $2^4 + 3^3 = 43$ $\quad 2^4 + 3^3 = 16 + 27 = 43$

34. $4^4 - 5^3 = 131$ $\quad 4^4 - 5^3 = 256 - 125 = 131$

35. $2^6 + 6^2 - 5^2 = 75$ $\quad 2^6 + 6^2 - 5^2 = 64 + 36 - 25 = 100 - 25 = 75$

36. 3.45698401×10^6 the decimal moves 6 places to the left

37. 8.6941×10^3 the decimal moves 3 places to the left

38. 9.45×10^{-3} the decimal moves 3 places to the right

39. 1.094659041×10^9 the decimal moves 9 places to the left

40. 6.356×10^1 the decimal moves 1 place to the left

41. 97 $\quad 3 \times 2^2 + 10 \times 5 + 2 \times 4 + 3^3 = 3 \times 4 + 10 \times 5 + 2 \times 4 + 27 = 12 + 50 + 8 + 27 = 97$

42. 32 $\quad 17 - 14 + 2 \times 2 + 5^2 = 17 - 14 + 2 \times 2 + 25 = 17 - 14 + 4 + 25 = 3 + 4 + 25 = 32$

43. 73 $\quad 24 + 8 \times 5 + 3^2 = 24 + 8 \times 5 + 9 = 24 + 40 + 9 = 73$

44. 59 $\quad 33 - 2^3 + 6 \times 2 + 5^2 - 3 = 33 - 8 + 6 \times 2 + 25 - 3 = 33 - 8 + 12 + 25 - 3 = 59$

45. (2, 3)

46. (3. –4)

47. (–3, –4)

48. (–4, 5)

49.

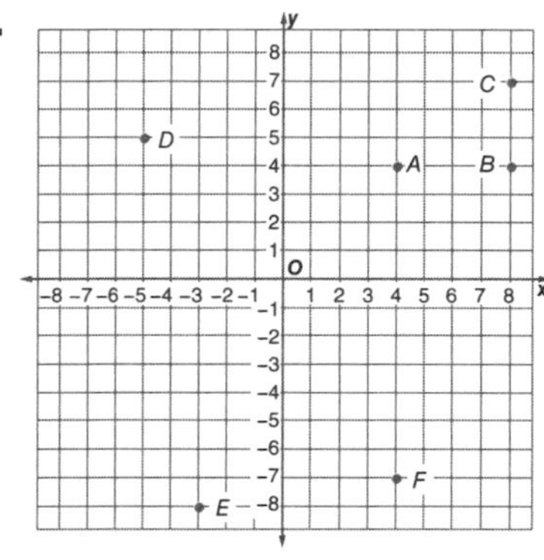

50. 8 $\quad 14 - 6 = 8$

Name ______________________

Understanding Variable Expressions

Sometimes you want to solve a problem to find an unknown number. The unknown number is called a **variable**. Variables are usually expressed as letters. Variables are used with numbers and symbols in **algebra**, a kind of math used to find the value of unknowns. An **algebraic expression** is a group of letters, numbers, and operations.

Examples:	$n + 19$	$(p - 72) \times 3$
$(36 \div g) + 9$	$\frac{b}{3}$	$12 \times m$

When you have a variable in a multiplication expression, you do not need to use the $\times$ symbol. So $12 \times m$ is usually written as $12m$. The 12 is called a **coefficient**, which is a number that multiplies a variable.

Exercises EXPRESS

Write each expression in word form.

1. $\frac{b}{6}$ ______________________

2. $x + 4$ ______________________

3. $2d + 10$ ______________________

4. $5q - 5$ ______________________

5. $\frac{(z - 5)}{33}$ ______________________

6. $(3h + 4)\ 10$ ______________________

7. What does $3x - 1$ mean?
   - **A.** Find the product of x times 3 and then subtract 1 from it.
   - **B.** Three times the sum of $x + 1$
   - **C.** Find $3 - 1$, then multiply it by x.
   - **D.** Find $x - 1$, then multiply it by 3.

8. Rilee needs to find out the cost for movie tickets that are \$8.50 each. She doesn't know how many tickets she needs to buy yet, so she wrote down $8.50 + x$. When she decides how many tickets to buy, will this expression give her the correct total?

   ____

Name ____________________

Writing Expressions and Equations

An important step toward learning algebra is learning to write expressions and equations using variables. In the real world, many problems can be solved with simple equations, but you have to know how to write them.

Examples: Write an algebraic expression that shows 4 subtracted from the sum of 2 and an unknown number.

Step 1: Choose a variable to represent the unknown number. Let's use x.

Step 2: Read the description carefully and figure out the order in which tasks are performed. Here you have 4 subtracted from the sum of 2 and x, but you have to find the sum of 2 and x before you can subtract 4 from it. Write $2 + x$. Now subtract the 4 from that: $2 + x - 4$.

Exercises WRITE EACH PHRASE AS AN ALGEBRAIC EXPRESSION

Write each phrase as an algebraic expression.

1. two times a number less three

   ____

2. a number minus twenty-two, times fourteen

   ____

3. twenty-two minus three, times a number, plus two

   ____

4. ten times a number minus three times another number

   ____

5. nine times a number divided by ten times the same number minus two

   ____

6. one-half of a number plus one-fourth of the same number

   ____

7. Which of the following shows the sum of a number plus 7?

   A. $7x$

   B. $7+x$

   C. $7-x$

   D. $\frac{7}{x}$

8. Which of the following shows two times a number?

   A. $2x$

   B. $2+x$

   C. x^2

   D. $x+2$

9.3

Name ______________________________

Equivalent Expressions

Equivalent expressions are expressions that mean the same thing but look different. If two algebraic expressions are equivalent, then the two expressions have the same value when you solve them.

Examples: Does $6(2+x)=12+6x$?

Step 1: Choose a number to use for the variable. Let's use 2 for x.

Step 2: Plug your number into each expression. Be sure to follow the order of operations (PEMDAS).

For the first expression:

$$6(2+x)=6(2+2)=6(4)=24.$$

For the second expression:

$$12+6x=12+6(2)=12+12=24.$$

They are equal.

Another way to find out if two expressions are equal is to put each one in its simplest form. In the example, the second expression can be simplified using the distributive property. Dividing out 6 from both terms in the second expression gives you $6(2+x)$!

Exercises DETERMINE WHETHER THE EXPRESSIONS ARE EQUIVALENT

1. Does $x+x+x=4x$?

2. Does $\left(\frac{1}{2}x\right)(6)=3x$?

3. Does $x+7+x=3x+7$?

4. Does $4.5x-9=4.5(x-2)$?

5. Does $\frac{6x}{3}=2x$?

6. Does $3x+8=6x+8-2x$?

7. Brie put 5 chairs in each of 4 rows and Henri put 10 chairs in each of 2 rows. Did they put out the same number of chairs?

8. Rachel wants to know how much money to take to the carnival. Admission is $10 and each ride costs x dollars. She wants to ride 5 rides. Select all of the following expressions that correctly show how much money she needs to bring.

   A. $5x+10$

   B. $5(x+10)$

   C. $5(x+2)$

   D. $x+x+x+x+10$

Name ________________________________

Solving Equations by Addition and Subtraction

You learned the Equality Properties of Addition and Subtraction, which say that if you add or subtract a number to one side of an equation, you must add or subtract the same number to the other side of the equation. This rule is important when you are trying to solve equations that use addition and subtraction.

Examples:

Problem: $z - 32 = 51$. Find z.
Can you add 32 to the left side of the equation to leave z by itself? You can do that, but you also have to add 32 to the right side of the equation.

Step 1: Add the same number to both sides of the equation. $z = 51 + 32$

Step 2: Add $51 + 32 = 83$. So $z = 83$

Problem: $d + 9 = 21$. Find d.
This time, you can subtract 9 from the left side of the equation to leave d by itself. But you have to subtract 9 from the right side of the equation, too.

Step 1: Subtract the same number from both sides of the equation. $d = 21 - 9$

Step 2: Subtract $21 - 9 = 12$. So $d = 12$

Exercises SOLVE

1. $w + 3 = 10$
2. $12 = q + 8$
3. $2 + y = 34$
4. $7 - e = 4$
5. $s + 17 = 50$
6. $d - 4 = 11$
7. $z + 10 = 25$
8. $23 = 5 + r$
9. $m + 45 = 54$
10. $15 + t = 33$
11. $45 - g = 30$
12. $3 - f = 1$
13. Chris scored 26 points more than Valerie did in their game of one-on-one basketball. The game ended with a total score of 108. Write an equation that can help you find the number of points Valerie scored. ______________________________

    How many points did Valerie score? ______________

    How many points did Chris score? ______________

Name ______________________

Solving Equations by Multiplication and Division

Before you begin to solve equations by multiplication and division, you should review some interesting things about numbers.

Division is the "opposite" of multiplication. Multiplication is the "opposite" of division. If you multiply an original number by a second number, and then divide the product by the second number, you are left with the original number. For example: $3 \times 5 \div 5 = 3$. If you divide an original number by a second number, and then multiply the quotient by the second number, you will be left with the original number. For example: $6 \div 3 \times 3 = 6$. That works because division is the same as multiplying by a reciprocal.

Examples:

$3 \times 5 \div 5 = 3 \times \left(5 \times \frac{1}{5}\right)$ $\quad 5 \times \frac{1}{5} = \frac{5}{5} = 1$

$6 \div 3 \times 3 = 6 \times \left(\frac{1}{3} \times 3\right)$ $\quad \frac{1}{3} \times 3 = \frac{3}{3} = 1$

Remember...

In an equation, you need to treat both sides in the same way. Whatever you do to one side, you must also do to the other side.

You know that if you have a fraction with the same number in the numerator and denominator, the fraction is equal to 1. So $\frac{5}{5} = 1$, $\frac{3}{3} = 1$, and $\frac{w}{w} = 1$. (You do not even need to know the value of w!)

Examples:

Problem: $\frac{k}{5} = 12$. Solve for k.
Since $\frac{k}{5} = k \times \frac{1}{5}$, you multiply the left side of the equation by 5. Then you would have $k \times 1$, which is equal to k alone. You can multiply the left side by 5 *only* if you *also* multiply the right side by 5.

Step 1: Multiply both sides by the same number.
$k = 12 \times 5$

Step 2: Multiply: $12 \times 5 = 60$. So $k = 60$

Problem: $7u = 56$. Solve for u.
Now, you divide the left side by 7 to get u. You must also divide the right side by 7.

Step 1: $u = 56 \div 7$

Step 2: Divide: $56 \div 7 = 8$. So $u = 8$

Exercises SOLVE

1. $3x + 10 = 19$
2. $4 + 7m = 32$
3. $10b + 8 = 118$
4. $12 + 2p = 88$
5. $\frac{y}{7} = 49$
6. $10 + 2u = 14 + u$
7. Lynda has twice as many cookies as Alex does. Together they have 12 cookies. Write an equation that can help you find the number of cookies Lynda has.

   ____

   How many cookies does Lynda have? ____________

   How many cookies does Alex have? ____________

Name ______________________

Evaluating Expressions

To evaluate an expression means to find out the value of the expression for a given value of each variable in the expression. In other words, you will solve an equation using the value of each variable in it.

Example: Evaluate $6(2 + x)$ for $x = -3$

Step 1: Plug the given value of the variable into the expression. $6(2 + -3)$

Step 2: Find the value of the expression. Be sure to follow the order of operations (PEMDAS). $6(2 + -3) = 6(-1) = -6$

Exercises EVALUATE THE EXPRESSIONS

Evaluate $x + 14$ when

1. $x = 3$ ______________

2. $x = -3$ ______________

Evaluate $2x - 3$ when

3. $x = 2$ ______________

4. $x = 1$ ______________

5. $x = 0$ ______________

6. $x = -1$ ______________

7. $x = -2$ ______________

Evaluate $x - 3y$ when

8. $x = 10; y = \frac{1}{2}$ ______________

9. $x = 3; y = 0$ ______________

Evaluate $\frac{1}{2}y - 4$ when

10. $y = -8$ ______________

11. $y = 2$ ______________

12. $y = 8$ ______________

13. $y = 9$ ______________

14. $y = 16$ ______________

10.1

Name ______________________________

Understanding Inequalities

An **inequality** is similar to an equation, but instead of telling you what a value equals, it tells you the relative size of two values. If you know a number is larger than 5, you can write $x > 5$. This means that any number larger than 5 can be the value of x.

Examples:

Write an inequality to show that a number plus 5 is larger than 12.

$$x + 5 > 12$$

Which of the following values could be the value of x if $x > 4$? Substitute each choice for x to see if it makes the inequality true.

A. 2 **B.** 3 **C.** 4 **D.** 5

Answer: Only choice D makes the inequality true, because x must be larger than 4.

An inequality can also be shown on a number line. Use a circle to show < or >. Use a solid dot to show ≥ or ≤.

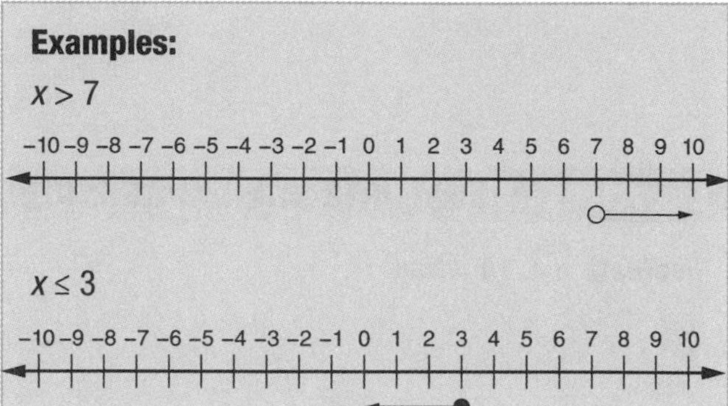

Exercises

Can x be equal to 5?

1. $x - 3 > 4$

____

2. $x + 1 > 3 - 2$

____

3. $4 + x \geq 9$

____

4. $4x - 1 < 15$

____

5. $x + 12 \leq 35$

____

Show the inequality on a number line.

6. $x > 0$

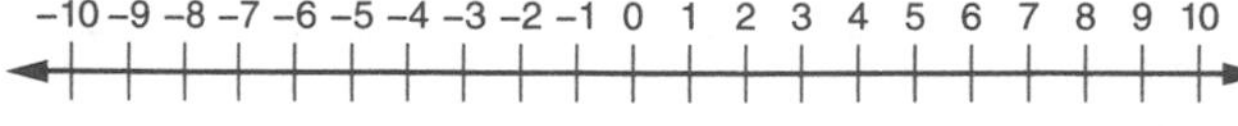

7. $x \geq 2$

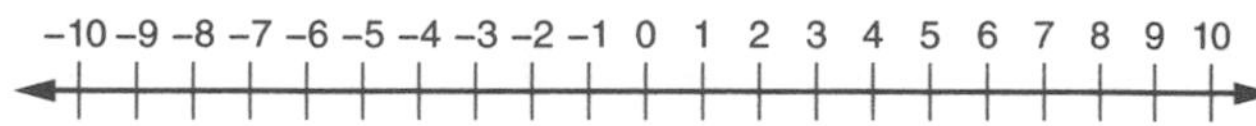

8. $x < 7$

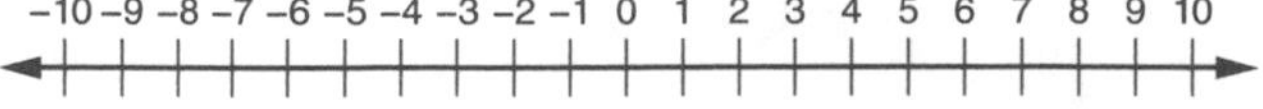

Name ______________________________

Solving Inequalities

Solving an equation or inequality is like answering a question: What could the value be? If you are given several options, you can just try each of them to see which ones, if any, make the equation or inequality true.

Examples:

If an elevator can hold a group of people weighing up to 2000 pounds, would it hold 8 people who weigh 200 pounds each?

Step 1: Find the weight of the people.
$8 \times 200 = 1600$ pounds.

Step 2: Compare. $1600 < 2000$, so the elevator can hold this group of people.

Exercises

1. Sydney has a dozen eggs. He wants to bake a cake, but his mother says she needs 9 of the 12 eggs. What equation could he write to see how many eggs he will be able to use for his cake?

____

2. If Sydney's cake recipe calls for 4 eggs, will he have enough eggs to bake the cake?

____

3. If Sydney decides instead to make brownies that require only 3 eggs, will he have enough eggs to make the brownies?

____

4. If $\frac{4}{k} > 2$, which of the following could be the value of k?

A. 1 B. 2

C. 3 D. 4

____

5. The Ferris wheel costs 4 tickets for each rider. Sarah and Sadie want to ride together. Sarah has only 3 tickets left. Sadie will need to have at least how many tickets for them to ride together?

____

6. Write the total number of tickets Sarah and Sadie need in question 7 as an inequality, using x for the number of tickets Sadie will need.

____

Unit 2 Test

Name ______________________

Solve for *x*.

1. $x - 5 = 12$
2. $29 - x = 25$
3. $x + 30 = 90$
4. $4x + 5 = 13$
5. $3x - 5 = 13$
6. $5x + 4 = 39$
7. $3x + 4 = 28$
8. $-4x + 4 = -28$
9. $\frac{x}{4} + 5 = 25$
10. $\frac{x}{2} - 5 = 30$
11. $\frac{2}{3}x - 4 = 26$

Solve the inequalities.

12. $2x \leq 14$
13. $x + 8 \geq 2$
14. $3 < \frac{x}{6}$
15. $x - 7 > 4$
16. $x + 3x > 16$

17. Elba has four tiles marked 1, 2, 3, and 4. If she needs to choose a tile that solves the equation $x - 1 > 2$, which one will she choose?

18. Vicki's mother tells her to pack at least 4 shirts for a trip. Write an inequality that expresses that command, using the letter x for the number of shirts.

Answers and Explanations

1. 17 $\begin{aligned} x-5 &= 12 \\ +5 &\quad +5 \\ \hline x &= 17 \end{aligned}$

2. 4 $\begin{aligned} 29-x &= 25 \\ +x &\quad +x \\ \hline 29 &= 25+x \\ -25 &\quad -25 \\ \hline 4 &= x \end{aligned}$

3. 60 $\begin{aligned} x+30 &= 90 \\ -30 &\quad -30 \\ \hline x &= 60 \end{aligned}$

4. 2 $\begin{aligned} 4x+5 &= 13 \\ -5 &\quad -5 \\ \hline \frac{4x}{4} &= \frac{8}{4} \\ x &= 2 \end{aligned}$

5. 6 $\begin{aligned} 3x-5 &= 13 \\ +5 &\quad +5 \\ \hline \frac{3x}{3} &= \frac{18}{3} \\ x &= 6 \end{aligned}$

6. 7 $\begin{aligned} 5x+4 &= 39 \\ -4 &\quad -4 \\ \hline \frac{5x}{5} &= \frac{35}{5} \\ x &= 7 \end{aligned}$

7. 8 $\begin{aligned} 3x+4 &= 28 \\ -4 &\quad -4 \\ \hline \frac{3x}{3} &= \frac{24}{3} \\ x &= 8 \end{aligned}$

8. 8 $\begin{aligned} -4x+4 &= -28 \\ -4 &\quad -4 \\ \hline \frac{4x}{-4} &= \frac{-32}{-4} \\ x &= 8 \end{aligned}$

9. 80 $\begin{aligned} \frac{x}{4}+5 &= 25 \\ -5 &\quad -5 \\ \hline (4)\frac{x}{4} &= 20(4) \\ x &= 80 \end{aligned}$

10. 70 $\begin{aligned} \frac{x}{2}-5 &= 30 \\ +5 &\quad +5 \\ \hline (2)\frac{x}{2} &= 35(2) \\ x &= 70 \end{aligned}$

11. 45 $\begin{aligned} \frac{2}{3}x-4 &= 26 \\ +4 &\quad +4 \\ \hline \left(\frac{3}{2}\right)\frac{2}{3}x &= 30\left(\frac{3}{2}\right) \\ x &= 45 \end{aligned}$

12. $x \le 7$ $\begin{aligned} \frac{2x}{2} &\le \frac{14}{2} \\ x &\le 7 \end{aligned}$

13. $x \ge -6$ $\begin{aligned} x+8 &\ge 2 \\ -8 &\quad -8 \\ \hline x &\ge -6 \end{aligned}$

14. $18 < x$ $\begin{aligned} (6)3 &< \frac{x}{6}(6) \\ 18 &< x \end{aligned}$

15. $x > 11$ $\begin{aligned} x-7 &> 4 \\ +7 &\quad +7 \\ \hline x &> 11 \end{aligned}$

16. $x > 4$ $\begin{aligned} x+3x &> 16 \\ \frac{4x}{4} &> \frac{16}{4} \\ x &> 4 \end{aligned}$

17. 4 $\begin{aligned} x-1 &> 2 \\ +1 &\quad +1 \\ \hline x &> 3 \end{aligned}$

18. $x \ge 4$ x must be equal to 4 or larger

11.1

Name ____________________

Understanding Ratios

A **ratio** compares two amounts and shows their relative sizes. A ratio is different from a fraction, which shows us how many parts there are out of the total number of parts. Ratios show us parts to parts rather than parts to whole. Percent is one type of ratio. Percent tells how many of something per 100.

There are several different ways to express a ratio. For example, if there is a class that has one teacher and 20 students, this can be written as a ratio of teachers to students:

- 1:20
- 1 to 20
- ratio of $\frac{1}{20}$ (also read as *one to twenty*)

Knowing that ratio can tell you several things. If you know there is a ratio of one teacher to 20 students, you can also say:

- the ratio of students to teachers is 20:1
- the ratio of teachers to the total number of people in the class is 1:21
- the ratio of students to the total number of people in the class is 20:21

Example: If a bowl of fruit has 6 apples and 3 pears, what is the ratio of apples to pears?

Step 1: Write the ratio like a fraction: $\frac{6 \text{ apples}}{3 \text{ pears}}$.

Step 2: Reduce the ratio just as you would a fraction: $\frac{6}{3} = \frac{2}{1}$

For every 2 apples, there is 1 pear. The ratio of apples to pears is 2:1.

Exercises WRITE THE RATIO

1. What is the ratio of circles to squares?

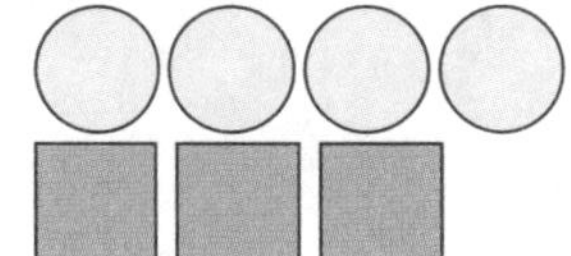

____

2. What is the ratio of squares to circles?

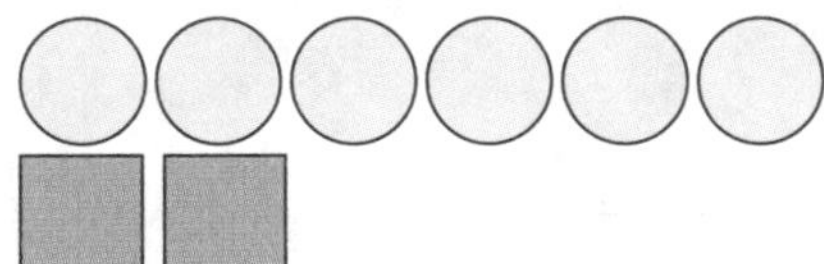

____

3. What is the ratio of girls to boys on the tennis team?

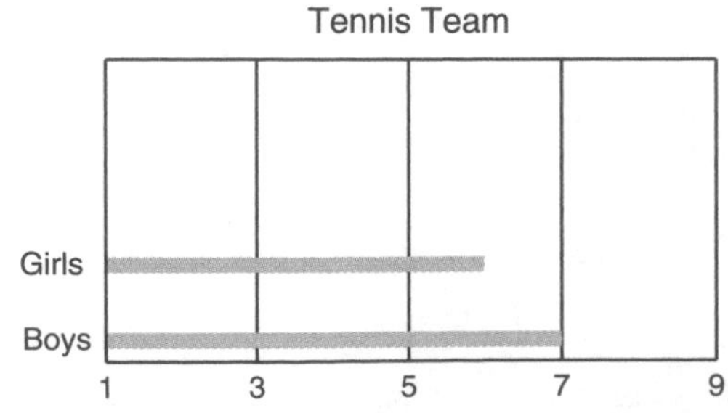

____

4. What is the ratio of cats to dogs?

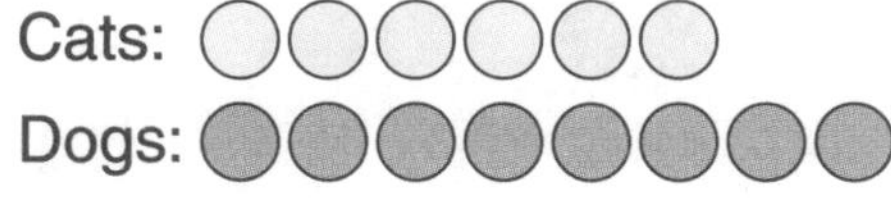

____

Name ______________________________

5 Audree is making cupcakes and the recipe calls for two cups of flour and one cup of sugar. What is the ratio of flour to sugar?

____

6 In a bag of marbles, there are 10 red marbles and 8 blue marbles. What is the ratio of blue marbles to red marbles?

____

7 In a box of candies, there are 5 peanut butter cups and 3 toffees. What is the ratio of toffees to peanut butter cups?

____

8 In a group of ten people, four are children and six are adults. What is the ratio of adults to children?

____

9 If there are 400 students and 32 teachers at a school, what is the ratio of students to teachers?

____

10 If there are 100 children and 80 adults at the park, what is the ratio of adults to children?

____

11.2

Name ___________________________

Part-to-Part and Part-to-Whole Relationships

A **ratio** compares two parts, but it can also tell you about the total number of parts. If there are 3 adults and 5 children in a room, then there are 8 total people in the room. You can form a ratio of parts to parts, or a ratio of one part to the whole.

Example: If a bowl of fruit has 6 apples and 3 pears, what is the ratio of pears to total pieces of fruit?

Step 1: Find the total of all the pieces of fruit. $6+3=9$.

Step 2: Write the ratio like a fraction: $\frac{\text{3 pears}}{\text{9 pieces of fruit}}$.

Step 3: Reduce the ratio just as you would a fraction: $\frac{3}{9}=\frac{1}{3}$

The ratio of pears to total pieces of fruit is 1:3.

Exercises **WRITE THE RATIO**

1. In a group of kittens, there are two white kittens and three tan kittens.

   A. What is the ratio of white kittens to tan kittens? ____________

   B. What is the ratio of tan kittens to white kittens? ____________

   C. What is the ratio of tan kittens to all kittens? ____________

   D. What is the ratio of white kittens to all kittens? ____________

2. Only cats and dogs are allowed as pets in the Lakeville Apartments. Cassie counted the number of cats and dogs and recorded them in this graphic.

   Cats: ○○○○○○

   Dogs: ●●●●●●●●

   A. What is the ratio of cats to dogs? _________

   B. What is the ratio of dogs to cats? _________

   C. What is the ratio of cats to the total number of pets? _________

   D. What is the ratio of dogs to the total number of pets? _________

Name ________________________________

3. Bethesda High School has a student to teacher ratio of 20:1 and there are 640 students. How many teachers should there be? ________________________________

____

4. If the ratio of chocolate chip cookies to sugar cookies is 2:1 and there are 13 sugar cookies, how many chocolate chip cookies will there be? ________________________________

____

5. If the ratio of boys to girls in a class is 3:4 and there are fewer than 20 total students in the class, what could the actual number of boys and girls be? ________________________________

____

11.3

Name ______________________________

Double Number Lines

A double number line is a set of two number lines, each with a different scale, one on top of the other. Double number lines can be helpful for visualizing ratios. Put the amount of one part on the top number line and the amount of the other part on the bottom number line.

Example: If 8 lemons cost $5.00, what is the cost for 4 lemons?

Step 1: Draw two number lines, one for number of lemons on top, and one for cost on the bottom. Make the tick marks on the lemon line go from 1 to 8. Put tick marks in the same spots on the bottom line and label the one underneath 8 lemons as $5.00.

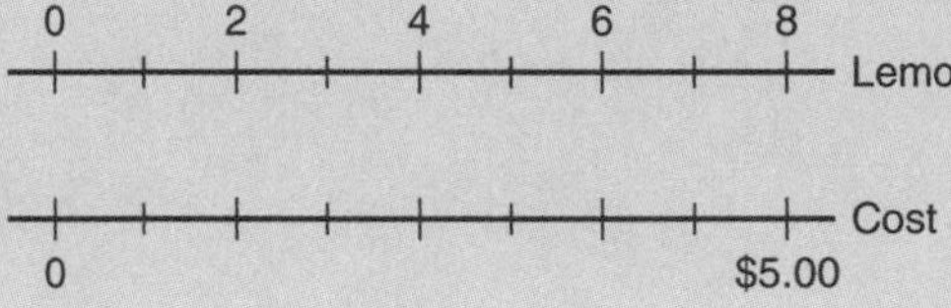

Step 2: Look at the place where 4 lemons is located. What position will that be on the cost line? It's halfway on the lemon line and halfway on the cost line. What is half of the total cost of $5.00? $5 \div 2 = 2.5 = \$2.50$

Exercises **SOLVE**

1 As shown on the double number line below, a car can drive 288 miles with 12 gallons of gas.

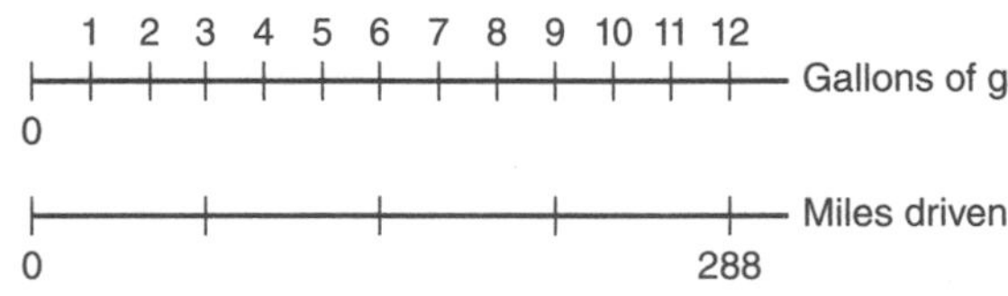

A. How far can the car drive with 6 gallons of gas? ________

B. How far can the car drive with 4 gallons of gas? ________

C. How far can the car drive with 1 gallon of gas? ________

D. How far can the car drive with 9 gallons of gas? ________

E. What is the ratio of miles to gallons?

____

2 Draw a double number line to show that the relationship between cups of flour and sugar needed for a recipe is in a ratio of 3:1. How many cups of flour will be needed with 3 cups of sugar?.

Name ______________________

12.1

Proportions: Equivalent Ratios

A **proportion** is a problem that contains two ratios that are equal. You saw many equal ratios on the double number lines in the last lesson. Now let's think of equivalent ratios in a slightly different way. We write proportions using the form of the ratio that looks like a fraction. In a proportion problem, one of the numerators or one of the denominators is not known. The method for finding the missing numerator or denominator is called **cross-multiplying**.

Example:

A recipe calls for 3 tablespoons of nuts in order to make nutty pancakes for 5 people. How many tablespoons of nuts do you need to make nutty pancakes for 15 people?

Step 1: Express a proportion problem that uses two ratios.

$$\frac{\text{3 tablespoons}}{\text{5 people}} = \frac{\text{(how many tablespoons?)}}{\text{15 people}}$$

Step 2: Remove the words. $\frac{3}{5} = \frac{?}{15}$

Let's use *t* (for tablespoons) for the number we do not know. $\frac{3}{5} = \frac{t}{15}$

Step 3: To cross-multiply, you must set up an **equation**. An equation is a mathematical statement that two things are equal.

Step 4: On one side of the equal sign, write the first numerator × the second denominator.
$3 \times 15 =$

Step 5: On the other side of the equals sign, write the multiplication of the first denominator × the second numerator. $3 \times 15 = 5 \times t$

Step 6: Multiply the side that does *not* have the unknown number. $45 = 5 \times t$

Step 7: Look at the side that has both a known number and the unknown number. Divide *both* sides of the equation by the known number. (In this equation, that number is 5.) You need 9 tablespoons of nuts to make nutty pancakes for 15 people.

Remember...

When you divide both sides of an equation by the *same* number, the expressions on both sides remain equal.

Exercises SOLVE FOR *z*

1. $\frac{4}{7} = \frac{z}{28}$
2. $\frac{3}{5} = \frac{12}{z}$
3. $\frac{8}{z} = \frac{36}{9}$
4. $\frac{2}{3} = \frac{z}{21}$
5. $\frac{z}{14} = \frac{2}{7}$
6. $\frac{10}{55} = \frac{z}{11}$
7. $\frac{8}{2} = \frac{2}{z}$
8. $\frac{3}{51} = \frac{1}{z}$

12.2

Name ______________________________

Problem-Solving with Proportions

There are many kinds of proportion problems that you may run across in real life. Just remember the basic steps:

Step 1: Express your proportion problem using two ratios.

Step 2: Use your proportion problem to set up an equation with cross-multiplication.

Step 3: To find the unknown number, divide both sides of the equation by the same number.

Exercises **SOLVE FOR *x***

1. If a car can travel 105 miles on 7 gallons of gas, how far can it travel on 9 gallons of gas?

   ____

2. Isabella runs 3 times per week. She ran for 15 minutes on Monday and 17 minutes on Wednesday. Her coach told her that she had run 80 percent of her goal that week. How many more minutes does she need to run to meet her goal for the week?

   ____

3. It takes Kenny 25 minutes to inflate the tires of 55 bicycles. How long will it take him to inflate the tires of 121 bicycles?

   ____

4. How many pizzas do you need for a party of 135 people if at the last party, 90 people ate 52 pizzas? (Assume the same rate of consumption.)

   ____

5. Jim spent $55 at the last yard sale when he bought 14 items. If he sees 24 items that he liked at the yard sale across the street, how much money should he expect to spend? (Assume he spends the same amount per item.)

   ____

6. Kim wants to expand her lawn mowing business. She presently mows 58 lawns with 6 workers. How many workers will she need if she plans to mow a total of 87 lawns?

   ____

7. At the apple orchard, each row of 7 apple trees yields 78 bushels of apples. If there are 112 trees in the orchard, how many bushels of apples should you expect to be harvested?

   ____

8. Each troop of 32 girl scouts eats 11 pounds of cereal a week. If there are 45 troops at the scout camp, how many pounds of cereal should be purchased?

   ____

Name ______________________________

Using Ratio Tables

Ratios of equivalent quantities, or proportions, can also be expressed in tables.

Example:

A chef normally prepares a lasagna recipe that serves 4 people, but tonight he will need to feed 16 people at a dinner party. To find out how much of each ingredient is needed, set up a ratio table.

Ingredient	Amount for 4 servings	Multiplier	Amount for 16 servings
Pasta	3 sheets		
Meat sauce	2 cups		
Cheese	10 ounces		

Step 1: Find the multiplier. The chef needs to feed 16 people rather than 4. Let the letter x stand in for the unknown multiplier. What number times 4 equals 16? You can also write $4x = 16$. The multiplier x is 4 because $4 \times 4 = 16$. You can fill that multiplier into the table.

Step 2: Use the multiplier to find the new quantities. Multiply each of the original quantities by 4 to find the new quantities.

Ingredient	Amount for 4 servings	Multiplier	Amount for 16 servings
Pasta	3 sheets	4	12 sheets
Meat sauce	2 cups	4	8 cups
Cheese	10 ounces	4	40 ounces

Exercises SOLVE

Fill in the missing values in the table.

1. Shortbread Cookie Recipe

Ingredient	Amount for 12 cookies	Multiplier	Amount for 36 cookies
Flour	3 cups		
Sugar	1 cup		
Butter	3 sticks		

2. The ratio of fifth graders to sixth graders at Lakeville Academy is 9:11.

	Fifth Graders	Sixth Graders	Total
Ratio	9	11	20
Multiplier			
Actual number	45		100

How many sixth graders are there? ____________

What percent of the students are fifth graders? ____________

12.4

Name ______________________________

Graphing Ratio Tables

Proportional relationships can also be shown graphically. Create a ratio table and then use the values for one part as x-coordinates and the corresponding other parts as the y-values to plot the points on a coordinate plane.

Example:

If for every pencil there are two erasers, show that relationship on the graph.

Step 1: Create a ratio table using the ratio given. Add several equivalent ratios.

Pencils	1	2	3	4
Erasers	2	4	6	8

Step 2: Use those values as x- and y-coordinates: (1, 2), (2, 4), (3, 6), and (4, 8).

Step 3: Plot those points on the graph.

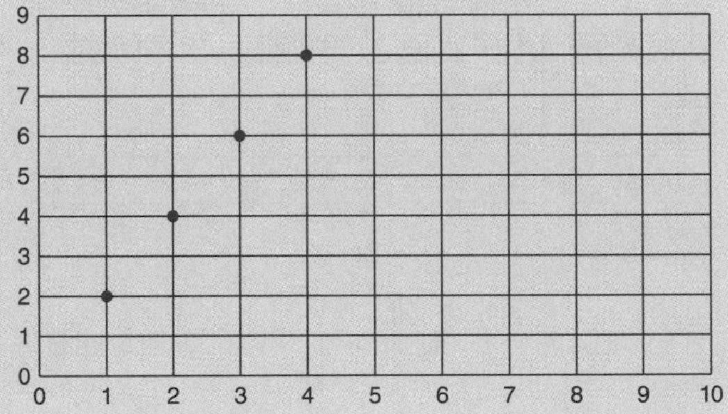

Exercises COMPLETE THE TABLE AND PLOT THE POINTS ON THE GRAPH

1 What is the multiplier?

x	3	4	5
y	6		10

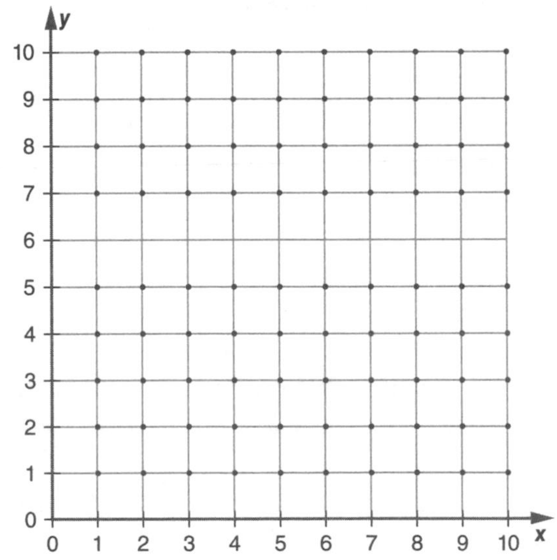

Name ____

2 What is the multiplier?

x	1	2	3
y	1.5		4.5

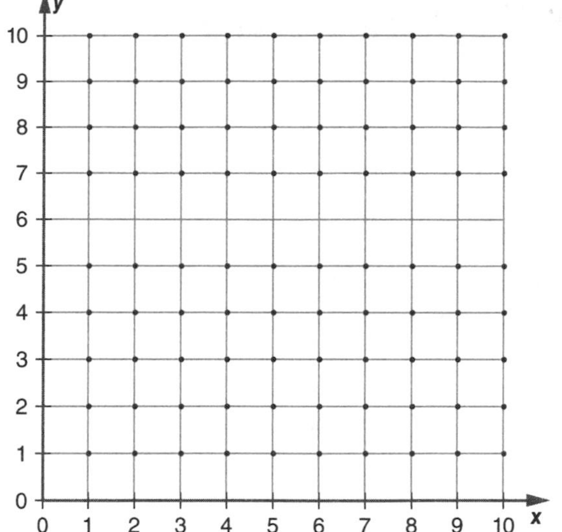

3 What is the multiplier?

x	1	2	3
y	3		9

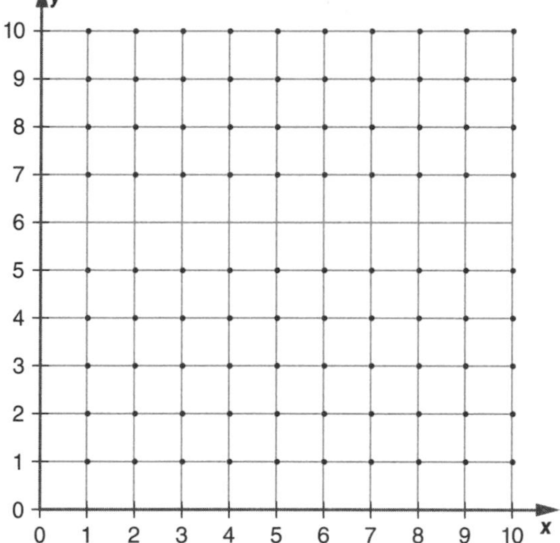

4 Every time Noah does a load of laundry, he makes $2.00. Make a table to find how much he could make for doing up to 4 loads and plot the values on the graph.

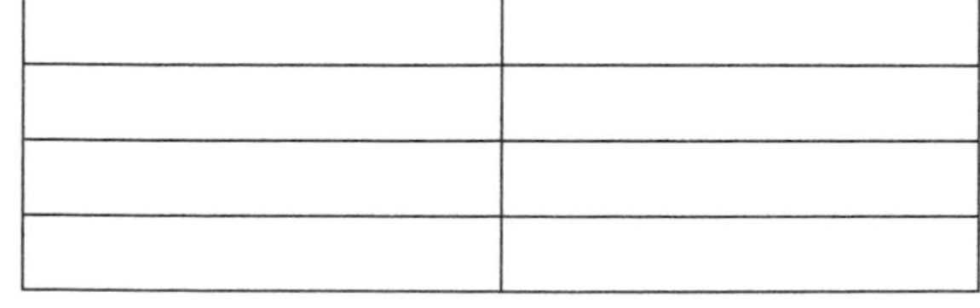

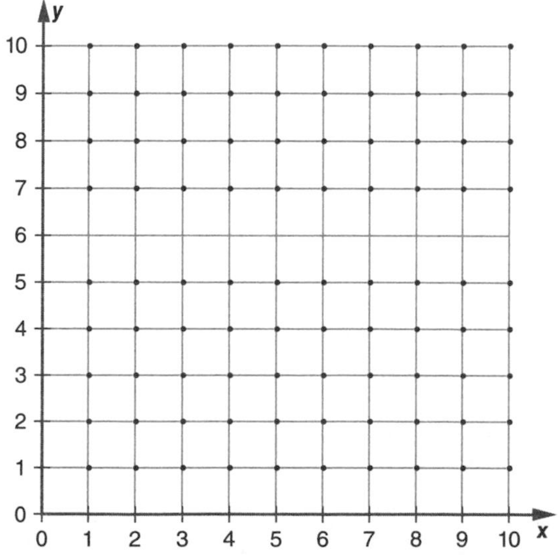

13.1

Name ______________________________

Understanding Rate

Sometimes, you will be asked to solve a problem about rates. A rate is a fixed ratio between two things. For example: Maria drives at a rate of 65 miles per hour. How many hours does it take her to drive 195 miles? Notice that this is really a proportion problem.

Example:

Step 1: Express the proportion problem using two ratios. In this problem, let's use h for the unknown number of hours. $\frac{1}{65} = \frac{h}{195}$

Step 2: Use the proportion problem to set up an equation. Then cross-multiply.
$195 = 65 \times h$

Step 3: Find the side of the equation with the unknown number. Then look at the known number on that side. (In this equation, it is 65.) Divide *both* sides of the equation by that known number. $195 \div 65 = h$

It will take Maria 3 hours to drive 195 miles!

Exercises **SOLVE**

1. Bob eats 6 apples in 2 days. How many days will it take for him to eat a basket of apples containing 51 apples?

____

2. Fay travels 56 kilometers in 8 hours. How many kilometers will she travel in a day?

____

3. Bob can paint the lines in the middle of the road at a rate of 18 miles in a 9-hour work day. How many miles can he paint on Saturday when he works 5 hours?

____

4. In the first 3 hours of a concert, 2100 people passed through the gates. How long will it take to fill a concert hall that has 2800 seats?

____

5. 5 horses can plow 20 acres of land in an hour. How many acres can 21 horses plow in an hour?

____

6. How many minutes will it take 5 people to stack 250 chairs if each person can stack 20 chairs a minute?

____

7. George can polish 240 square feet of floor in 2 hours. How many square feet can he polish in 7 hours?

____

8. It took 35 minutes for the first 45 people to pass through customs at the airport. If it takes the same amount of time for each person, how long will it take for the whole plane of 135 people to pass through customs?

____

Name ______________________________ 13.2

Unit Rate

A unit rate is the amount per one unit of something, such as miles per hour or the cost of 1 pencil in a pack of 12. You can find unit rate by setting up a proportion with the known ratio and using an equivalent ratio with a unit of 1.

Example:

If 3 students use 72 pieces of paper per week, how many pieces does 1 student use?

Step 1: Set up a proportion using the ratio given.

$$\frac{72 \text{ pieces}}{3 \text{ students}} = \frac{p \text{ pieces}}{1 \text{ student}}$$

Step 2: Solve the proportion for the unknown quantity. $3p = 72 \times 1; \frac{3p}{3} = \frac{72}{3}; p = 24$

Notice that you divided the number of pieces of paper by the number of students. You can find any unit rate by simply dividing. Think of it this way: if you divided 72 pieces of paper equally among 3 students, how would you find the number each student gets? You would divide 72 by 3!

Exercises FIND THE UNIT RATE

1. $\frac{300 \text{ students}}{12 \text{ teachers}} = \frac{x \text{ students}}{1 \text{ teacher}}$ $x =$ ________

2. $\frac{150 \text{ heartbeats}}{2 \text{ minutes}} = \frac{x \text{ heartbeats}}{1 \text{ minute}}$ $x =$ ________

3. $\frac{\$2.25}{10 \text{ ounces}} = \frac{x}{1 \text{ ounce}}$ $x =$ ________

4. $\frac{\$280}{40 \text{ hours}} = \frac{x}{1 \text{ hour}}$ $x =$ ________

5. If Kai can run 7 miles in 28 minutes, how many miles does he run per minute?

   ____

6. If an office building has 6 floors and 36 equally sized offices, how many offices are on each floor?

   ____

7. Jacques used 8 cups of flour to bake 3 loaves of bread. How many cups of flour are in each loaf?

   ____

8. If a car drives 25 miles in $\frac{1}{2}$ hour, what is the unit rate in miles per hour?

   ____

13.3

Name ______________________________

Graphs of Rates

You can graph rates just as you did with ratios. Each equivalent ratio provides the x- and y-coordinates for your graph. If you are shown a graph of rate, you can easily find the unit rate by looking at the value of the one coordinate when the other is 1.

Example: After 2 hours, Ron has walked 1 mile. After 3 hours, he has walked 1.5 miles. Graph his rate and determine the unit rate.

Step 1: Use the equivalent rates given as points to plot. 2 hours/1 mile becomes the point (2, 1) and 3 hours/1.5 miles becomes the point (3, 1.5).

Step 2: Plot the points and draw a straight line on the graph going through the points.

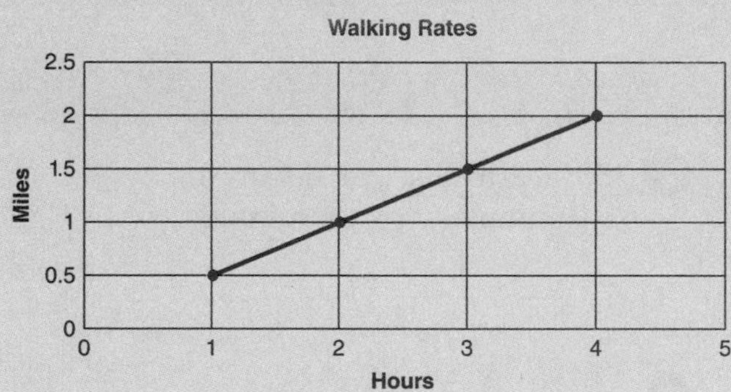

Step 3: To find the unit rate, look at how far he has walked after 1 hour. At the point for 1 hour, the number of miles is 0.5. That means Ron's unit rate is 0.5 miles per hour.

Exercises

1. What is the unit rate for the graph below?

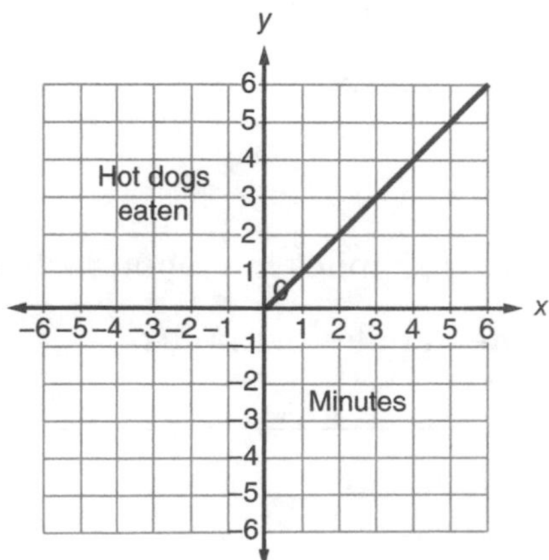

Name ____________________

2 Draw a graph for the rates shown in the table. What is the unit rate?

2 candies	3 cents
4 candies	6 cents
6 candies	9 cents

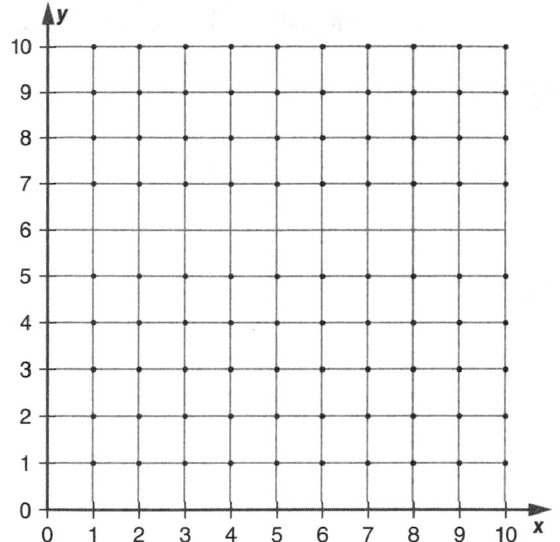

Unit 3 Test

Name ______________________________

Create a ratio and reduce to simplest form.

1. 8 people want to share a large pizza. Use a ratio to express how much of the pizza each person will receive if the pizza is divided equally. ______________________________

2. In the school parking lot, there are 5 red cars and 25 black cars. Express this as a ratio. ______________________________

   What percent of the cars are red? ______________________________

Determine if the following proportions are equal. (Write Yes or No.)

3. $\frac{4}{5} = \frac{25}{20}$ __________

4. $\frac{7}{12} = \frac{28}{36}$ __________

5. $\frac{2}{19} = \frac{38}{4}$ __________

6. $\frac{3}{4} = \frac{18}{24}$ __________

7. Wally rides his bicycle at an average speed of 13 miles per hour. How many miles will he travel in $4\frac{1}{2}$ hours? ______________________________

8. Jasmine can make 49 cupcakes in a batch. How many batches of cupcakes does she need to make 323 cupcakes? ______________________________

9. Phillip drinks $\frac{2}{3}$ pint of water for each mile he runs. How many pints of water will he drink if he runs $4\frac{1}{2}$ miles? ______________________________

10. Perry texts his friends 2337 times in 21 days. Will he go over his limit of 3000 texts in the 30-day billing period? ______________________________

11. Glenn's car burns 2 quarts of oil every 1750 miles. How many quarts of oil should he buy if he plans to take a trip of 3275 miles? ______________________________

Name ______________________

Fill out the ratio table and plot the values on the graph.

12

x	2	4	6
y	3	5	

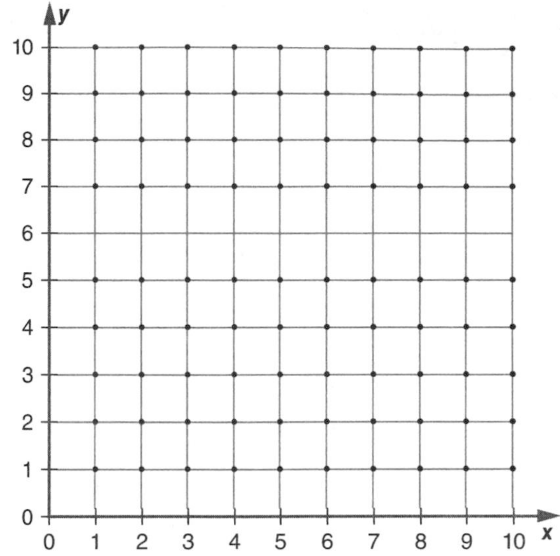

Name ______________________

Answers and Explanations

1. $\frac{1}{8}$ of a pizza	Each gets 1 of the 8 pieces.
2. 1:5 or $\frac{1}{5}$; 16.67%	$5:25 = 1:5$; $\frac{5}{25} = \frac{1}{5}$; $\frac{5 \text{ red}}{30 \text{ total}} = \frac{1}{6} = 0.1667 = 16.67\%$
3. No	$\frac{25}{20} = \frac{5}{4} \neq \frac{4}{5}$
4. No	$\frac{28}{36} = \frac{7}{9} \neq \frac{7}{12}$
5. No	$\frac{38}{4} = \frac{19}{2} \neq \frac{2}{19}$
6. Yes	$\frac{18}{24} = \frac{3}{4} = \frac{3}{4}$
7. 58.5 miles	$\frac{13 \text{ miles}}{1 \text{ hour}} = \frac{y \text{ miles}}{4.5 \text{ hours}}$; $13 \times 4.5 = 1 \times y$; $58.5 = y$
8. 7 batches	$323 \div 49 = 6.59$, so she needs to make 7 batches
9. 3 pints	$\frac{\frac{2}{3} \text{ pint}}{1 \text{ mile}} = \frac{y \text{ pints}}{\frac{9}{2} \text{ miles}}$; $\frac{2}{3} \times \frac{9}{2} = 1 \times y$; $\frac{18}{6} = y$; $3 = y$
10. Yes, he will	$\frac{2337 \text{ texts}}{21 \text{ days}} = \frac{y \text{ texts}}{30 \text{ days}}$; $2337 \times 30 = 21 \times y$; $70{,}110 = 21y$; $\frac{70{,}110}{21} = \frac{21y}{21}$; $3338.57 = y$; $3338.57 > 3000$
11. 4 quarts	$\frac{2 \text{ quarts}}{1750 \text{ miles}} = \frac{1 \text{ quart}}{875 \text{ miles}}$; $3275 \div 875 = 3.74$, so he should buy 4 quarts
12. 7	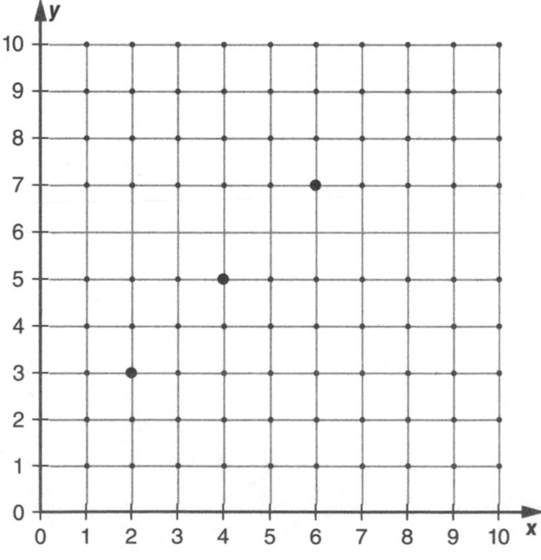

Name ______________________________

14.1

Length Measurements

Customary Units of Length

The customary units of length are inches (in.), feet (ft), yards (yd), and miles (mi).

1 foot = 12 in.

1 yard = 3 ft

1 mile = 1760 yd

You can compare these units to each other.

Example:

How many feet are in a mile?

Step 1: You know that there are 1760 yards in a mile and there are 3 feet in a yard, so multiply the number of yards × 3.

Step 2: 1760 × 3 = 5280. There are 5280 feet in a mile.

Remember...

You do *not* have to add the plural *s* when you abbreviate units of measure.

Metric Units of Length

The metric units of length are millimeters (mm), centimeters (cm), meters (m), and kilometers (km).

1 centimeter = 10 mm

1 meter = 100 cm

1 km = 1000 m

You may have noticed that metric units are based on the powers of 10. So they are easy to work with. For example: 1 meter = 1000 mm = 100 cm = 0.001 km.

Remember...

Learn these prefixes:

milli = thousandth

centi = hundredth

kilo = thousand

Examples:

How many cm = 35 m?

Step 1: Think: 100 cm = 1 m

Step 2: Multiply the number of meters × 100.

You can do this by regular multiplication.
35 × 100 = 3500

However, it is much easier to move the decimal point two places to the right.

35 m = 3500 cm

How many m = 465 mm?

Step 1: Think: 1000 mm = 1 m

Step 2: Divide: 465 ÷ 1000 = $\frac{465}{1000}$

You can also do this calculation by moving the decimal point three places to the left.

456 mm = 0.456 m

14.1

Name ______________________________

Exercises CONVERT

1. 3.5 feet is how many inches?

____

2. 10.5 yards is how many feet?

____

3. 7.25 miles is how many inches?

____

4. 3.75 yards is how many inches?

____

5. 125 miles is how many yards?

____

6. 53 yards is how many miles?

____

7. 235 cm = ________ m

8. 4235 mm = ________ m

9. 5.7 km = ________ cm

10. 625 km = ________ mm

11. 5 cm + 5 mm = _____ m

12. 11 km = ________ m

Name ________________________________

14.2

Liquid Volume Measurements

Customary Units of Liquid Volume

Liquid volume is the amount of liquid a container can hold. The customary units of liquid volume are cups (c), pints (pt), quarts (qt), and gallons (gal).

1 pint = 2 c
1 quart = 2 pt
1 gallon = 4 qt

You can compare these units to each other.

Metric Units of Liquid Volume

The basic metric unit of liquid volume is the **liter** (L). There are also milliliters (mL), centiliters (cL), and kiloliters (kL).

You can probably figure out that:

1 liter = 1000 mL
1 kiloliter = 1000 liters

Remember...

All metric units are powers of 10.

Example:

How many cups are in a gallon?

Step 1: You know that there are 4 quarts in a gallon, and there are 2 pints in a quart. So multiply the number of quarts × 2 to find out how many pints are in a gallon.

Step 2: 4 × 2 = 8 pints in a gallon.

Step 3: You know that there are 2 cups in a pint. So multiply the number of pints × 2.

Step 4: 8 × 2 = 16 cups in a gallon.

Example:

How many milliliters are in 3.5 liters?

Step 1: Think: 1000 mL = 1 liter

Step 2: Multiply: 1000 by 3.5 = 3500 mL

Exercises CONVERT

1. 54 quarts is how many gallons?

   ____

2. 57 gallons is how many pints?

   ____

3. 21 quarts is how many cups?

   ____

4. 32 pints is how many gallons?

   ____

5. 88 pints is how many quarts?

   ____

6. 125 cups is how many pints?

   ____

7. If a water cooler holds 30 liters of water, and each cup of water holds 250 milliliters, how many cups can you fill before the water cooler is empty?

   ____

8. If there are 35 students and each expects to drink 10 half-liter bottles of water in a week, how many total liters is this?

   ____

9. A half-liter bottle of soda is a common size. How many bottles of soda would it take to fill a 10-liter container?

   ____

10. If a reservoir holds 100,000,000 liters of water, then how many kiloliters of water does it hold?

   ____

14.3

Name ____________________

Weight and Mass Measurements

Customary Units of Weight

The **customary units of weight** are ounces (oz), pounds (lb), and tons.

1 pound = 16 oz
1 ton = 2000 lb

You can compare these units to each other.

Example:

How many ounces are in three pounds?

Step 1: You know that there are 16 oz in one pound. So multiply the number of ounces in one pound by three.

Step 2: $16 \times 3 = 48$ ounces in three pounds.

Metric Units of Mass

The basic metric unit of mass is the **gram** (g). There are also milligrams (mg), centigrams (cg), and kilograms (kg).

Since you know about metric prefixes, you could probably make the following list yourself!

1 cg = 10 mg
1 g = 100 cg
1 kg = 1000 g

Example:

How many grams are in an object that has a mass of 4.25 kilograms?

Step 1: Think: 1000 grams = 1 kilogram

Step 2: Multiply: $4.25 \times 1000 = 4250$ grams

Exercises CONVERT

1. 10 pounds is how many ounces?

   ____

2. 14 tons is how many ounces?

   ____

3. 60,000 ounces is how many tons?

   ____

4. A 250-pound man weighs how many tons?

   ____

5. A $\frac{3}{4}$ ton truck can carry $\frac{3}{4}$ of a ton of materials. How many pounds is that?

   ____

6. If there are 850 students at school and each eats 4 ounces ($\frac{1}{4}$ pound) of hamburger for lunch, how many pounds of hamburger, in total, do the students eat every day?

   ____

7. 15 kg = ________ mg

8. 550 g = ________ kg

9. 5600 mg = ________ g

10. 2.3 kg + 0.66 kg = ________ g

11. 42 g + 100 mg = ________ cg

12. 35 g + 3500 g = ________ kg

Name ______________________________

Changing from Customary Units to Metric Units

Use the chart below to help you convert customary units to metric units. The values may not be exact in all cases, but your answers will be close to correct.

Milk and fruit juices in the United States often include labels that express their liquid volume in **fluid ounces**. 1 fluid ounce = 29.574 milliliters.

Length	Liquid Volume	Weight
1 inch = 2.54 centimeters	1 cup = 0.237 liters	1 ounce = 28.35 grams
1 foot = 0.305 meters	1 pint = 0.473 liters	1 pound = 0.454 kilograms
1 yard = 0.914 meters	1 quart = 0.946 liters	1 ton = 907.18 kilograms
1 mile = 1.609 kilometers	1 gallon = 3.785 liters	

Remember...

A zero is often placed in front of a decimal point to avoid confusion. The zero does not change the value of the number that follows the decimal point!

Example:

3 yards = how many millimeters?

Step 1: Find yards on the chart above. 1 yard = 0.914 meters.

Step 2: Multiply $0.914 \times 3 = 2.742$

Step 3: Multiply meters × 1000 to find millimeters. $2.742 \times 1000 = 2742$

So 3 yd = about 2742 mm.

Exercises CALCULATE

1. 3 feet is how many meters? ______________________________

2. A $\frac{1}{2}$ gallon is how many liters? ______________________________

3. Which is larger, a pint of milk, or a $\frac{1}{2}$ liter soda bottle? ______________________________

4. A 200-pound person weighs how many kilograms? ______________________________

5. If the highway exit sign says it is 2 miles to the next exit, how many kilometers is that? ______________________________

6. Which race should take longer, the 100-yard or 100-meter dash? ______________________________

7. If a tank has a 105.68 gallon capacity, how many liters is that? ______________________________

8. Which is heavier, a 16-ounce steak or a 0.5-kilogram steak? ______________________________

9. A 2-ton truck weighs how many kilograms? ______________________________

10. If a man is 6.56 feet tall, how many meters tall is he? ______________________________

Name ______________________

Changing from Metric Units to Customary Units

Use the chart below to help you convert metric units to customary units. The values may not be exact in all cases, but your answers will be close to correct.

Length	Liquid Volume	Weight
1 millimeter = 0.039 inches	1 liter = 1.056 quarts	1 gram = 0.035 ounces
1 centimeter = 0.394 inches	1 kiloliter = 263.2 gallons	1 kilogram = 2.205 pounds
1 meter = 39.37 inches		
1 kilometer = 0.621 miles		

Example:

4 meters = *about* how many feet?

Step 1: Find meters on the chart above.
1 meter = 39.37 inches

Step 2: Multiply 39.37 × 4 = 157.48 inches

Step 3: Divide inches by 12 to find feet.
157.48 ÷ 12 = 13.1225 feet

So 4 meters = *about* 13.1233 feet.

You might be asked to round this to the nearest whole number. 4 meters = *about* 13 feet

Exercises CALCULATE

1. Which is larger, a 2-liter bottle of soda or a 2-quart bottle?

   ____

2. A 2-meter long snake is how many inches long?

   ____

3. A man weighs 91 kilograms. How many pounds is that?

   ____

4. The police officer said that you were traveling at a speed of 100 kilometers an hour. How many miles per hour were you traveling?

   ____

5. The weight limit on a bridge is 15,000 kilograms. How many tons is that?

   ____

6. 100 meters is how many yards?

   ____

7. Is $5.00 a gallon for gas more than $1.75 a liter?

   ____

8. 7 liters of water is about how many quarts?

   ____

9. Which is shorter, 15 millimeters or 0.75 inches?

   ____

10. Which is larger, a 200 gram steak or a $\frac{1}{2}$ pound one?

   ____

Name ______________________________

14.6

Time Measurements

You already know most of the units of time. They are seconds, minutes, hours, days, weeks, months, and years. Sometimes people also talk about decades and centuries.

1 minute = 60 seconds

1 hour = 60 minutes

1 day = 24 hours

1 week = 7 days

1 month = 28 or 29 or 30 or 31 days. (Months can vary in length. Some have 30 days, while others have 31. February has only 28 days, except in a leap year when it has 29.)

1 year = 12 months = 52 weeks = 365 days. (A leap year has 366 days. The extra day is added to February.)

a decade = 10 years   a century = 100 years

Example:

How many days are in a three-year span of time that has a leap year?

Add 2 times 365 + 366 = 1096 days

Remember...

To speak accurately about time, you need to know two other terms.

a.m. = *ante meridiem*, which means "before the middle of the day." So a.m. hours are between midnight and noon.

p.m. = *post meridiem*, which means "after the middle of the day." So p.m. hours are between noon and midnight.

Exercises SOLVE

1. 24 hours = ________ seconds
2. 35 days = ________ hours
3. 365 days = ________ minutes
4. 12 hours = ________ days
5. 52 weeks = ________ days
6. 51 hours = ________ minutes
7. 24 days = ________ weeks
8. 200 years = ________ decades
9. 3000 years = ________ centuries
10. 42 days = ________ minutes
11. 2 weeks = ________ seconds
12. 45 minutes = ________ hours
13. If you got paid $800 and you worked 2.92 days, approximately how much did you make per hour?

    ____
14. How much do you have to pay a rock band that will play for 2 hours and wants to be paid $15/second?

    ____
15. 3 decades = ________ hours
    Assume 365 days per year.
16. A man tells you he is 2,270,592,000 seconds old. How many years old is he if you assume 365 days per year?

    ____

14.7

Name ______________________________

Temperature Measurements

The unit of temperature is the degree. It is written as a small circle above the number.
$65° = 65$ degrees

Customary degrees are measured on the Fahrenheit scale. However, there are other scales, so you must add the letter **F**, or the word Fahrenheit, to make it clear that you are measuring on the customary scale.

$65°$ F = 65 degrees Fahrenheit

In customary units, the freezing point of water is $32°$ F. The boiling point of water is $212°$ F.

Exercises CONVERT

For this exercise F will be the symbol for the temperature in degrees Fahrenheit. C will be for the temperature in degrees Celsius. To convert from one scale to the other, you use one of the following formulas:

$(F - 32) \times (\frac{5}{9}) = C$ and $C \times (\frac{9}{5}) + 32 = F$

1. $32°$ F = ________ C

2. $100°$ C = ________ F

3. $-149°$ F = ________ C

4. $0°$ C = ________ F

5. $100°$ F = ________ C

6. $72°$ F = ________ C

7. $32°$ C = ________ F

8. $212°$ C = ________ F

9. When Kaveri was very ill, the nurse wrote down a temperature of 40°C. What was Kaveri's temperature in degrees Fahrenheit?

   ____

10. The average low temperature in Chicago in January is 22°F and in London it is 4.4°C. Which is colder?

   ____

Name ______________________

Perimeter

Sometimes you want to know the **perimeter**. The perimeter is the distance around a figure. To find the perimeter of a figure, add the lengths of all of its sides.

Examples: The perimeter of this triangle is $6 + 8 + 10 = 24$ in.

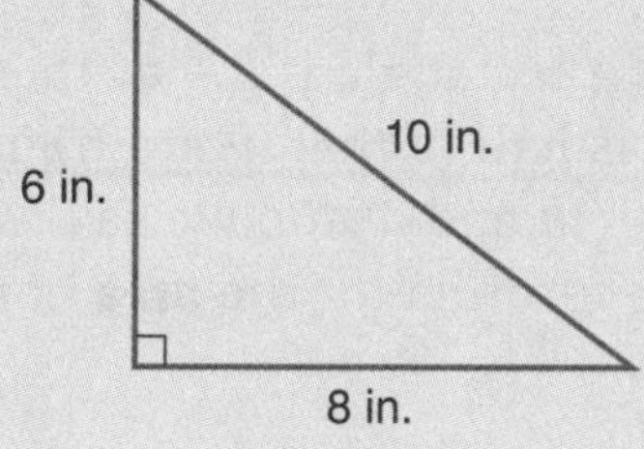

Find the figure's perimeter.

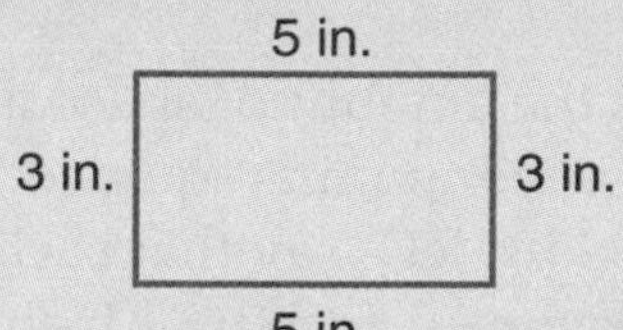

Step 1: Add the lengths of all sides.
$5 + 3 + 5 + 3 = 16$

Step 2: Write your answer using the correct unit.
16 in.

Step 3: If you need to, you can change the unit to a larger or smaller one. Since 12 inches = 1 foot, you can change the answer into feet by dividing by 12.

Step 4: $16 \div 12 = \frac{16}{12}$

Step 5: You may simplify the fraction and change it into a mixed number.
$\frac{16}{12} = \frac{4}{3} = 1\frac{1}{3}$

So the perimeter of the rectangle is $1\frac{1}{3}$ ft.

Exercises SOLVE

1. What is the perimeter of a 2-inch square?

____

2. A right triangle with sides measuring 3, 4, and 5 feet has what perimeter?

____

3. Which has a longer perimeter, a 7-foot square or a rectangle with sides of 5 feet and 8 feet?

____

4. A farmer is building a fence and wants to save fencing material. So he builds a rectangular fence with sides of 30 feet and 45 feet. One of the shorter sides of the fence will be the side of the barn. How many feet of fencing material will the farmer need?

____

5. Which has a longer perimeter, a 14-foot square or an equilateral triangle with sides of 10 feet?

____

6. A triangle has one side of 5 inches and two sides of 7 inches. What is its perimeter?

____

7. A triangle has 3 equal sides of 200 feet. What is its perimeter?

____

8. A building has a rectangular base with sides of 200 feet and 450 feet. What is its perimeter?

____

15.2

Name ______________________________

Area

Area means the amount of space inside a figure and is measured in units squared. In the rectangle below, let's say that each of the equal squares measures 1 inch by 1 inch. You can count the number of squares to find the area of the rectangle. Since there are 20 equal squares, the area of the rectangle is 20 square inches.

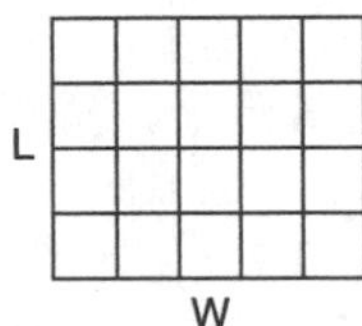

An easier way to find the area of a rectangle is to multiply the length of the rectangle times its width. For the rectangle above, since there are 5 columns that each have 4 equal squares, the length is 5 and the width is 4. $5 \times 4 = 20$. The formula for **area of a rectangle** is $\boldsymbol{A = l \times w}$.

For a square, since the length and width are the same, we use the term "side" of the square. The formula for the **area of a square** is $\boldsymbol{A = s^2}$.

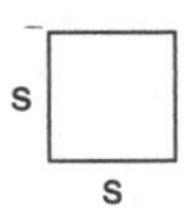

For a triangle, the area formula can also be derived from the formula for the area of a rectangle. Think of a triangle as half of a rectangle.

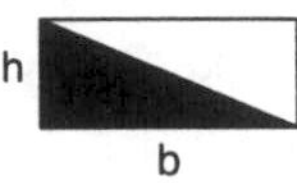

If the area of a rectangle is $l \times w$, then the area of a triangle is half of that. For a triangle, instead of *length* and *width*, we say *base* and *height*, so the formula for the **area of a triangle** is $\boldsymbol{A = \frac{1}{2} b \times h}$.

Remember...

Be careful! A square foot *does not equal* 12 square inches. It equals 144 square inches. A square yard *does not equal* 3 square feet. It equals 9 square feet.

Examples:

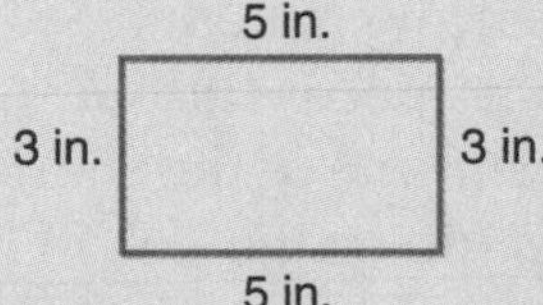

To find the area of a rectangle or a square, multiply the length × the width. In a rectangle and a square, both lengths and both widths are the same, but use only *one* of *each* when you multiply.

Area = 5 in. (length) × 3 in. (width) = 15 square inches.

To find the area of a triangle, multiply its length (also called its base) × its height × $\frac{1}{2}$.

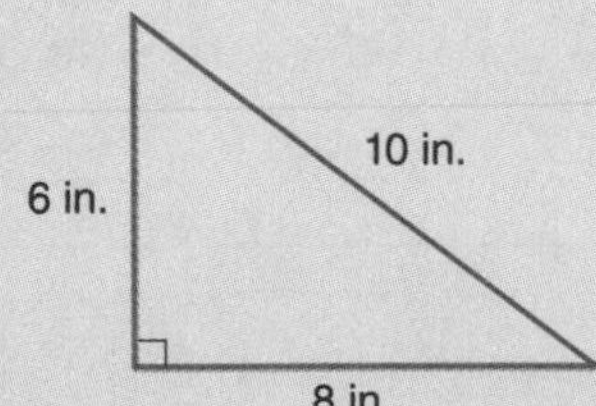

Find the area.

Multiply $6 \times 8 \times \frac{1}{2} = 24$ square inches.

What is the area of a rectangle with a length of 6 and a width of 7?

$6 \times 7 = 42$

What is the area of a triangle with a base of 6 and height of 7?

$\frac{1}{2}(6 \times 7) = \frac{1}{2} \times 42 = 21$

Exercises **SOLVE**

1. What is the area of a square with 4 ft sides?

____

2. If a rectangle has sides of 2 ft and 12 ft, what is its area?

____

3. There are 9 sq ft in one square yard (3 ft × 3 ft). How many square feet are in a 3-yd by 4-yd rug?

____

4. How much will the area decrease if you take away 3 feet from each side of a square with 10-ft long sides?

____

5. John walks west 20 ft, then 10 ft to the south, then 20 ft to the east, and then returns to his starting point to form a rectangle. What is the area of that rectangle?

____

6. If a square that has sides of 25 ft is split in half, what is the area of each of the pieces?

____

7. A right triangle has sides of 7 ft, 24 ft, and 25 ft. What is its area?

____

8. Which has a larger area, a triangle with a base of 15 ft and a height 25 ft or a square with sides of 14 ft?

____

9. What is the area of a rectangle that is 3.2 inches by 4.8 inches?

____

10. 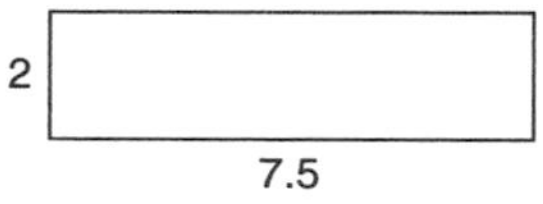 2

7.5

____

Name ______________________________

11. Kim wants to put carpet on her bedroom floor and needs to find the total area of the floor. If the floor measures 13.5 feet by 12 feet, what is the total area of the floor?

____

12. What is the area of a square with sides of 0.7 inches?

____

13. 5

5

____

14. If Aaron wants to lay a tile floor in a room that is 12 feet long and 9 feet wide, how many 1 ft. square tiles will he need?

____

15. What is the area of a triangle with base 3 and height 5?

____

16.

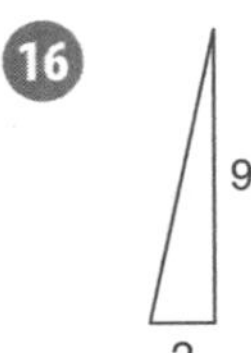

____

17. A sailboat has a triangular sail with an area of 12 ft^2. If the height of the sail is 6 feet, how long is the base?

____

18. What is the area of the figure below?

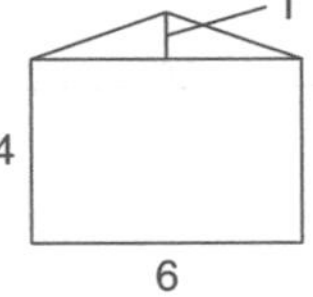

____

19. Erlene needs 5 square feet of fabric to make a jacket. If she buys a square of blue fabric that is 2 feet long and 2 feet wide and a triangular piece of red fabric for the hood that measures 2 feet across the base and is 1 foot high, will she have enough fabric?

____

20. The total area of a square is 9 $inches^2$. If the square is cut in half diagonally, what is the area of one of the triangles?

____

Name ______________________________

15.3

Volume of a Solid

You learned the units for measuring liquid volume in a container. However, if you want to know how many units a solid figure contains, or its **volume**, the units are called cubic inches, cubic feet, or cubic yards.

Since volume is a measurement of the space within a three-dimensional figure, you can find the volume of a rectangular box by packing the box with unit cubes. If each unit cube measures $1 \times 1 \times 1$, then the volume of a unit cube is 1. Count how many units it will take to fill the box.

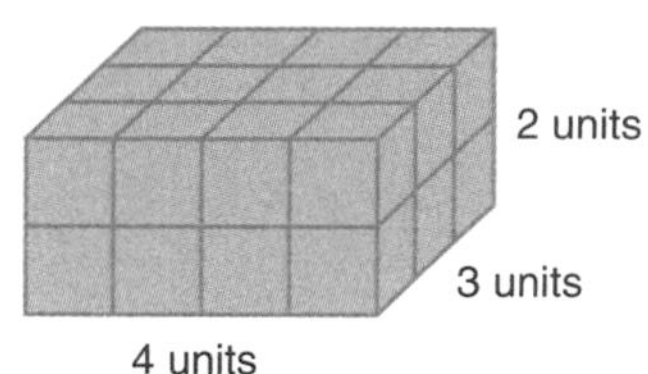

If you count the number of unit cubes, you get 24. 24 cubes times a volume of 1 per unit cube equals 24. This is the same as if you multiply the dimensions of the box (the length times the width times the height): $4 \times 3 \times 2 = 24$. That is why the formula for a right rectangular prism is $l \times w \times h = V$.

Example:

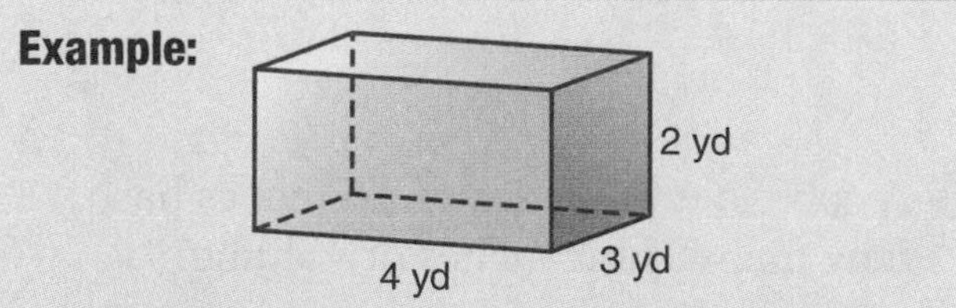

To find the volume of a rectangular solid, multiply its length $\times$ its width $\times$ its height.

Volume $= 4 \times 3 \times 2 = 24$ cubic yards

What if the unit cubes are fractional units? Finding the volume works the same way. Find the volume of the unit cube, then count the number of unit cubes in the figure. Multiply the number of unit cubes by the volume of 1 unit cube.

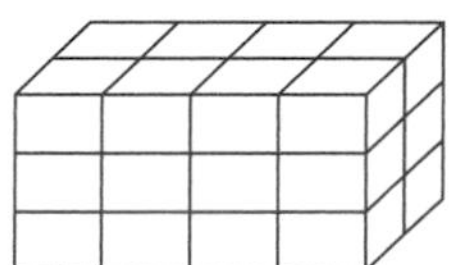

If each unit cube measures $\frac{1}{2}$, then the volume of each unit cube is $\frac{1}{2} \times \frac{1}{2} \times \frac{1}{2} = \frac{1}{8}$

You can find the volume in the same way, by counting the unit cubes, but you must remember that each one has a volume of only $\frac{1}{8}$. Count the unit cubes. There are 24. $24 \times \frac{1}{8} = 3$.

This is the same as multiplying the length times the width times the height: $\frac{4}{2} \times \frac{2}{2} \times \frac{3}{2} = \frac{24}{8} = 3$.

15.3

Name ______________________________

Exercises SOLVE

1 A football field measures 360 ft long and 165 ft wide. If a construction company is told that they need to have 3 feet of gravel under the field for proper drainage, how many cubic feet do they need to order?

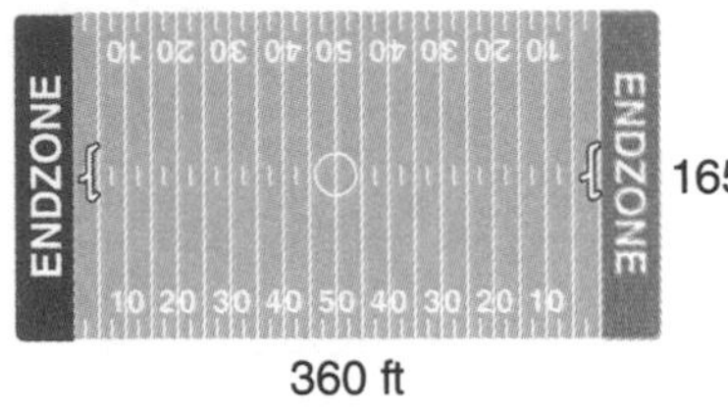

____

2 A shoe box has dimensions of 12 inches by 10 inches by 7 inches. How many cubic inches is it?

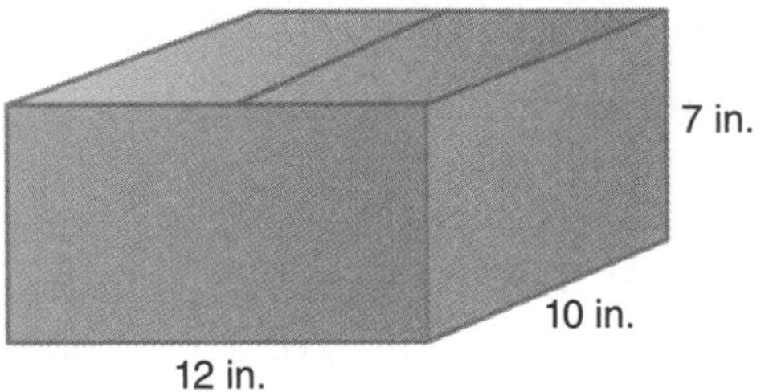

____

3 What is the volume of a cube with sides of 5 ft?

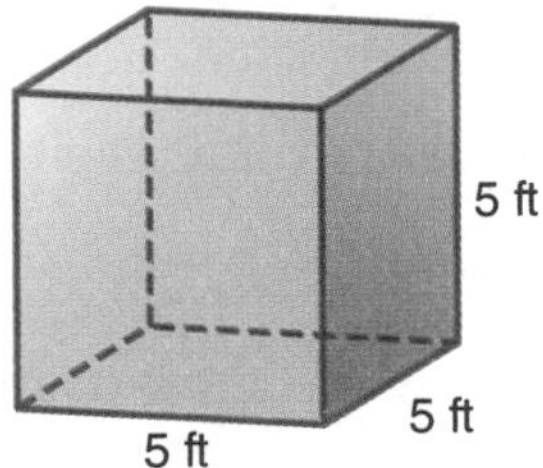

____

4 A shipping box has dimensions of 6 in. by 5 in. by 8 in. If a pound of granola takes up a cubic inch, how many pounds of granola can you put in the box?

____

5 A rectangular solid with sides of 8 ft by 4 ft by 11 ft has what volume?

____

6 A cube that has sides of 2.5 inches has how many cubic inches of volume?

____

7 Jim built a rectangular prism out of $\frac{1}{2}$-inch cubes. The prism is 5 cubes long, 2 cubes wide, and 2 cubes tall. What is the volume of the prism?

____

8 Bob is packing a rectangular box with sugar cubes. If the box measures 4.5 inches by 3.5 inches by 2 inches, how many $\frac{1}{2}$-inch sugar cubes will fit in the box?

____

Name ______________________________

16.1

Points and Lines

A **point** is a specific location in space. It has no dimensions, and you cannot measure it. Since it would be impossible to see anything with no dimensions, we usually represent a point with a dot. Points are usually identified by a capital letter.

A **line** is a straight path that goes in both directions and never ends. It has only one dimension, length. However, when we draw a line, it actually has a tiny bit of width—the width of a pencil point—or we would not be able to see it! A line can be identified by any two points located anywhere on it.

You can identify a line in either direction. Line $\overleftrightarrow{AB}$ = Line $\overleftrightarrow{BA}$

Some lines intersect. **Intersecting lines** cross each other at a specific point. Line $\overleftrightarrow{AB}$ and Line $\overleftrightarrow{CD}$ intersect at Point E.

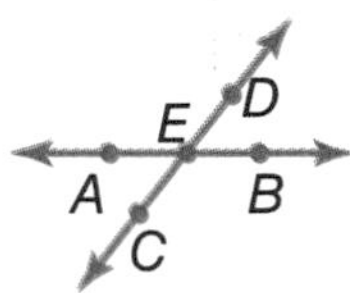

Remember...

A line extends in *both* directions. It does not come to an end in *either* direction. Its only dimension is length.

Exercises SOLVE

1 Use a symbol to name this figure.

____

2 Identify the following figure.

M

____

3 Using symbols, give two names for this figure.

____

4 Is the following figure a line? Explain your answer.

F J

____

____

5 What is the point of intersection in this figure?

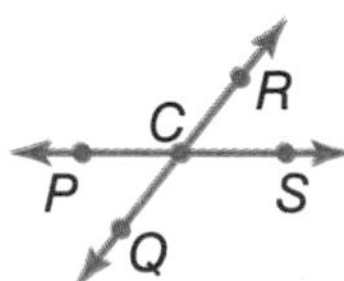

____

6 Is AY a line? Explain your answer.

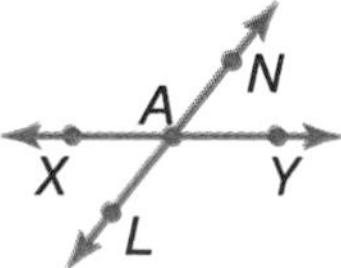

____

____

16.2

Name ____________________

Line Segments and Rays

A **line segment** is a specific part of a line. It ends at two identified points.

A line segment is named by its two endpoints. segment $\overline{FG}$ = segment $\overline{GF}$. $\overline{FG} = \overline{GF}$

A **ray** is a part of a line that extends from a specific point in only one direction. The specific point of a ray is called a **vertex** or an **endpoint**.

However, to identify a ray, you must use one other letter along the line's path.

Ray $\overrightarrow{HI}$ *does not equal* ray $\overleftarrow{IH}$, because the first point named in a ray shows the vertex, and ray $\overleftarrow{IH}$ goes in the opposite direction of ray $\overrightarrow{HI}$.

Exercises SOLVE

1. For the figure below, call the point of intersection of the diagonals E. List all the line segments in the figure.

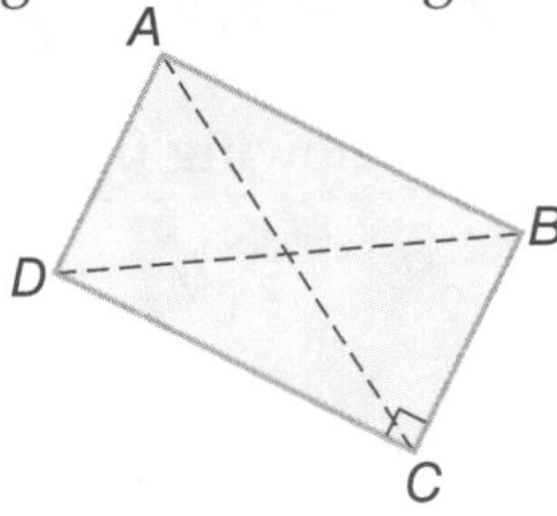

____

____

2. For the figure below, count how many line segments there are. Do not include line segments that contain another point. For example, the line segment $\overline{EH}$ contains the point I.

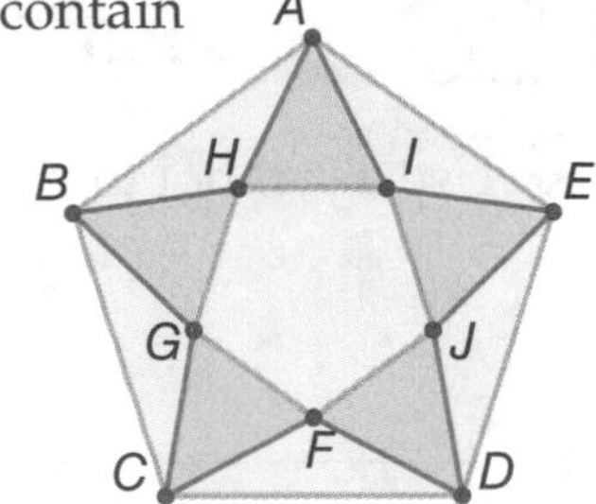

____

____

3. Name two rays from the image below.

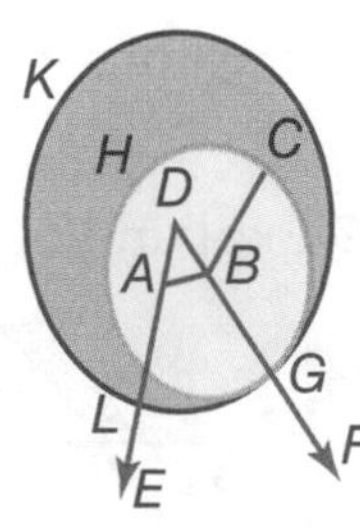

____

____

4. List three rays that contain the point N.

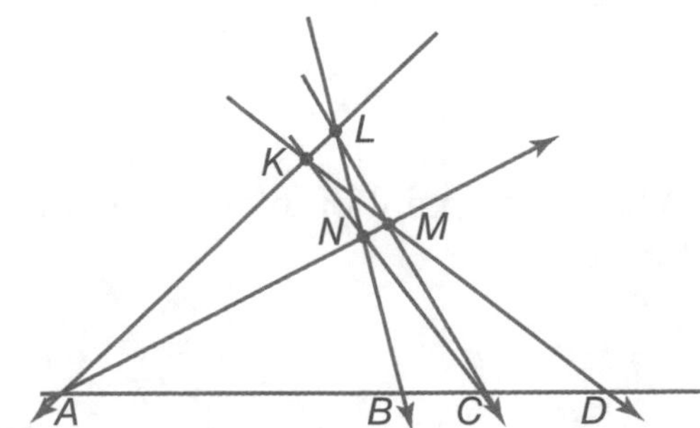

____

____

Name ____________________

Measuring Angles

An **angle** is formed by the rays of two intersecting lines, when the rays have the same vertex. An angle is named by both of its lines, with the vertex *in the middle* of its name.

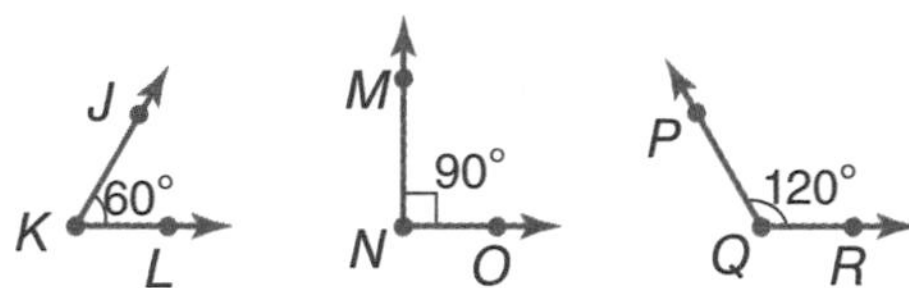

Rays KJ and KL intersect at Point K, a shared vertex, to form angle JKL.

Angles are measured in degrees. A straight line is 180°, so an angle will always be less than that. Angles that are less than 90° are called **acute angles**. Angles that are more than 90° are called **obtuse angles**. Angles that are *exactly* 90° are called **right angles**. Right angles are often indicated with a very small square at the point where the two lines meet.

In the angles shown on the left:
Angle JKL is an acute angle. Angle MNO is a right angle. Angle PQR is an obtuse angle.

Exercises IDENTIFY

1. Is the angle acute or obtuse?

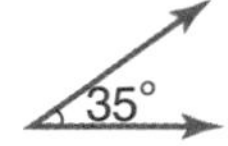

____

2. Is the angle acute or obtuse?

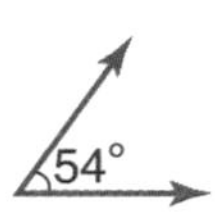

____

3. Is the angle acute, obtuse, or right?

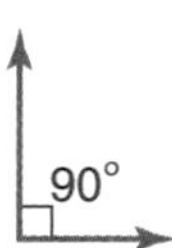
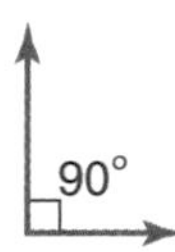

____

4. Is the angle acute, right, or obtuse?

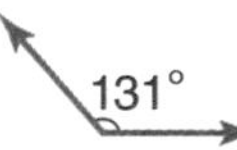

____

5. Is the angle acute, right, or obtuse?

____

6. How many degrees do you need to subtract from the angle to make it acute?

____

7. How many more degrees would you have to add to the angle to make it an obtuse angle?

46°

____

8. Can you subtract one obtuse angle from another and still have an obtuse angle?

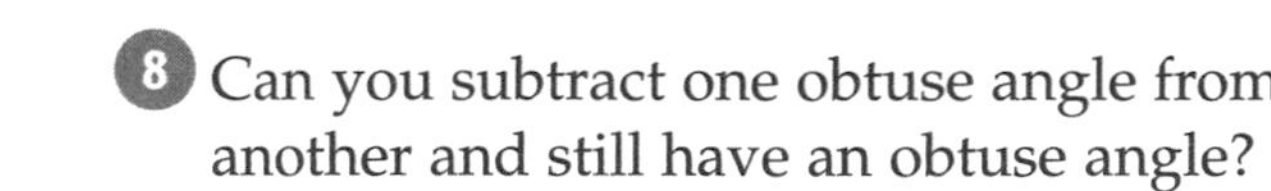

____

9. What three angles below could you add together and not get an obtuse angle?

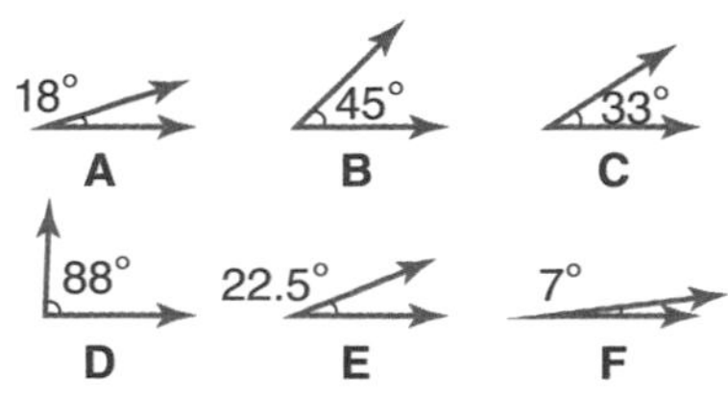

____

10. Are either of the angles below a right angle?

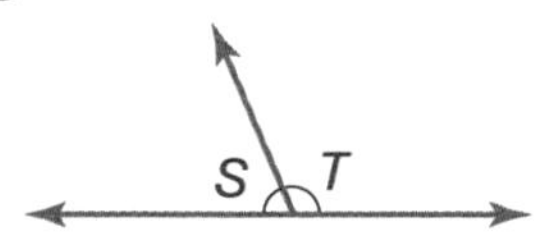

____

16.4

Name ______________________________

Types of Angles

Sometimes, two angles can be defined by their relationship to each other.

Supplementary angles are two angles that form a line. Their sum will be 180°, so if you know the measure of one, you can figure out the other. Note that angles can sometimes be called by just one letter, placed near the vertex.

Example:

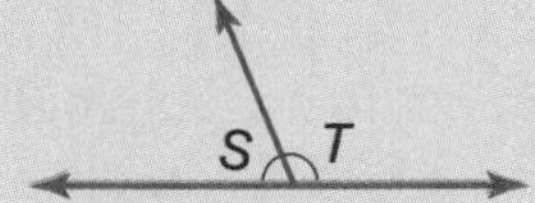

If angle S = 113°, what is the measure of angle T?

Step 1: Think: A straight line = 180°

Step 2: Subtract: 180 − 113 = 67
So angle T = 67°

Remember...

You can easily *prove* that vertical angles are equal. Angle *W* and angle *X* form a straight line. So angle *W* = 180° − angle *X*. Angle *Y* and angle *X* also form a straight line. Angle *Y* = 180° − angle *X*. So angle *W* = angle *Y*!

Complementary angles are two angles that form a right angle. Their sum will be 90°.

Example:

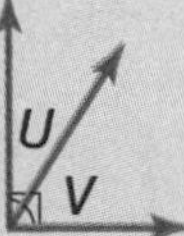

If angle U = 32°, what's the measure of angle V?

Step 1: Think: A right angle = 90°

Step 2: Subtract: 90 − 32 = 58
So angle V = 58°

When two lines intersect, the angles opposite each other are called **vertical angles**.

Those angles are equal.

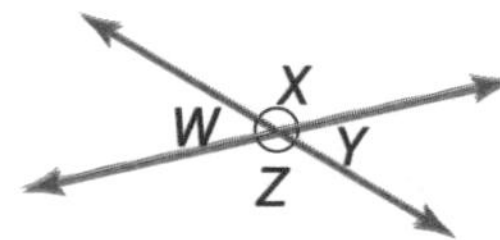

Exercises IDENTIFY

1. Are the two angles shown below supplementary?

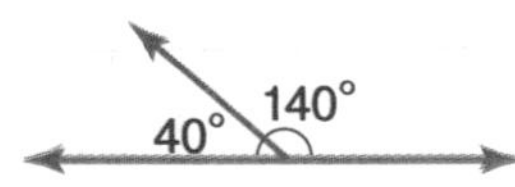

____

2. Are the two angles below complementary?

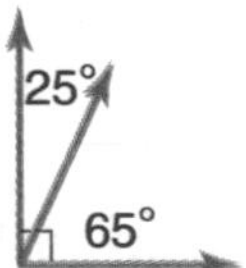

____

3. Are the two angles A and B supplementary?

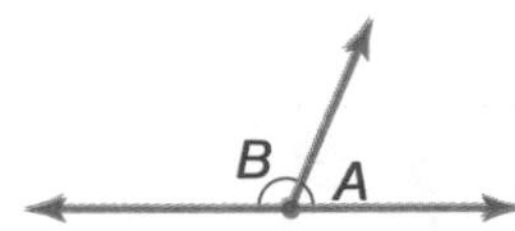

____

4. Are the two angles supplementary?

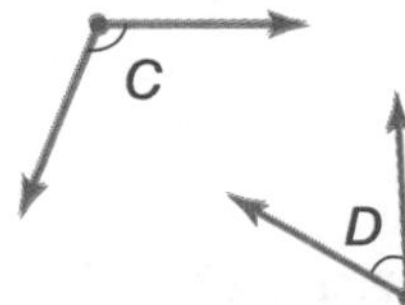

____

Name ______________________________

5 Are the two angles CFD and DFE complementary? Why, or why not?

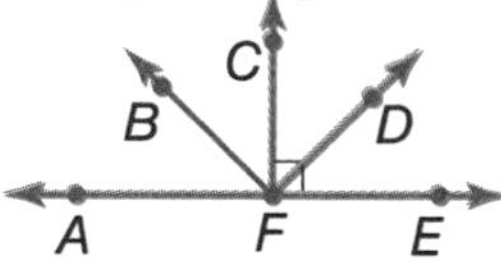

____

6 Name the two angles below, and determine if they are supplementary.

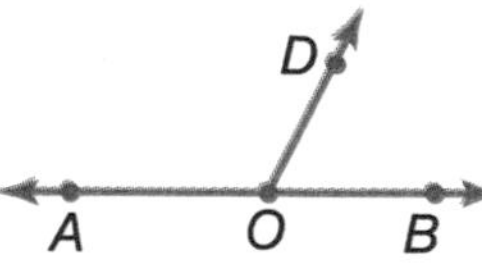

____

7 Determine if the two angles are complementary.

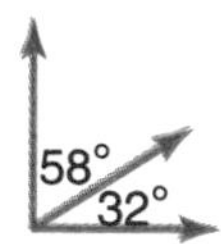

____

8 What size angle would you have to add to make this a right angle?

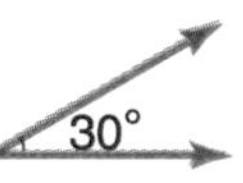

____

9 In the figure below, list three sets of vertical angles.

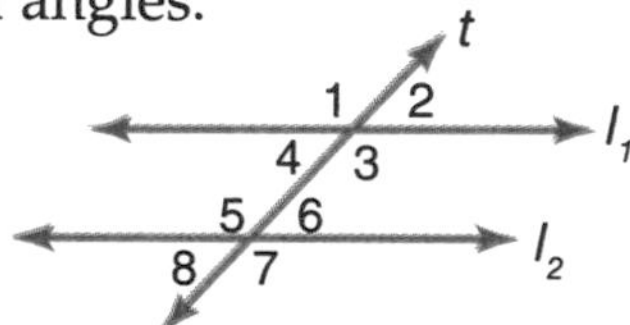

____

10 Of the angles labeled below, which ones are supplementary?

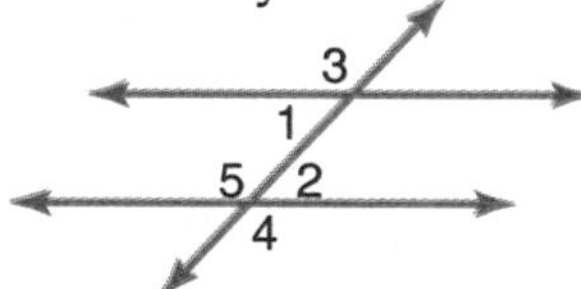

____

11 List two pairs of vertical angles in the figure.

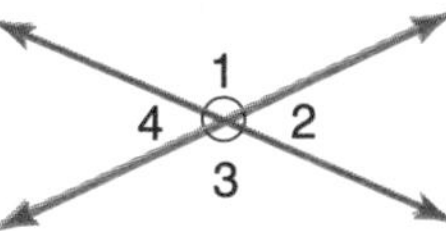

____

12 What type of angles are C and B?

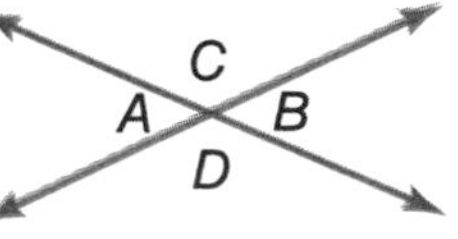

____

____

13 List two pairs of vertical angles in the figure below.

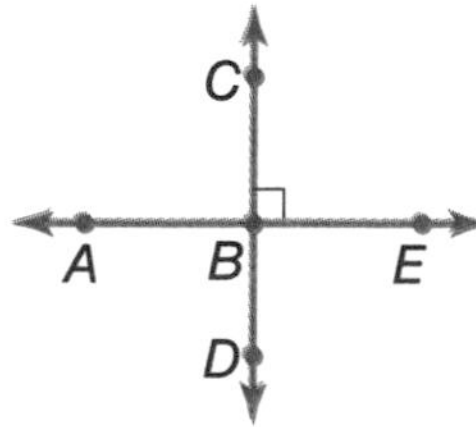

____

14 What are the two angles in the figure below? Are the angles complementary? Assume that angle ACB is 90 degrees.

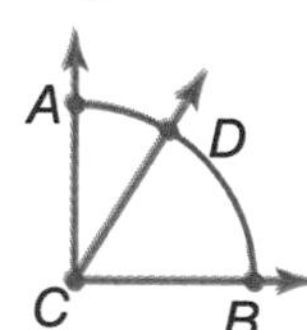

____

17.1

Name ____________________

Triangles

A two-dimensional figure with three sides is a triangle. A triangle has three angles that *always* add up to 180°. This is one way that you can classify triangles.

A triangle with *only* acute angles—angles less than 90°—is called an **acute triangle**. A triangle with one right angle is called a **right triangle**. A triangle with one obtuse angle is called an **obtuse triangle**.

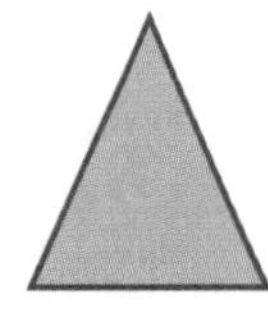
acute triangle

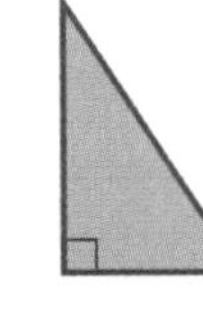
right triangle

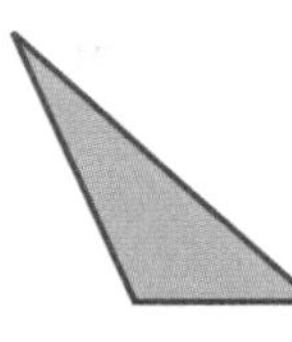
obtuse triangle

Since the measures of the angles in a triangle add up to 180°, a triangle can have at most only one right angle or one obtuse angle. Can you figure out why? Ask yourself: How many degrees are in two right angles? What is the smallest number of degrees that two obtuse angles could total?

Another way of thinking about a triangle is to look at the length of its sides. If all three sides are the same length, the triangle is **equilateral**. If two sides are the same length, but the third is different, the triangle is **isosceles**. And if all three sides have different lengths, the triangle is **scalene**.

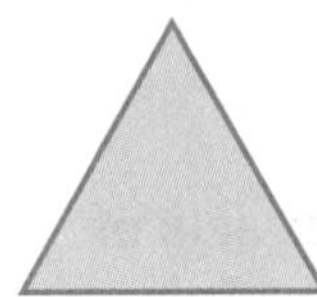
equilateral triangle

isosceles triangle

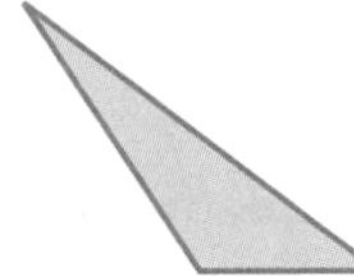
scalene triangle

Exercises IDENTIFY

Determine if the triangle is acute, right, or obtuse.

1
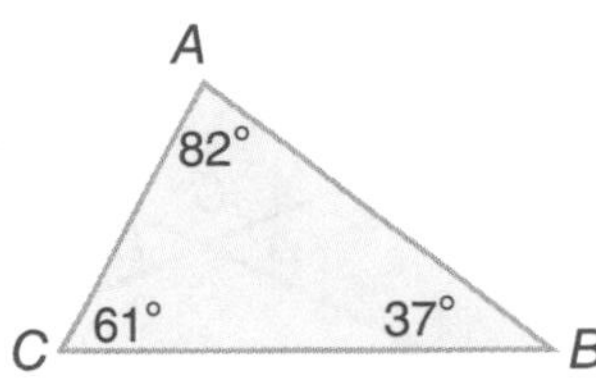

____

2
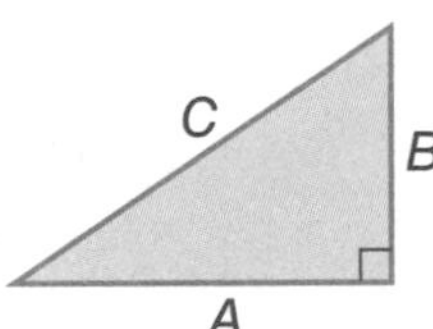

____

3
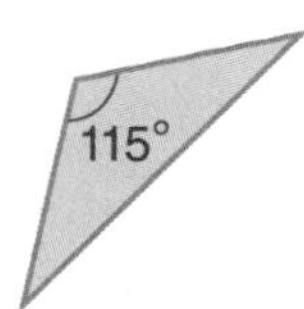

____

Determine if the triangle is isosceles, equilateral, or scalene.

4
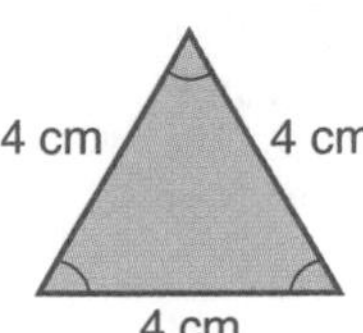

____

5
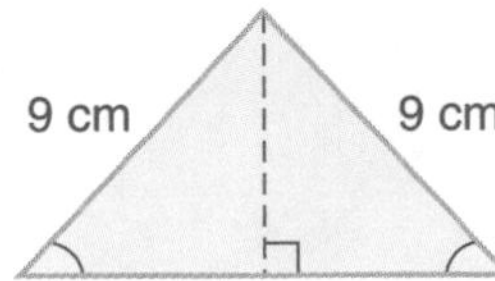

____

6
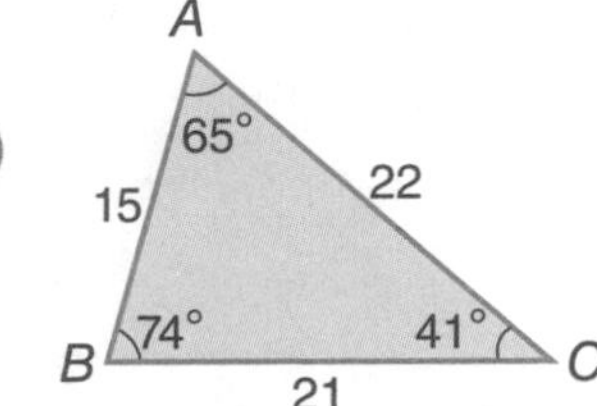

____

Name ______________________________

17.2

Quadrilaterals

A **quadrilateral** is a two-dimensional figure with four sides—and four angles.

A rectangle has four right angles and two sets of opposite sides that are parallel, and equal in length. The lengths of the sides that meet at the right angle are not equal.

rectangle

square

A square is a special kind of rectangle. *All* of its sides are of equal length.

A **rhombus** does *not* have four right angles. However, like a rectangle, both sets of opposite sides are parallel and have the same length.

A **trapezoid** has two parallel sides, while the other two sides are not parallel to each other.

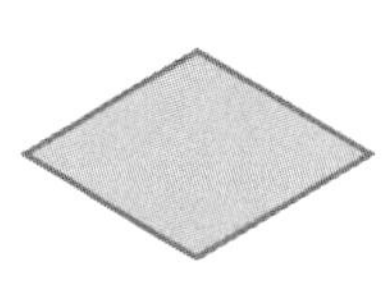

rhombus

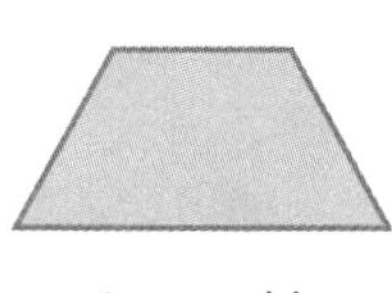

trapezoid

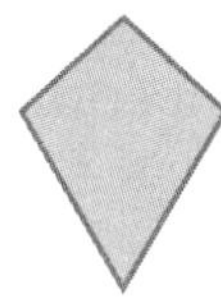

kite

A **kite** looks like a typical toy kite. Two angles in a kite are equal. Two *touching* sides are equal in length, and the other two *touching* sides are equal in length.

Exercises IDENTIFY

Determine what type of shape the figure is: square, rectangle, rhombus, trapezoid, or kite.

1. 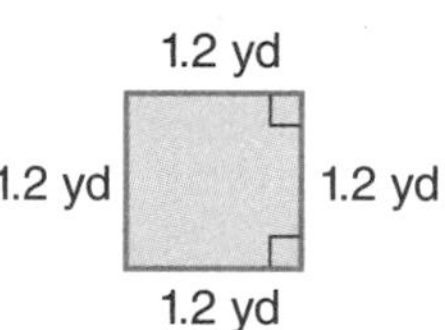

____

2. 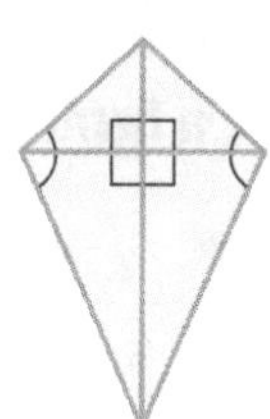

____

3.
18	15
14, 4, 7, 8, 10, 9	

____

4. 

____

5.
6 cm
3 cm
3 cm
11 cm

____

6. 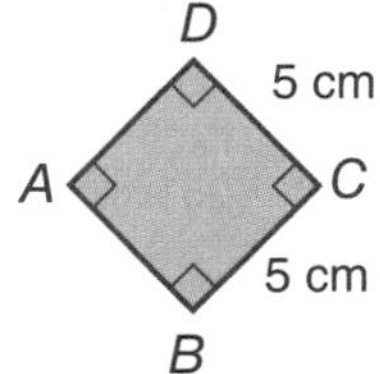

____

7. 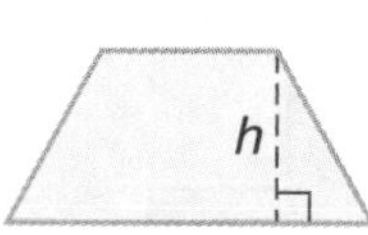

____

8. 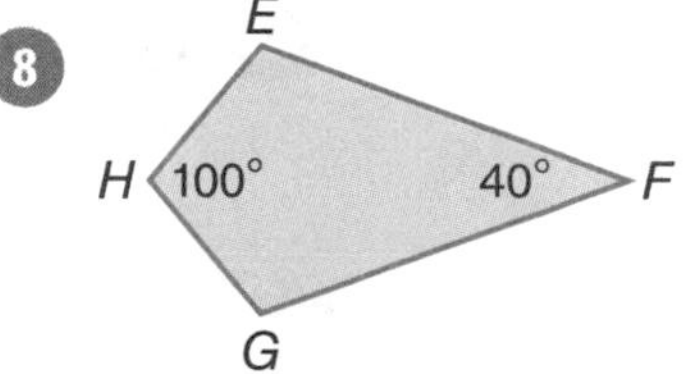

____

9. 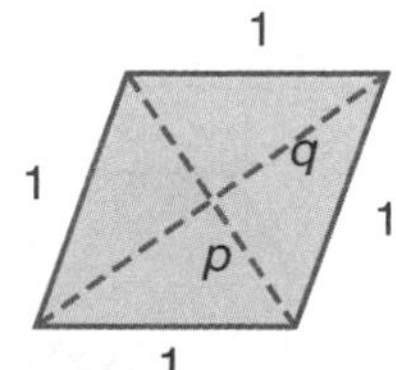

____

17.3

Name ______________________________

Polygons

A **polygon** is any closed 2-dimensional figure that is made up of line segments. Triangles and quadrilaterals are polygons. However, a polygon can have any number of sides greater than 2. The number of sides = the number of angles. Many polygons are named for the number of sides.

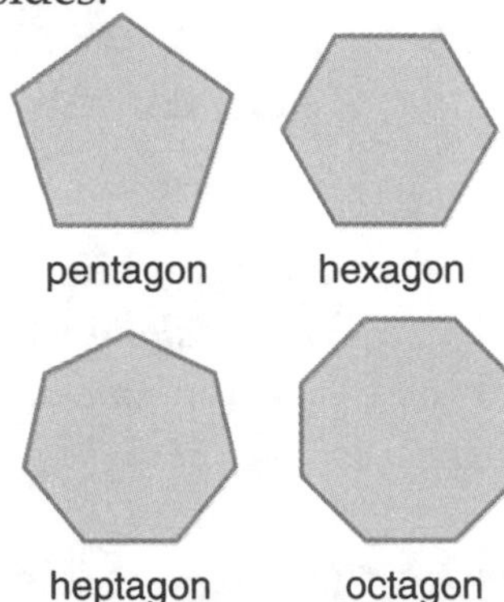

penta = 5, **hexa** = 6, **hepta** = 7, **octa** = 8

Two polygons are **congruent** if their shape and size are the same. The sides and angles in one polygon must exactly equal the sides and angles in the other. Congruent polygons do *not* have to face in the same direction. The best way to find out if two polygons are congruent is to measure the sides and angles of both.

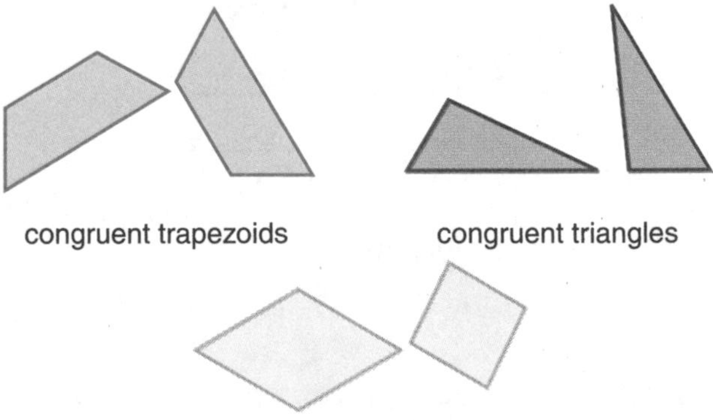

not congruent rhombuses

Exercises IDENTIFY

Determine if the figure is a pentagon, a hexagon, a heptagon, or an octagon.

1. 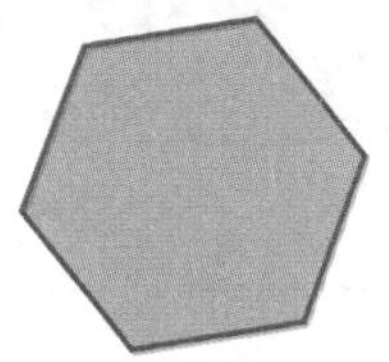

____

2. 

____

3. 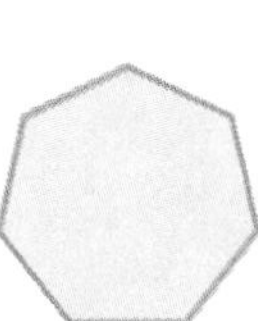

____

4. 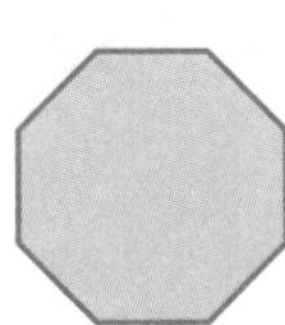

____

5. 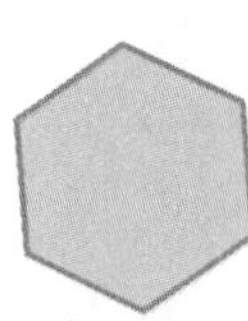

____

6. 

____

7. 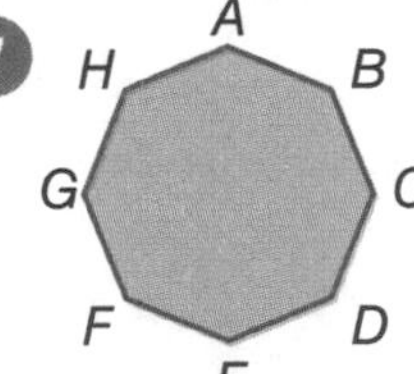

____

8. 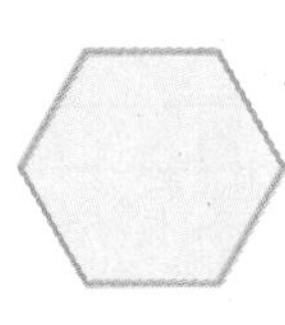

____

9. Are these two figures congruent?

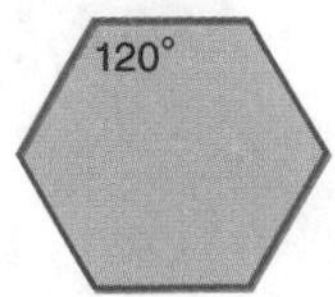

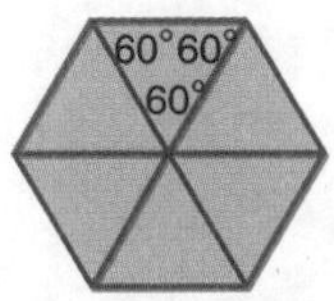

____

10. Are these two figures congruent?

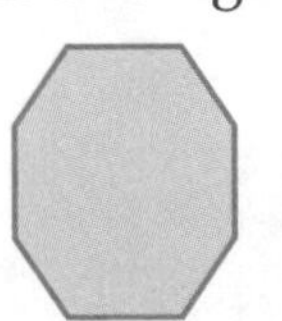

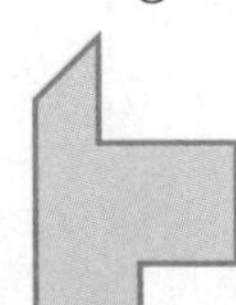

____

Name ______________________________

Circles

A **circle** is a 2-dimensional figure with every point on its circumference an equal distance from its center point, or **origin**. A circle's **circumference** is its perimeter, the distance around it.

A line segment that starts at a circle's origin and extends to its circumference is called a **radius**. The plural of *radius* is **radii**. In a circle, all radii are equal in length.

A **chord** is a line segment that has both endpoints on the circumference. A **diameter** is a special kind of chord that passes through the origin. It is always equal in length to 2 radii.

Exercises IDENTIFY

1. What is the radius of the circle, if the diameter is 11 cm?

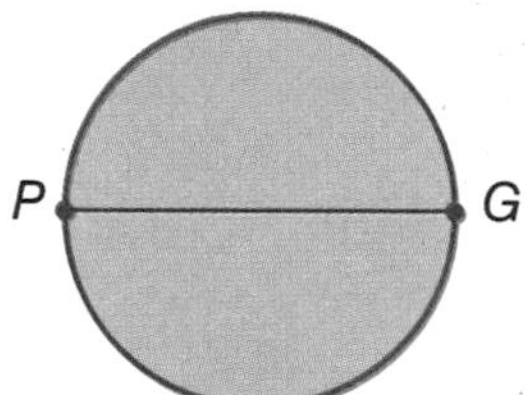

____

2. Identify the chord in the figure below.

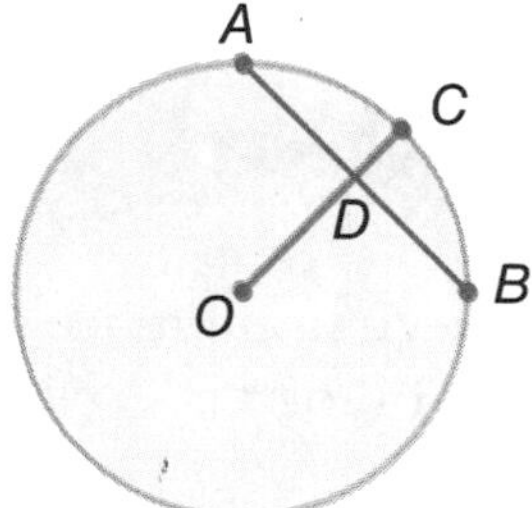

____

3. Identify the 2 radii below.

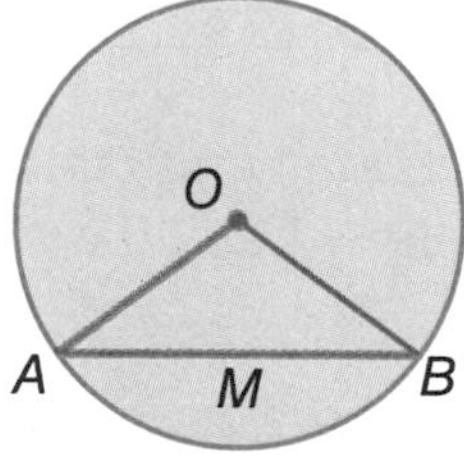

____

4. What are the 5 chords formed by inscribing the pentagon inside of the circle?

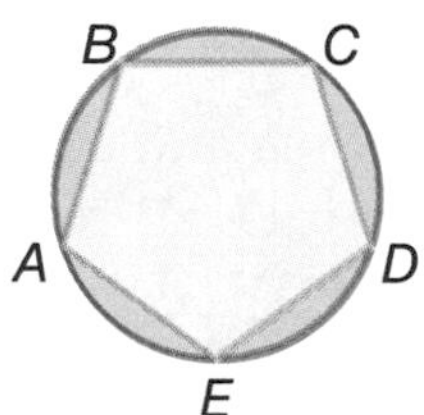

____

5. Describe the two line segments from the connected points on the circle.

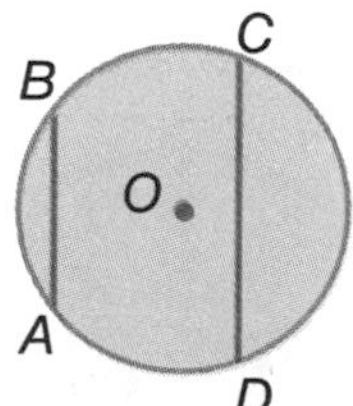

____

6. Identify the diameter.

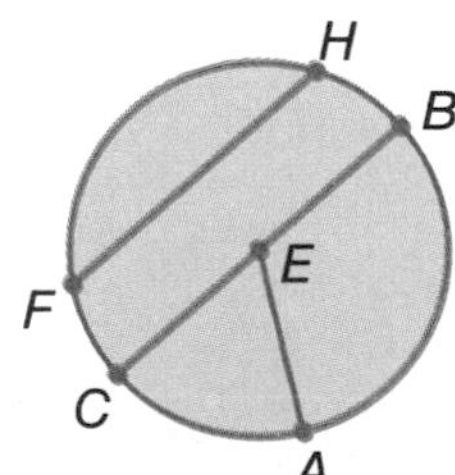

____

17.4

Name ______________________________

Circles (cont.)

A circle's circumference and area are calculated by using a special long decimal, written as the Greek letter π, pronounced ***pi***. To make calculations easier, pi is often rounded to 3.14. Pi is the ratio of a circle's diameter to its circumference—a ratio that is exactly the same for every circle.

Calculating the circumference and area of a circle is actually fairly easy to do. A circle's circumference = pi times its diameter (πd). A circle's area = pi times the square of its radius (πr^2).

Example:

If a circle has a radius of 3 inches, you can find its circumference by multiplying the radius $\times$ 2 and then multiplying that number $\times$ π.

Its circumference $= (2 \times 3)\ \pi$ inches

$= 6\pi = 18.84$ inches

To find this circle's area, you have to raise its radius to the second power and then multiply that times π. In this example, its area $= (3 \times 3)$ times π square inches $= 9$ times $\pi = 28.26$ square inches.

Exercises **CALCULATE**

7. Calculate the circumference of the circle below. Use 3.14 for π.

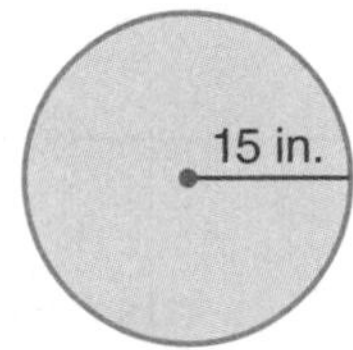

____

8. Calculate the area of the circle below. Use 3.14 for π.

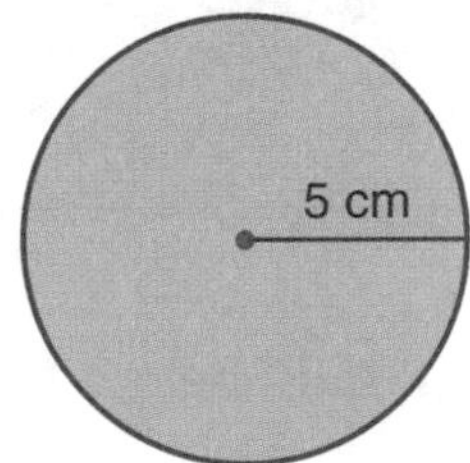

____

9. Calculate the area and circumference of the circle below. Use 3.14 for π.

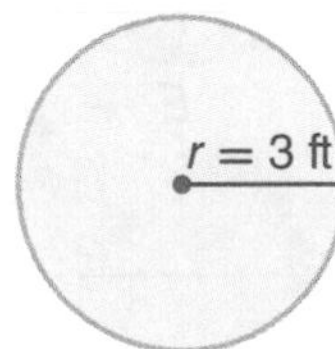

____

10. Calculate the area and circumference of the circle below. Use 3.14 for π.

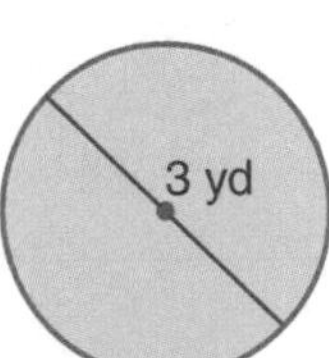

____

11. Calculate the area and circumference of the circle below. Use 3.14 for π.

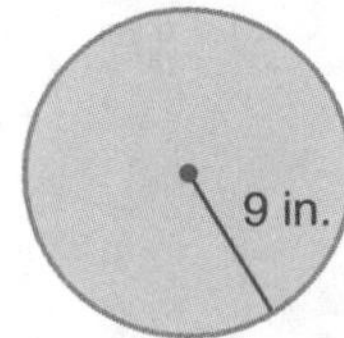

____

12. Name the two chords that have been drawn in the figure below.

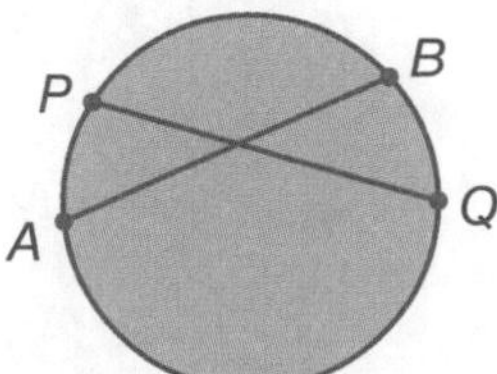

____

Name ______________________

17.5

Solid Figures

A **solid figure** is a figure that has three dimensions. These are some common solid figures:

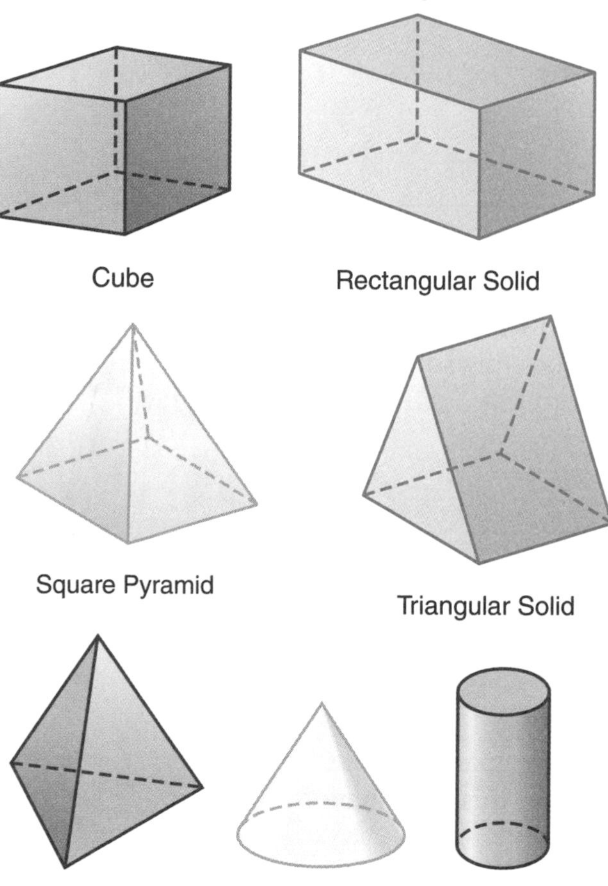

Here are some terms that are used to describe solid figures:

Face: The flat surface of a solid figure. Each face looks like a two-dimensional figure.

Edge: The line where two faces meet.

Vertex of a solid: A specific point at which *more than* 2 faces meet, or a point where a curve begins.

Base: The face on the bottom of a solid figure.

Examples:

Look at the solid figures drawn on this page.

A cube and a rectangular solid have 6 faces each. Any of the bases can be the base.

A square pyramid has 5 faces. The base is square and the other 4 faces are triangular.

A triangular solid has 5 faces. Two of them are triangular. Three are rectangular.

A cone has a circular base and 1 vertex. A cylinder has 2 circular faces and *no* vertex.

A triangular pyramid has a triangular base, 4 vertices, 4 faces, and 6 edges.

Exercises IDENTIFY

1. How many faces does this figure have?

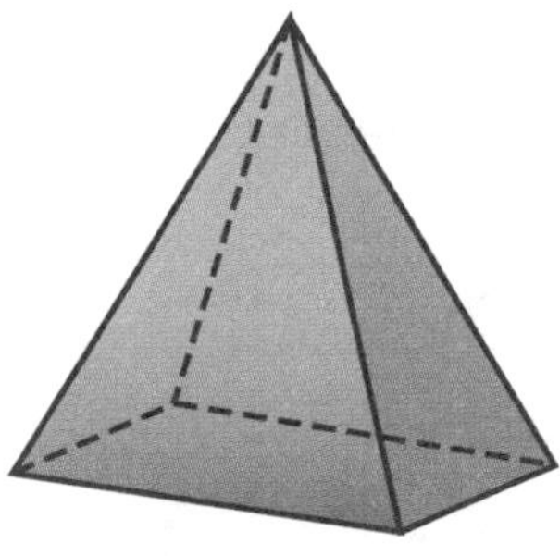

____

2. How many faces does this figure have?

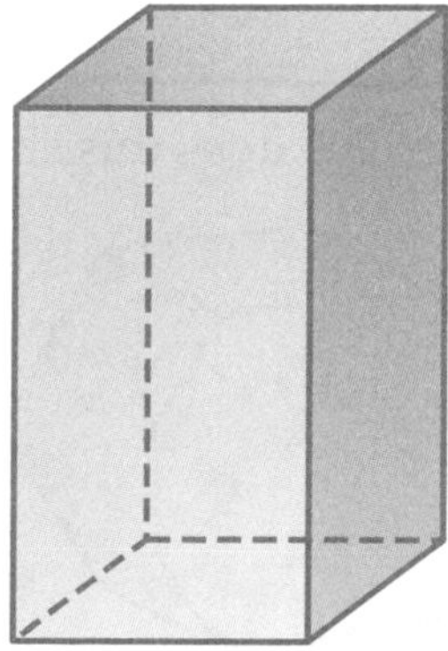

____

Name ___________________________

3 What shape is the base of this figure?

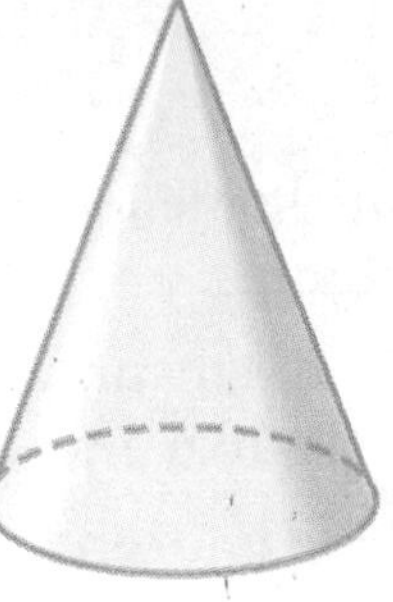

____

4 How many faces does this figure have?

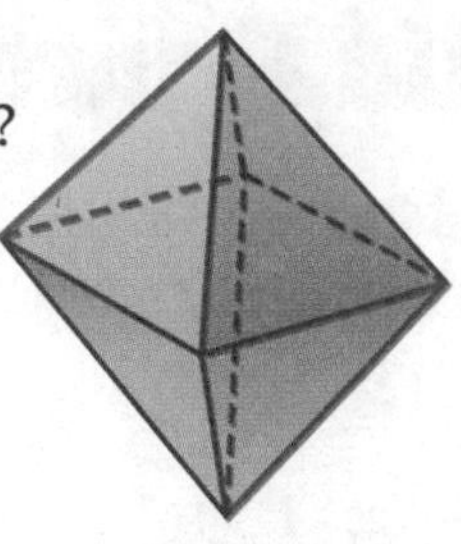

____

5 How many edges does this solid have?

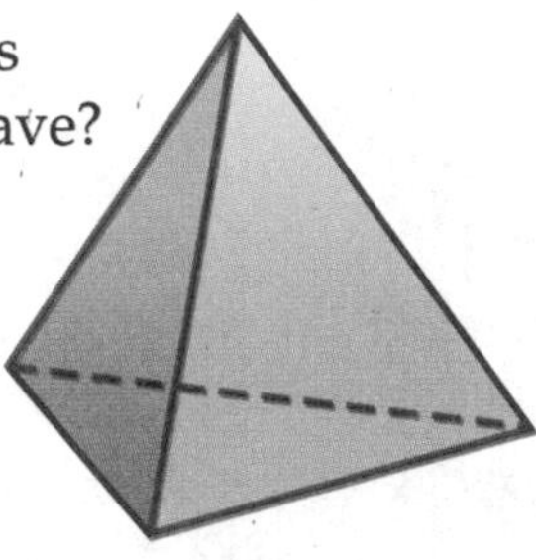

____

6 How many faces does this solid have?

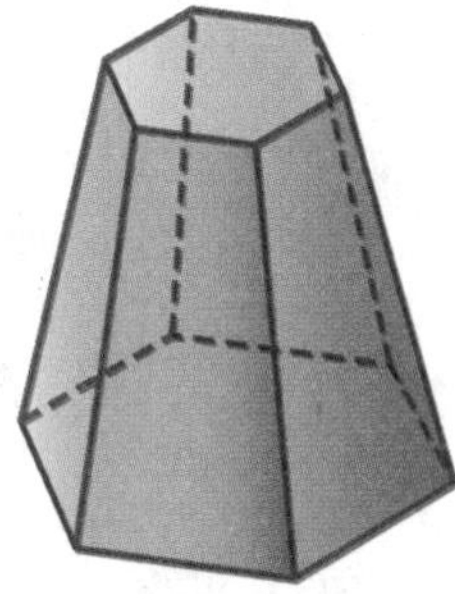

____

7 How many vertices does this solid have?

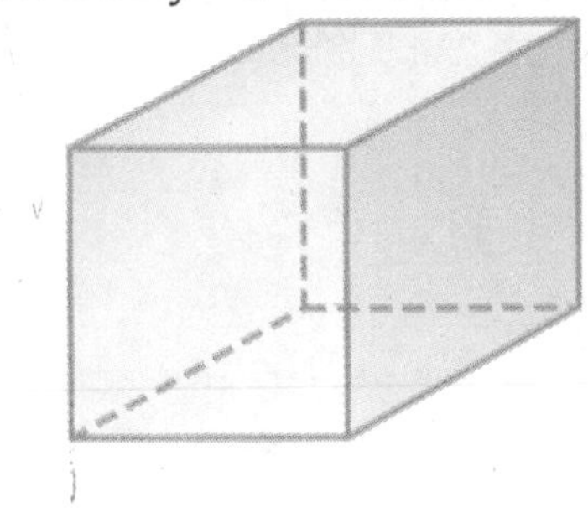

____

8 How many vertices does this solid have?

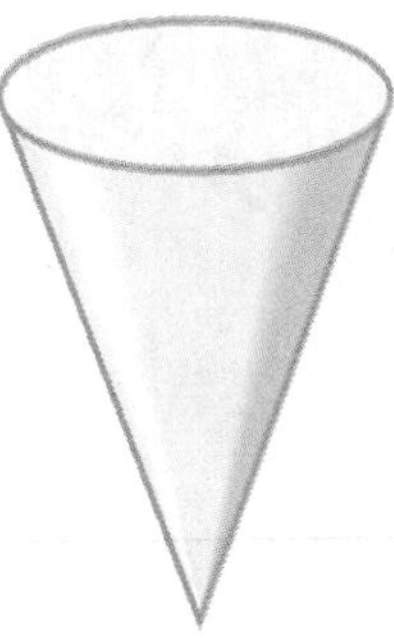

____

9 How many edges does this solid have?

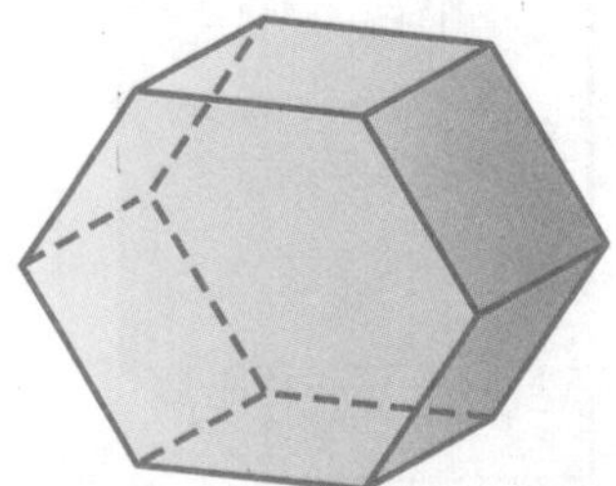

____

10 How many edges and vertices does this cube have?

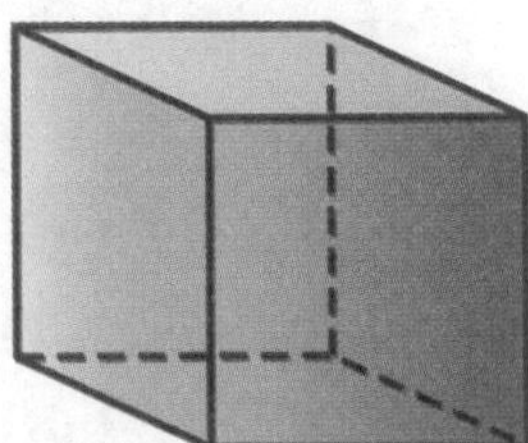

____

Surface Area

Surface area is the sum of the areas of all the faces on a three-dimensional object. Think about a rectangular box. It has 6 faces: top, bottom, front, back, left end, and right end.

To find the surface area of a box, you need to find the area of each of the 6 faces and then add those areas together. Picture the rectangular box broken down into a flat net. Now it is easier to see that you have four rectangles and two square ends.

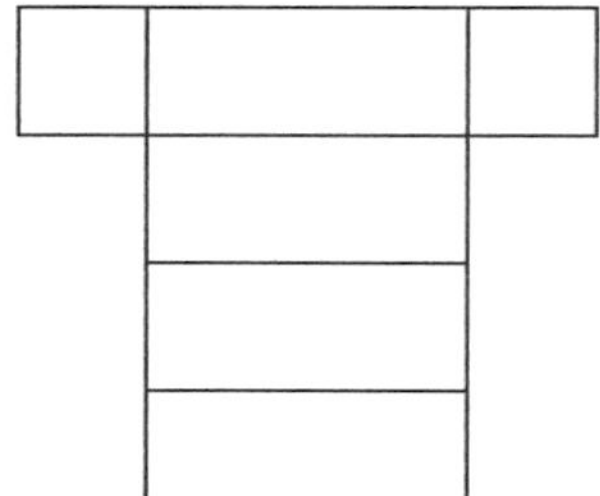

The same is true for any three-dimensional figure such as a square cube or a triangular pyramid: find the area of each face and then add them together.

Example:

What is the surface area of a cube with sides of 2 inches?

Step 1: Picture the cube broken apart.

Step 2: Find the area of one face. $2 \times 2 = 4$

Step 3: Multiply by the number of faces.

The total surface area is $4 \times 6 = 24$ in.^{2}

Exercises FIND THE SURFACE AREA

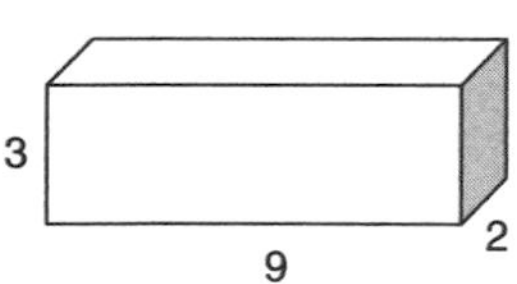

____

2 Laura wants to cover a box in fabric for an art project. If the box is a square with 4-inch sides, how much fabric will she need to completely cover all the sides?

____

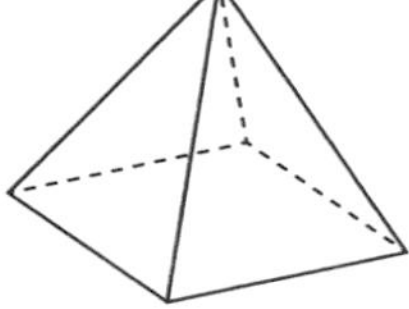

What is the surface area of the pyramid above if the base is a square with sides of 5 and each triangular side has an area of 10π?

____

17.7

Name ___________________________

Graphing Figures

You have already learned to plot ordered pairs on the coordinate plane and how to find the area of figures. Let's put these two skills together and learn to graph figures on the coordinate plane. You can use coordinates to plot points and then draw lines between those points to form shapes such as squares, rectangles, and triangles.

Examples:

Draw a rectangle using the coordinates (2, 3), (6, 3), (2, 1), and (6, 1).

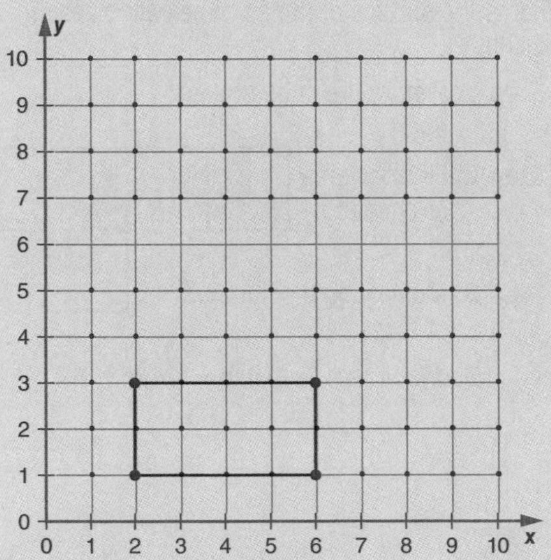

Find the length of the side formed by coordinates (6, 3) and (6, 1).

Count the spaces in between those coordinates along the right side of the rectangle. The length is 2. You can also find this without a graph by looking at the values that differ—in this case the *y*-coordinates—and subtracting the smaller coordinate from the larger: 3 – 1 = 2.

What figure is formed by connecting vertices at points (1, 8), (1, 3), and (4, 3)?

Step 1: Plot the points on a coordinate grid.

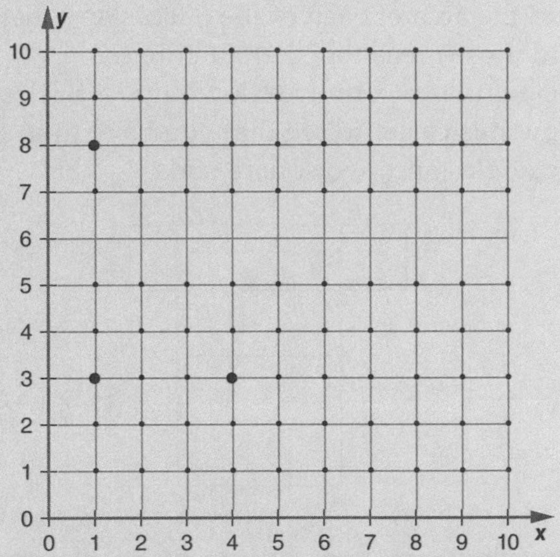

Step 2: Draw straight lines between the points.

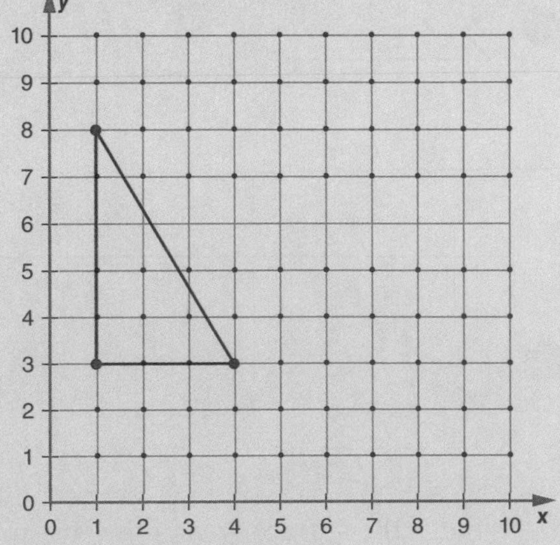

The figure is a right triangle.

Name ______________________

17.7

Exercises SOLVE

1 Plot the coordinates (2, 5), (2, 2), (4, 2), and (4, 5).

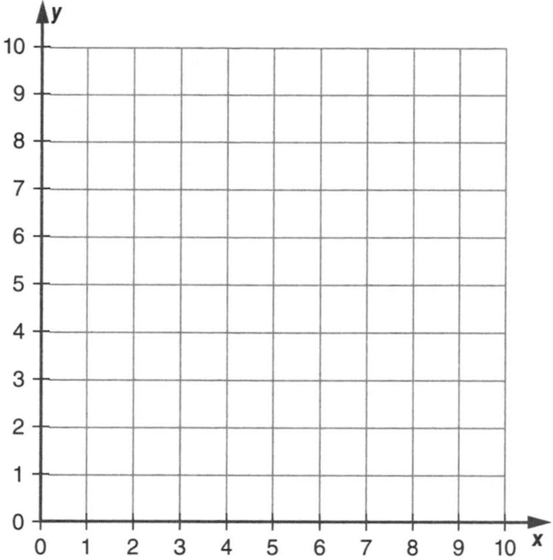

____

2 Draw lines between the points. What shape is formed?

____

3 Write in the length of each side.

____

4 What is the perimeter of the figure?

____

5 What is the area of the figure?

____

6 Robert is going to walk from his house at the corner of Elm and 1st to his friend Jack's house at the corner of Birch and 4th. If Robert walks 3 blocks south on Elm Street, what does he need to do next to get to Jack's house?

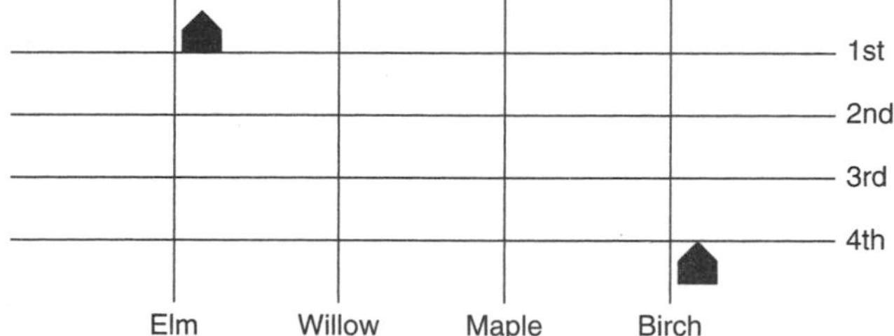

____

Unit 4 Test

Name ______________________________

Solve.

1. Wilfredo is replacing the trim around all of the windows in his house. The perimeter of each window measures 124 inches and he has 9 windows.

   How many feet of trim does Wilfredo need to replace? ______________________

2. Ainsley wants to fill a fish tank with water for her new fish. The fish tank holds 176 quarts and she is adding the water with a one-gallon container.

   How many gallon containers will she need to fill the tank? ______________________

3. Sally wants to build a fence in her garden to keep the rabbits out, and she needs to know how much fencing to buy. The garden has an irregular shape with sides of $15\frac{1}{4}$ feet, 660 inches, 12 yards, one foot, $\frac{1}{160}$ of a mile, and 6 feet. How much fence material does she need (in feet)? ______________________

4. What is the area of a rectangle with a length of 20 ft and a width of 144 inches? ______________________

5. What is the area of a right triangle with lengths of 3 feet, 4 feet, and 60 inches? ______________________

6. A modern spacecraft travels 4.9 miles per second to maintain enough speed to stay in orbit around the earth. How far does the spacecraft travel

   in a minute? ______________________

   in an hour? ______________________

   in a day? ______________________

7. If the earth is 24,000 miles in circumference, how much time would it take the spacecraft in Exercise 8 to orbit the earth once? ______________________

   How many times a day would the spacecraft orbit the earth? ______________________

   How many times in a week? ______________________

   How many times in a year? ______________________

8. What is the area of a triangle with sides of 6 cm, 6 cm, a base of 9 cm, and a height of 4 cm? ______________________ sq cm

Name ______________________________

Unit 4 Test

9 How much corn feed can fit into a rectangular bin that measures 4.6 meters in width, 14.5 meters in length, and 5.5 meters high?

______________________ cu meters

10 The average player on the basketball team is 6 feet 4 inches tall.

About how tall is that in centimeters? ______________

11 The average US car has a gas tank that holds 65 liters of gasoline.

How much is that in gallons? ______________________

12 Paulie was looking for lawn mowing jobs. He surveyed the people in his neighborhood and found out that the average lawn measured 54 feet by 30 feet.

What is the total area in square feet? ______________

In square yards? ______________________

About how much is the total area in square meters? ______________________

13 The oil company suggests that people set the temperature in their homes at between 20 and 22 degrees Celsius during the winter.

What is that range in Fahrenheit? ______________

14 What is the volume of the triangular solid?

____

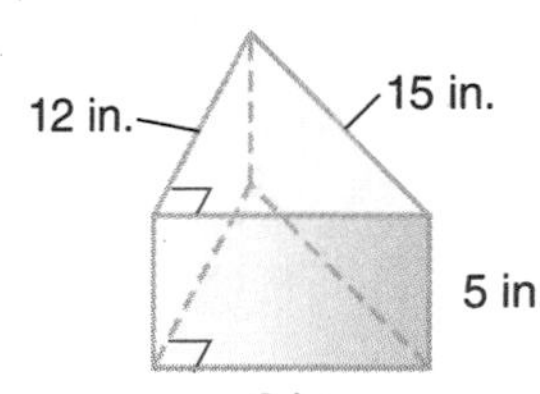

Identify each angle as obtuse, acute, or right.

15

____

16

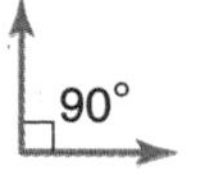

____

17

____

Unit 4 Test

Name ______________________________

Identify each pair of angles as supplementary or complementary, and explain why.

18 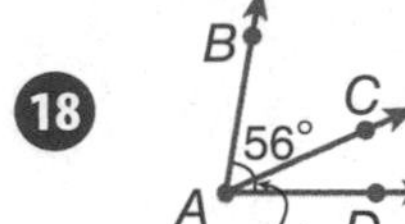

____

19 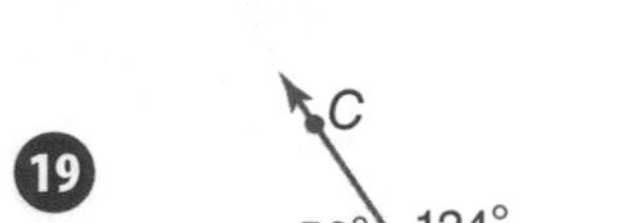

____

Identify each triangle as scalene, equilateral, or isosceles.

20 

____

21 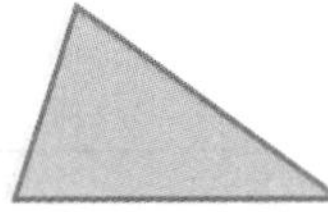

____

22 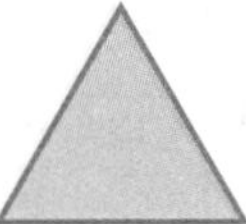

____

Identify each triangle as obtuse, right, or acute.

23 

____

24 

____

25 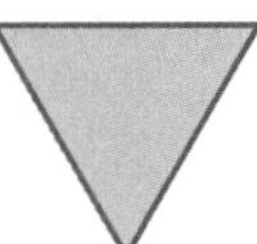

____

Identify the following quadrilaterals.

26 

____

27 

____

28 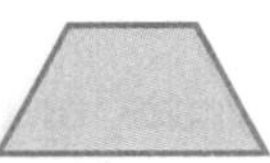

____

29 

____

30 Which segments are chords? 

31 Which segments are radii? 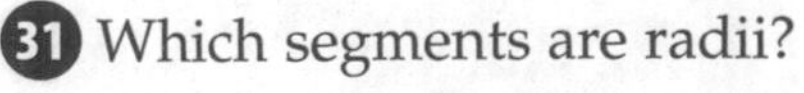 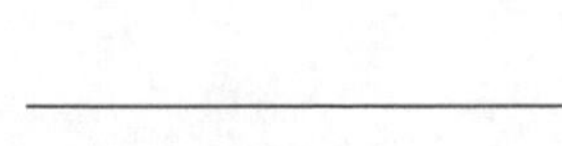

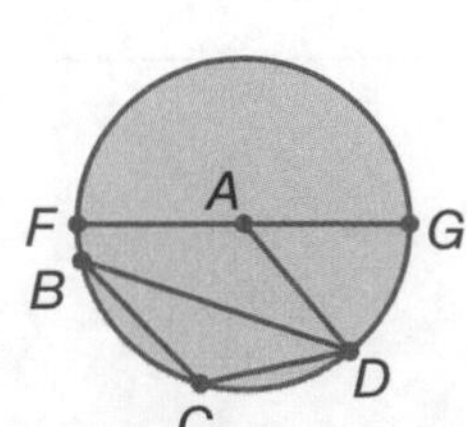

Name ____________________

Unit 4 Test

Identify each figure and fill in the information requested.

32 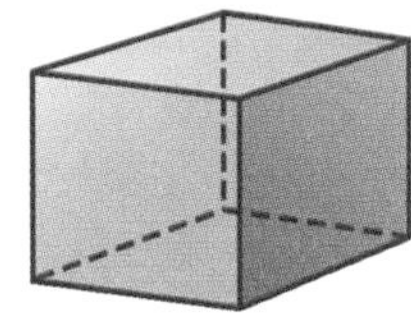

Figure ______________
Base is ______________
Number of faces ______
Number of edges ______
Number of vertices ____

33 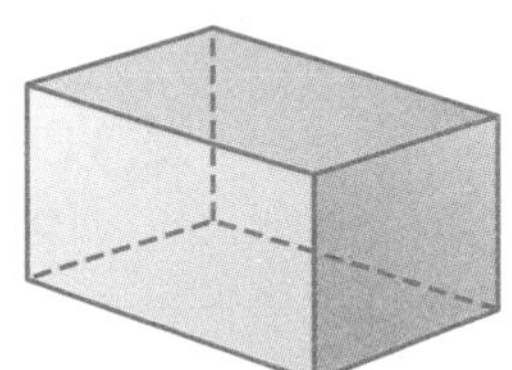

Figure ______________
Base is ______________
Number of faces ______
Number of edges ______
Number of vertices ____

34 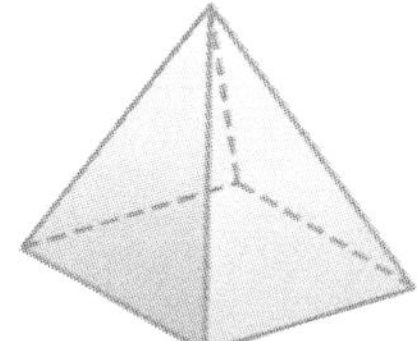

Figure ______________
Base is ______________
Number of faces ______
Number of edges ______
Number of vertices ____

35

Figure ______________
Base is ______________
Number of faces ______
Number of edges ______
Number of vertices ____

36 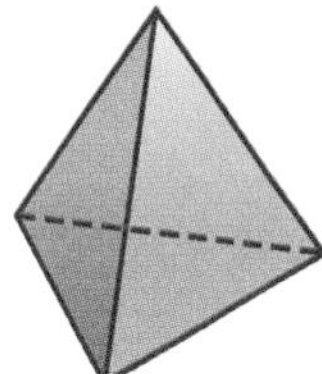

Figure ______________
Base is ______________
Number of faces ______
Number of edges ______
Number of vertices ____

37 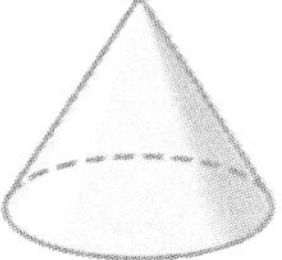

Figure ______________
Base is ______________
Number of faces ______
Number of edges ______
Number of vertices ____

38 Figure ______________
Base is ______________
Number of faces ______
Number of edges ______
Number of vertices ____

Unit 4 Test

Name ______________________________

Find the surface area of each figure.

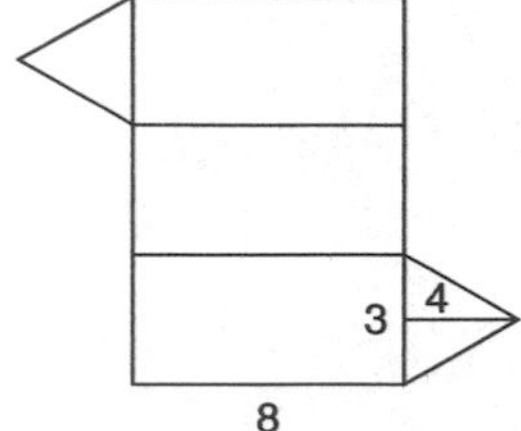

____

40 Plot the coordinates (1, 1), (6, 1), (1, 6), and (6, 6). Write in the length of each side.

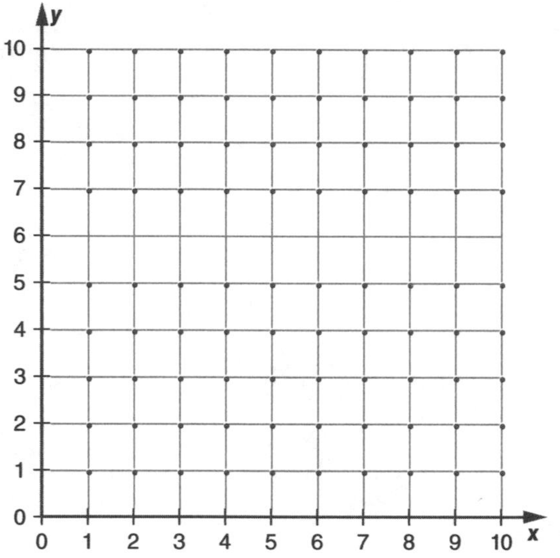

The figure is a ______________________________

The perimeter is ______________________________

The area is ______________________________

Name ______________________________

Unit 4 Test

Answers and Explanations

1. 93 feet — $124 \times 9 = 1116$ in.; $1116 \div 12 = 93$ ft

2. 44 gallons — $176 \div 4 = 44$

3. 146.25 feet — $15.25\text{ ft} + \dfrac{660\text{ in.}}{12} + (12\text{ yd} \times 3) + 1\text{ ft} + \left(\dfrac{1}{160\text{ miles}} \times 1760 \times 3\right) + 6$

$= 15.25 + 55 + 36 + 1 + 33 + 6 = 146.25$

4. 240 sq ft — 144 in. $= 12$ ft; $12 \times 20 = 240$ sq ft

5. 6 sq ft — 60 in. $= 5$ ft so that is the longest side; $A = \frac{1}{2}bh; A = \frac{1}{2}(3)(4) = \frac{1}{2}(12) = 6$

6. 294 miles; — $\dfrac{4.9\text{ miles}}{1\text{ second}} \times 60\text{ seconds} = \dfrac{294\text{ miles}}{1\text{ minute}}$;

17,640 miles; — $\dfrac{294\text{ miles}}{1\text{ minute}} \times 60\text{ minutes} = \dfrac{17{,}640\text{ miles}}{1\text{ hour}}$;

423,360 miles — $\dfrac{17{,}640\text{ miles}}{1\text{ hour}} \times 24\text{ hours} = \dfrac{423{,}360\text{ miles}}{1\text{ day}}$

7. 1.36 hours; — $\dfrac{17{,}640\text{ miles}}{1\text{ hour}} = \dfrac{24{,}000\text{ miles}}{y\text{ hours}}; 17{,}640 \times y = 1 \times 24{,}000; y = \dfrac{24{,}000}{17{,}640} = 1.36$ hours;

17.6 times per day; — $\dfrac{1.36\text{ hours}}{1\text{ orbit}} = \dfrac{24\text{ hours}}{y\text{ orbits}}; 1.36y = 24; y = \dfrac{24}{1.36} = 17.6$ orbits per day

123 times per week; — $\dfrac{17.6\text{ orbits}}{1\text{ day}} = \dfrac{y\text{ orbits}}{7\text{ days}}; y = 17.6 \times 7 = 123.2$ orbits per week

6406 times per year — $\dfrac{123.2\text{ orbits}}{1\text{ week}} = \dfrac{y\text{ orbits}}{52\text{ weeks}}; y = 123.2 \times 52 = 6{,}406.4$ orbits per week

8. 18 sq cm — $A = \frac{1}{2}bh; A = \frac{1}{2}(9)(4) = \frac{1}{2}(36) = 18$

9. 366.85 cubic m — $4.6 \times 14.5 \times 5.5 = 366.85$

10. 193 cm — 6 ft $= 72$ in. $+ 4 = 76$ in.; $76 \times 2.54 = 193.04$ cm

11. 17.2 gal — $65\text{ L} \div 3.785 = 17.17$

12. 1620 sq ft; 180 sq yd; 150 sq m — $54 \times 30 = 1620$ sq ft; $1620 \div 3^2 = 180$ sq yd; $180 \times (0.914)^2 = 150.37$ sq m

13. $68° - 72°$F — $20°\text{C} \times \frac{9}{5} + 32 = 68°\text{F}$; $22°\text{C} \times \frac{9}{5} + 32 = 71.6°\text{F}$

14. 270 cubic in. — $A = \frac{1}{2}bhl = \frac{1}{2}(12)(9)(5) = 270$

15. Obtuse — $128° > 90°$

16. Right — $90°$

17. Acute — $55° < 90°$

18. Neither — $\angle DAC + \angle CAB = 24° + 56° = 80°$

19. Supplementary — $\angle DAC + \angle CAB = 124° + 56° = 180°$

20. Isosceles — 2 sides are equal

21. Isosceles — 2 sides are equal

22. Equilateral — all sides are equal

Unit 4 Test

Name ______________________

23. Obtuse — one angle is greater than 90°

24. Right — one angle equals 90°

25. Acute — all angles are less than 90°

26. Rectangle — opposite sides are equal and all angles are 90°

27. Rhombus — angles are not 90°, but opposite sides are equal

28. Trapezoid — two parallel sides

29. Kite — two equal angles and touching sides are equal

30. $\overline{BD}$, $\overline{DC}$, $\overline{CB}$ — these are straight lines that do not go through the center

31. $\overline{AG}$, $\overline{AF}$, $\overline{AD}$ — these go from the center to the outside edge

32. cube, square, 6, 12, 8

33. rectangular prism, rectangle, 6, 12, 8

34. rectangular pyramid, rectangle, 5, 8, 5

35. triangular prism, rectangle, 5, 9, 6

36. triangular pyramid, triangle, 4, 6, 4

37. cone, circle, 2, 0, 1

38. cylinder, circle, 3, 0, 0

39. 84 — 3 equal rectangles + 2 equal triangles:

$$8 \times 3 = 24; 24 \times 3 = 72; A = \frac{1}{2}bh = \frac{1}{2}(3)(4) = \frac{1}{2}(12) = 6; 6 \times 2 = 12; 72 + 12 = 84$$

40.

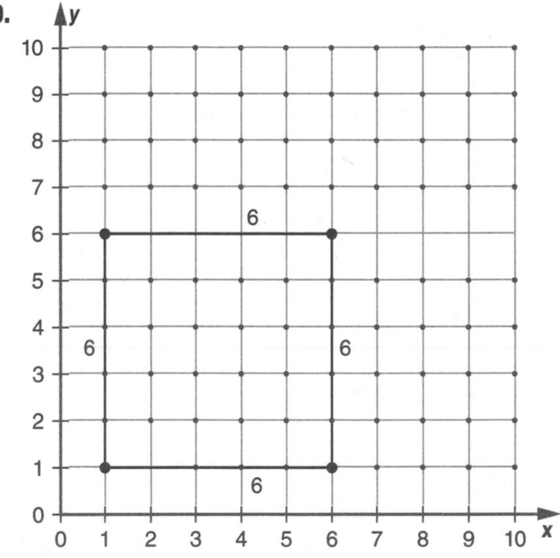

Square; 24; 36

Name ______________________

Bar Graphs

Graphs are useful ways to display information, or **data**. A **bar graph** uses bars to compare two or more people, places, or things. The bars in this type of graph may be horizontal or vertical, but not both. Each bar represents a number. Because the data are shown visually, the bars can be compared to one another. Sometimes, different colored bars that represent different kinds of people or things are used.

Examples:

Each student at Centertown Middle School voted for his or her favorite kind of pie.

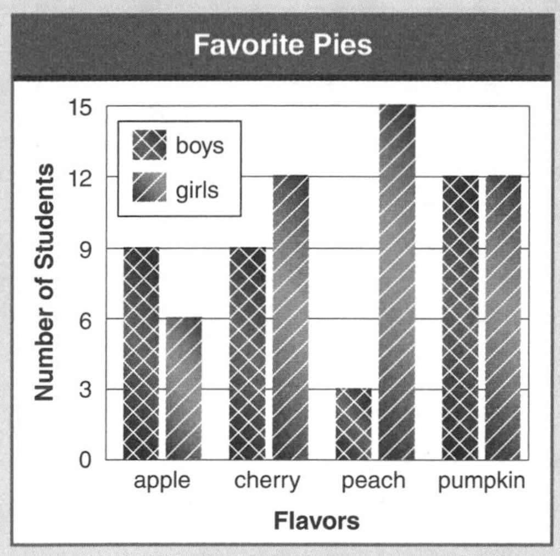

The key tells you that the bars that are cross-hatched stand for boys and the bars with slashes stand for girls. The horizontal line, or **axis**, at the bottom of the graph names different kinds of pie. The vertical axis tells you how many boys and how many girls voted for that kind of pie.

How many students voted for either apple or peach?

Step 1: Find "apple" on the horizontal axis. Look at the top of each bar in the "apple" section, and follow that line back to the vertical axis to find out how many girls voted for apple pie, and how many boys voted for apple pie. 9 boys + 6 girls = 15 students voted for this kind of pie.

Step 2: Find "peach" on the horizontal axis. Repeat the process. 3 boys + 15 girls = 18 students

Exercises INTERPRET

1. Use the graph below to identify the second most-liked fruit.

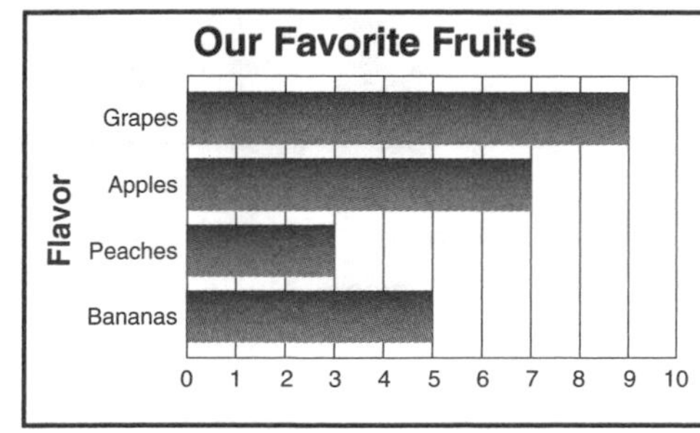

____

2. According to this bar graph, what was the least favorite color for students' favorite juices?

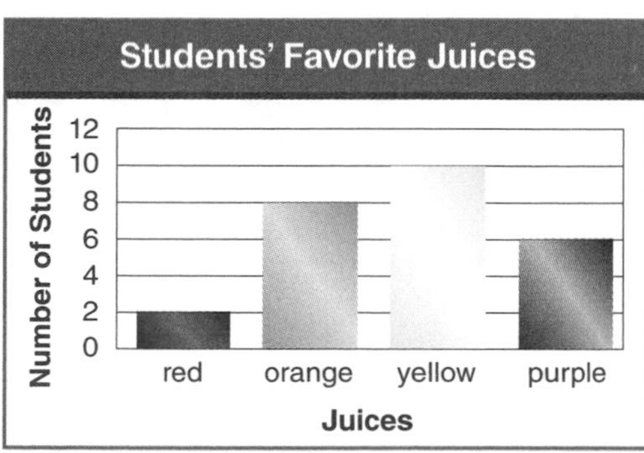

____

18.1

Name ______________________________

3 Ignoring "Other," what is the least common means for students to get to school according to the bar graph below?

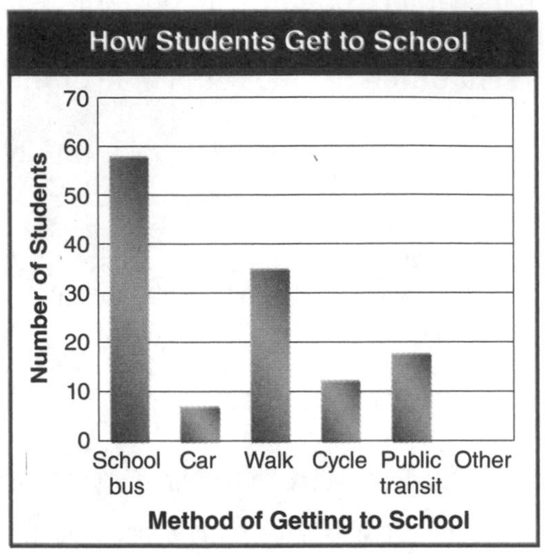

____

4 A class survey asked each student his or her birth month. The graph below displays this data. What month had the most student birthdays?

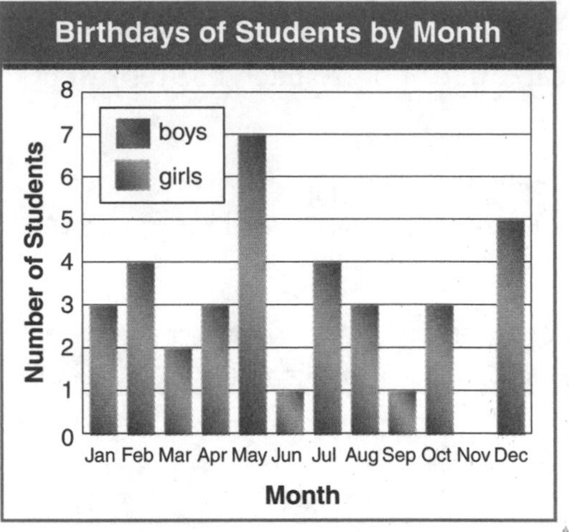

____

5 Which Canadian province has the third highest Average Annual Income?

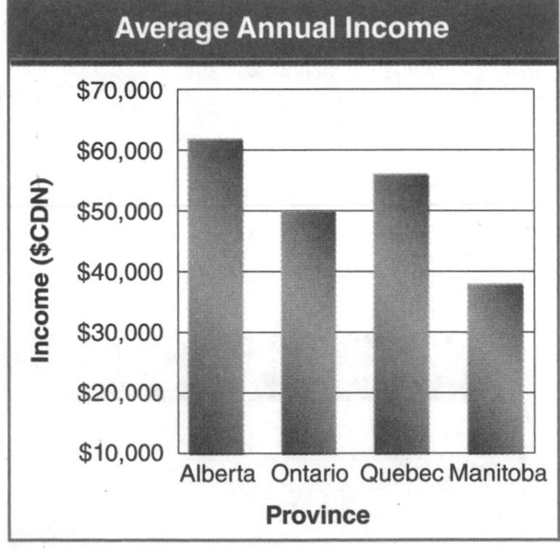

____

6 How many more students prefer jazz music than prefer rock music?

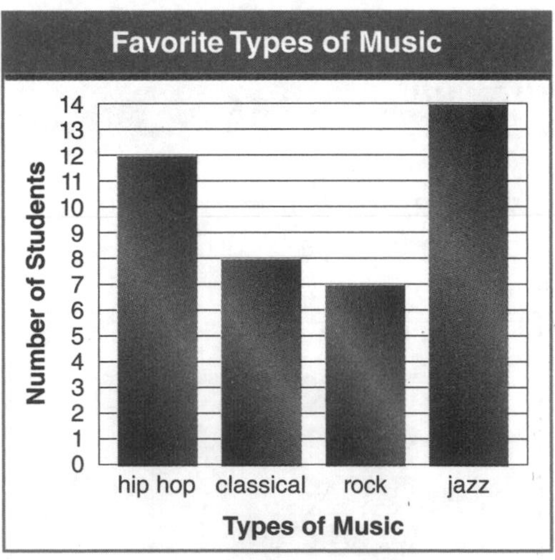

____

Name ______________________________

18.2

Line Graphs

A **line graph** often shows how information changes as time passes. Each number on the horizontal axis represents a specific time. The distance from one time to another is called an **interval**. In a line graph, the steeper a line segment is, the more change there has been during that interval.

Example:

During what interval did Amy send the most messages? About how many messages did she send during that interval?

Step 1: Look for the steepest line segment between intervals. That segment is between 4:00 P.M. and 7:00 P.M.

Step 2: Look along the horizontal axis for the time at the beginning of that interval. Then look at where the line is at that time on the vertical axis to find out how many text messages Amy sent by then. By 4:00, Amy had sent 20 text messages.

Step 3: Look for the time at the end of that interval. Find out how many text messages Amy had sent by then. By 7:00, Amy had sent 40 messages.

Step 4: Subtract. $40 - 20 = 20$. So between 4:00 and 7:00, Amy sent 20 text messages.

Exercises **INTERPRET**

1. Between what two years did the number of dolphin sightings increase the most?

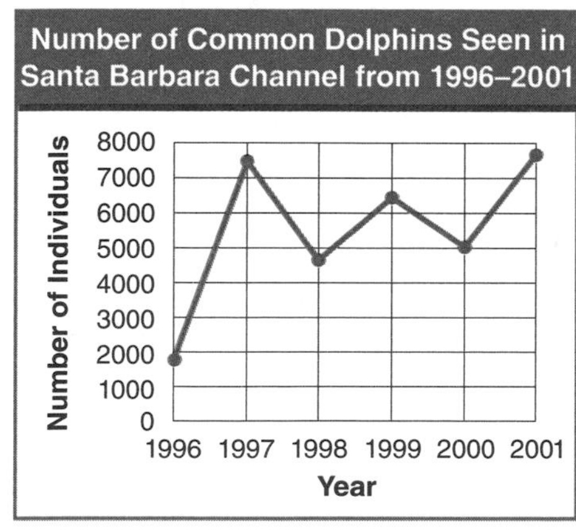

____

2. What number of students could locate materials in 20 minutes?

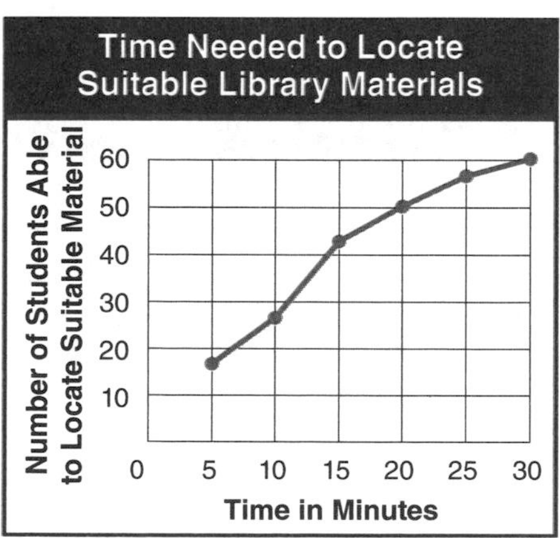

____

Name ______________________________

3 Looking at the line graph below, what two days would you try to avoid going to the Registration office?

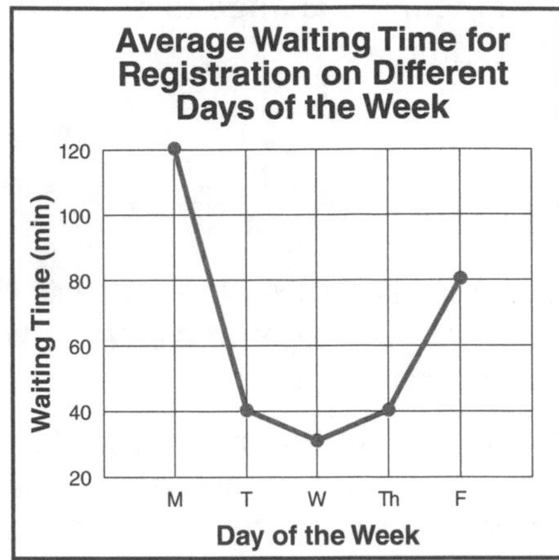

____

4 Between which two days did the number of correct facts increase the most?

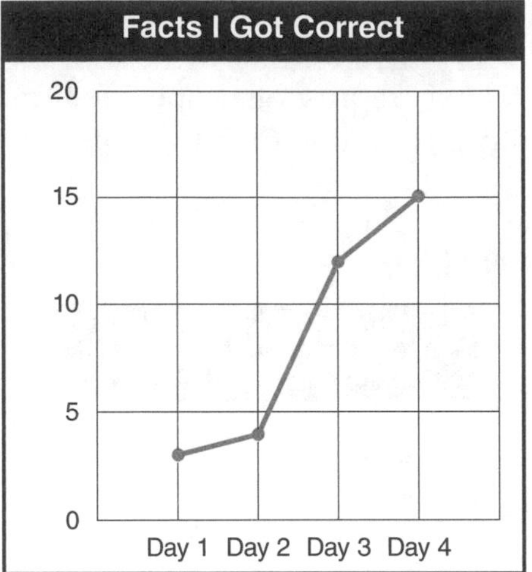

____

5 What are the two most popular days for consuming potatoes, according to the line graph?

____

____

How many kilos of potatoes are consumed on those two days?

____

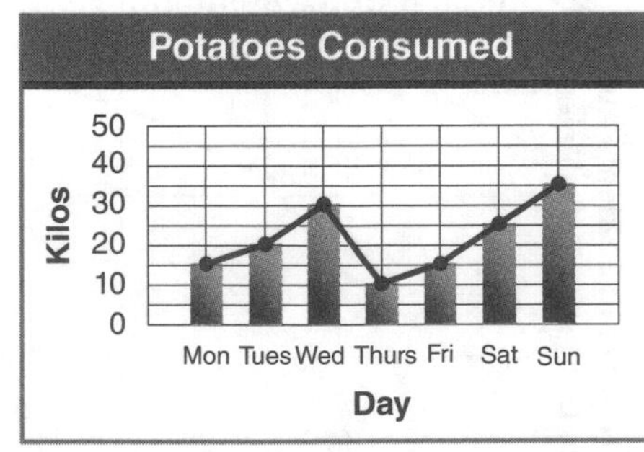

6 From the line graph below, describe the levels of ozone between January and March.

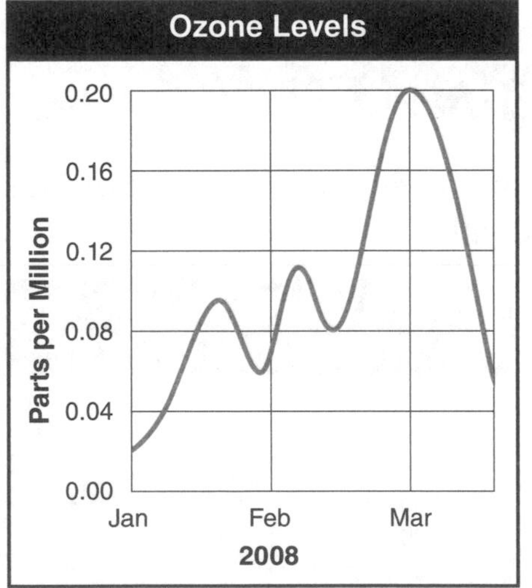

____

____

Name ______________________________

Double-Line Graphs

A **double-line graph** often compares how information changes *for two or more* people, places, or things as time passes.

Example:

When did Amy and Jim both send exactly the same total number of messages? How many total messages did each of them send?

Step 1: Look for a point on the graph where the lines touch one another. Then follow that point down to the horizontal axis to see what time it was. At 7:00 P.M., they had each sent 40 messages.

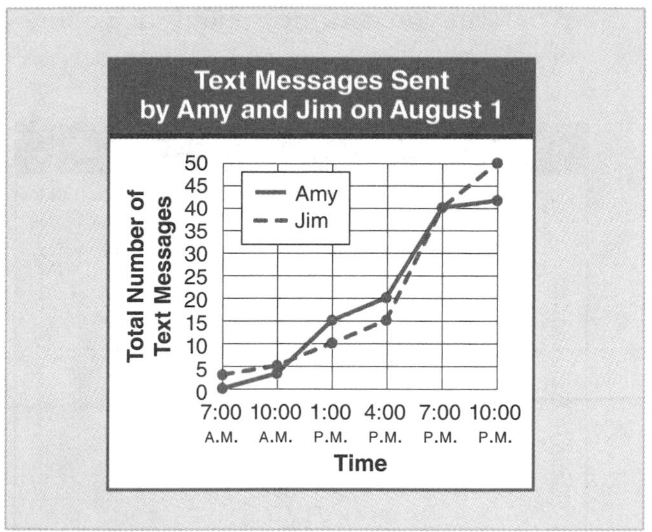

Exercises INTERPRET

1. What can you say about the supply and demand of chocolates from the double-line graph?

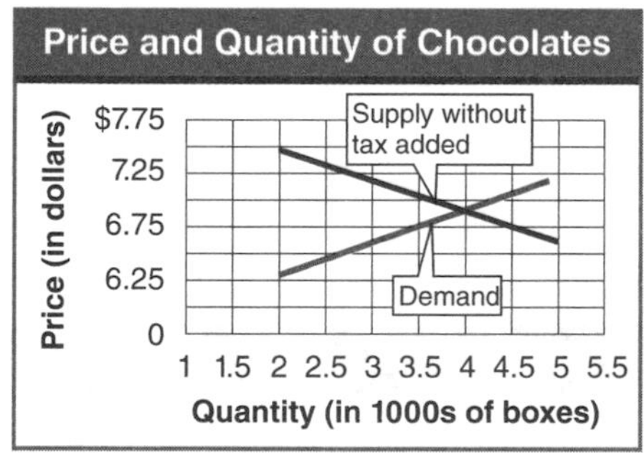

____

____

2. What conclusion can you draw from the double-line graph about grades and how much television is watched?

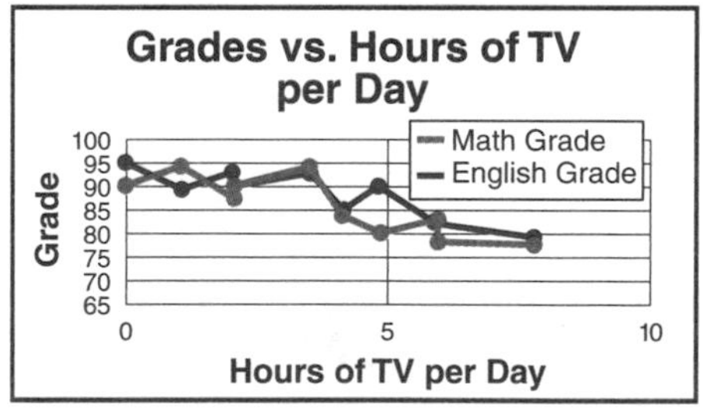

____

____

3. What conclusion can you draw about the temperatures in Hawaii and Wisconsin by looking at the double-line graph?

____

____

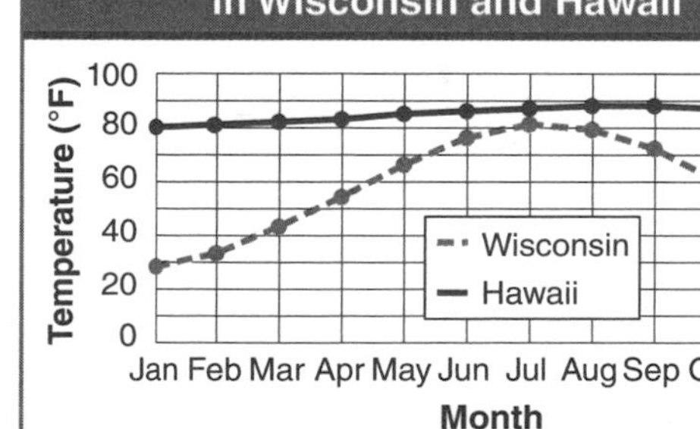

18.3

Name ____________________

4 The graph displays the volume (number) of calls for Europe and the United States. What can you conclude about the volume of calls between January to December?

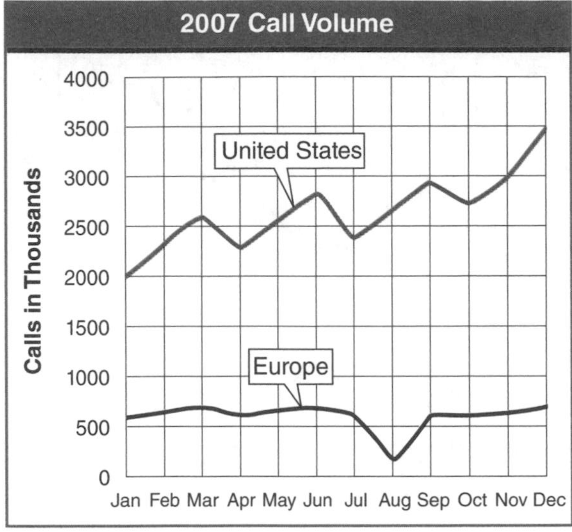

____

____

5 The double-line graph shows the amount of time that a single family house and a condominium stay on the market before they are sold. What conclusion can you make about the relationship?

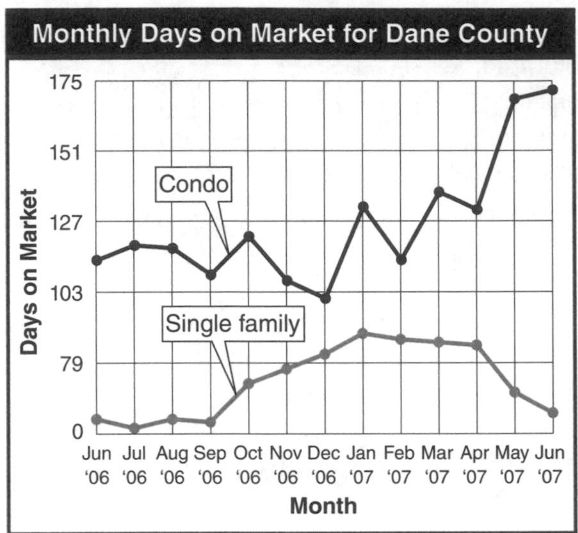

____

____

6 What can you determine about the sales figures for Harry and Kate?

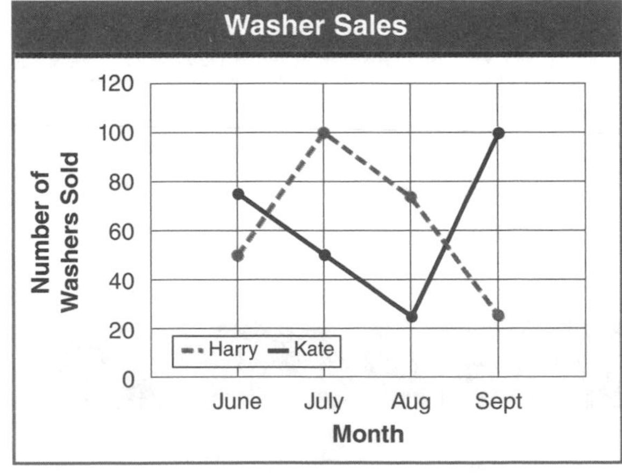

____

____

7 What can you conclude from the double-line graph about Lisa's Book Collection between January and May?

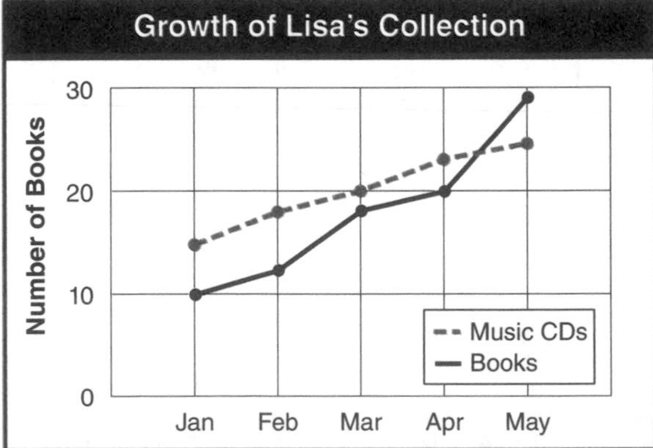

____

____

Name ______________________________

18.4

Circle Graphs

A **circle graph** compares parts of a whole to the whole. Some people refer to a circle graph as a pie chart, because it looks like a pie that is sliced up. When you read a circle graph, it does not always matter how big the whole is, because you are comparing parts to each other and to the whole. However, sometimes you can calculate a part exactly.

Examples:

Which kind of coin did Pat save the most?

Step 1: Find the biggest **segment** of the graph.

Step 2: Read the label for that segment. Pat saved more quarters than any other kind of coin.

Coins in Pat's Bank

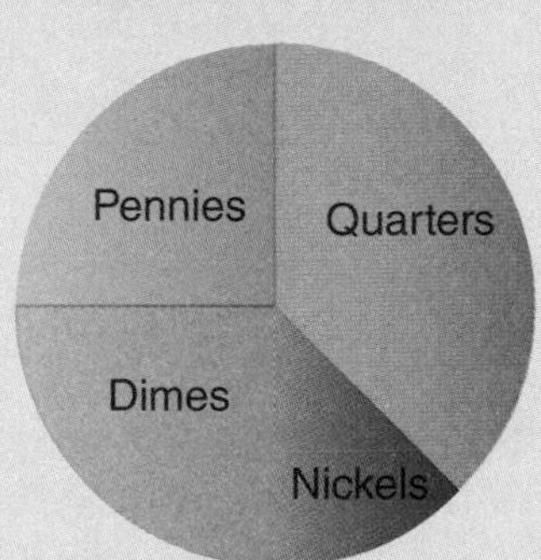

Pat saved a total of 64 coins. How many of them were pennies?

Step 1: Look at the whole circle. You may not be able to tell exactly how big each part is. However, you can estimate. If you compare pennies and dimes to the whole circle, those two **segments** account for half the circle.

Step 2: Multiply $\frac{1}{2} \times 64 = 32$. Altogether there are 32 pennies and dimes.

Step 3: Now compare the pennies and the dimes to each other. The segments look the same. So $\frac{1}{2}$ of those 32 coins are pennies and $\frac{1}{2}$ are dimes.

Step 4: Multiply $\frac{1}{2} \times 32 = 16$. There are 16 pennies.

Exercises INTERPRET

1. In the circle graph, which is the smallest department in terms of new hires for the year?

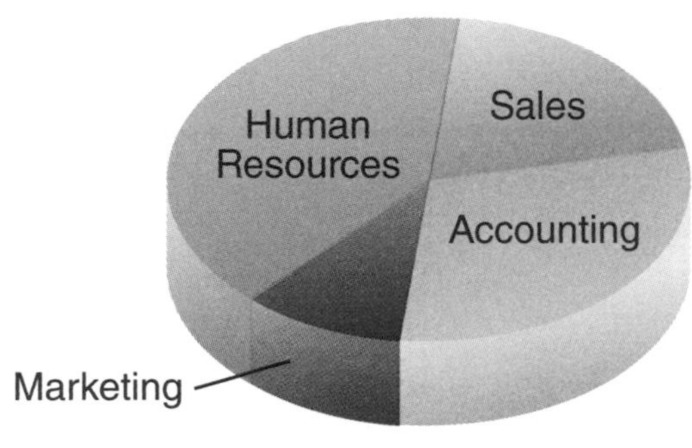

____

2. The circle graphs display how people in a company communicated in 2004 and 2008. What information can you gather from the two graphs?

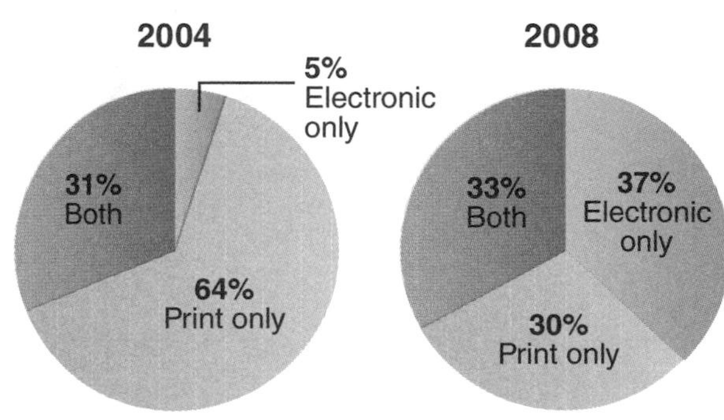

____

Name ________________________________

3 Is the total of items A, E, and B more than C and D?

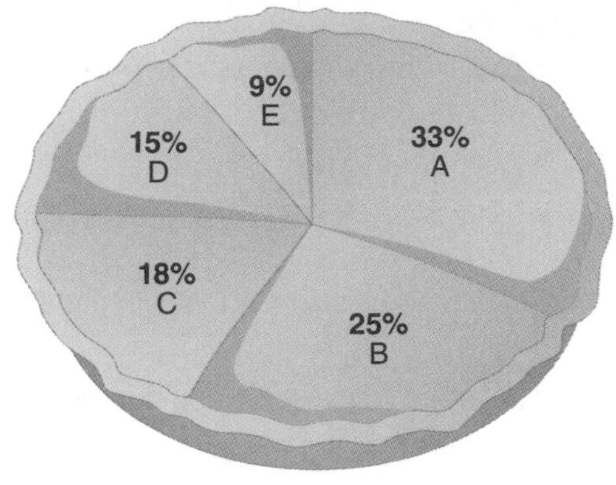

____

4 Do the Americas represent more than 50% of the total?

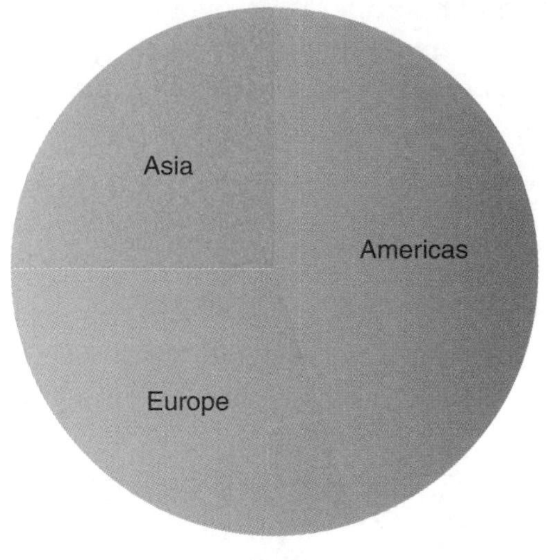

____

5 According to the circle graph, are the combined sales for Atlanta and Sydney more than sales for Paris?

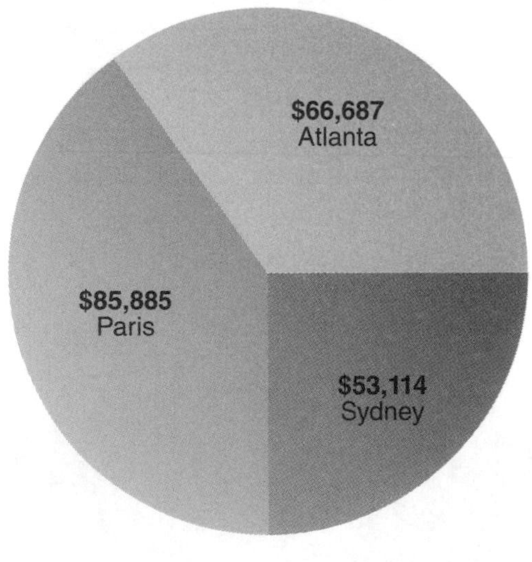

____

6 In the circle graph, which age group makes up the majority of students who attend Basic Skills Summer School?

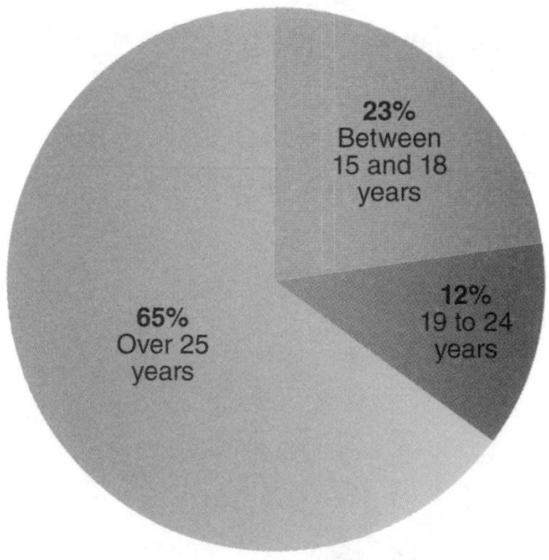

____

Name ______________________________

Mean

Statistics is a branch of math that studies data expressed in numbers. In the data, the numbers answer questions like: How many? How long? How far? How big?

The **mean** (sometimes called the average) is the total of the whole collection divided by the number of addends.

Let's say you have this set of numbers: 21, 10, 18, 10, 14, 7, 10, 14

The mean is the total of all the numbers added up, which is 104, divided by the number of addends, 8. $104 \div 8 = 13$.

Example:

Find the mean of 5, 3, 6, 10, 5, 2, 4

Step 1: Add the numbers:
$5 + 3 + 6 + 10 + 5 + 2 + 4 = 35$

Step 2: Divide by the number of addends:
$35 \div 7 = 5$

Exercises FIND THE MEAN

1. What is the average for this set of numbers?

   2, 2, 3, 3, 4, 6, 6, 10

   ____

2. What is the mean for the data below?

   5, 8, 11, 4

   ____

3. What is the mean for this set of numbers?

   10, 20, 30, 69, 79, 89, 3

   ____

4. George earns tips of \$10 for Sunday, \$15 for Monday, and \$35 for Tuesday. What is the average of his tips for the three days?

   ____

5. If a group of 20 students in a class has an average age of 13 years, what would happen to the average if a student who was 12 years old was replaced with a student who was 14 years old? Would the average go up, go down, or stay the same?

   ____

6. Brooke wants to know her current grade in social studies. Her grade is the average of her unit-test scores. Her scores are: 75, 80, 90, 83, and 87. What is her average?

   ____

7. Brooke takes her sixth unit test and scores a 92. Her other scores are: 75, 80, 90, 83, and 87. What is her new grade average?

   ____

8. What is the arithmetic mean (average) of this data set?

   15, 9, 23, 8, 42, 6, 35, 8

   ____

19.2

Name ____________________

Median and Mode

In addition to mean, there are a couple of other things we can find out about a data set that can tell us about the center of the data: median and mode.

The **median** is the number in the middle when the values are put in order. If your collection has an even number of addends, the median is the average of the two middle ones.

The **mode** is the number that appears most often in the collection.

Example:
What are the median and mode for this set of numbers:

21, 10, 18, 10, 14, 7, 10, 14

To find the median, first put the data in order:

7, 10, 10, 10, 14, 14, 18, 21.

Since there is an even number of addends, the median is the average of the two middle ones.

$(10 + 14) \div 2 = 24 \div 2 = 12$

The mode is the number that appears most often in the collection: 10

Exercises

1. What is the mode for this set of numbers?

   2, 2, 3, 3, 4, 6, 6, 6, 10

   ____

2. What is the median for the data below?

   5, 8, 11, 4

   ____

3. What is the median for this set of numbers?

   10, 20, 30, 69, 79, 89, 3

   ____

4. What is the median of this set of numbers?

   2, 5, 10, 15, 6, 5, 6, 2, 5

   ____

5. What is the mode of this set of numbers?

   2, 5, 10, 15, 6, 5, 6, 2, 5

   ____

6. What is the median for this set of numbers?

   3, 7, 2, 8, 9, 4, 6

   ____

7. What is the median of this data set?

   15, 9, 23, 8, 42, 6, 35, 8

   ____

8. What is the mode of this data set?

   15, 9, 23, 8, 42, 6, 35, 8

   ____

Name ______________________

19.3

Range

The **range** of a data set shows how far the data spreads out. You find the range by subtracting the smallest number from the greatest number.

Example: What is the range for this data set:

21, 10, 18, 10, 14, 7, 10, 14

Step 1: Begin by arranging the values in order:

7, 10, 10, 10, 14, 14, 18, 21

Step 2: Subtract the smallest number from the greatest number:

$21 - 7 = 14$

Remember...

The range, mean, median, and mode numbers may all be different! Or some of them may be identical.

Exercises

1. What is the range for this set of numbers?

   1, 8, 14, 22, 13, 19

   ____

2. What is the range for this set of numbers?

   2, 4, 9, 34, 35, 42, 15, 14

   ____

3. Aniyah wants to know how much progress she has made during the semester, so she looks at her test scores from her first test to her last. Her scores are: 79, 78, 80, 83, 87, and 92. What is the range of her scores?

   ____

4. In a group of 16 children, what is the range of their ages? The boys are ages 13, 4, 16, 7, 6, 12, and 15. The girls are ages 12, 3, 6, 11, 14, 9, 7, 15, and 5.

   ____

5. What is the range of the first 8 positive even numbers?

   ____

6. Andres made a list of the heights of his cousins. What is the range of their heights?

Anna	60 inches
Inez	59 inches
Camila	52 inches
Cesar	71 inches
Rafael	63 inches

____

19.4 Name ______________________________

Mean Absolute Deviation

Range gives the spread of the data from smallest to largest value, but that doesn't always give a good mental picture of how the data points are distributed. Deviation means how far a data point is away from the average. **Mean absolute deviation (MAD)** is the average of the distance away from the average (the deviation) for each data point.

Finding the mean absolute deviation takes a bit of time, but it is very helpful for evaluating data distribution. The measures of central tendency don't always give us a good mental picture of the data distribution. The mean and median of {49, 50, 51} are both 50, but so are the mean and median of {1, 50, 100}. Those are very different distributions! Finding the range of those values would help you see that. The range of {49, 50, 51} is 3, while the range of {1, 50, 100} is 99. Even knowing both the mean and the range doesn't always give the whole picture though. Mean absolute deviation can give a more thorough idea of how the data is spread.

Example: What is the mean absolute deviation (MAD) for these two data sets:

A: 49, 50, 51

B: 1, 50, 100

Step 1: Find the average of each data set.

A: $49+50+51=150; 150 \div 3=50$

B: $1+50+100=151; 151 \div 3=50$

Step 2: Subtract each data point from the mean to find the deviation. Use the absolute value for any negative results.

A: $50-49=\mathbf{1}; 50-50=\mathbf{0}; 50-51=|-1|=1$

B: $50-1=\mathbf{49}; 50-50=\mathbf{0}; 50-100=|-50|=\mathbf{50}$

Step 3: Find the average of the deviations (MAD).

A: $1+0+1=2; 2 \div 3=0.67$

B: $49+0+50=99; 99 \div 3=33$

Now you can see that the distribution of the two data sets is actually very, very different! The values in Set A are very close together, while the values in Set B are spread widely apart.

Exercises

Use the chart for questions 1–3.

Student	Test 1	Test 2	Test 3	Test 4	Test 5
Jamal	85	87	91	89	92
Nico	96	73	86	90	75

1. What is the mean absolute deviation for Jamal's scores? ______________________

2. What is the mean absolute deviation for Nico's scores? ______________________

3. Which student has the more consistent performance? ______________________

Name ______________________________

Stem-and-Leaf Plots

A **stem-and-leaf plot** organizes data and helps you compare it. Think of the plot as a plant with stems. Each stem may have a different number of leaves.

Example:

To read this, attach each leaf to its stem. In Mrs. Levy's math class, the test scores were 66, 67, 68, 74, 75, 75, 82, 84, 86, 88, 88, 90, 90, 92, and 98. You will notice that the data is organized from least to greatest.

In this stem-and-leaf plot, the stems are the scores (in tens) and the leaves are the ones of the scores. To find the **range** in a stem-and-leaf plot, look at the first leaf on the first stem and the last leaf on the last stem. Subtract the smaller number from the larger one.

Range = 98 − 66 = 32

Math Test Scores in Mrs. Smith's Math Class

Stems	Leaves
6	6 7 8
7	4 5 5
8	2 4 6 8 8
9	0 0 2 8

Exercises INTERPRET

1. What are the data points in this stem-and-leaf plot? What is the range?

Stems	Leaves
1	9
2	2 5 6
3	0
4	
5	2 3 5
6	2

____

____

____

Range: ______________________

2. Make a stem-and-leaf plot from the following data:
55, 75, 77, 79, 82, 83, 84, 88, 89, 90, 95

Stems	Leaves

19.6

Name ______________________________

Box-and-Whisker Plots

A **box-and-whisker plot** allows you to look at data to tell where most of the numbers lie. Thus, this type of plot shows the medians in the data.

Example:

You have recorded the heights, in inches, of the 13 children you baby-sit for. You arranged these numbers in order:
21, 23, 26, 30, 34, 34, 36, 36, 37, 38, 40, 48, 52

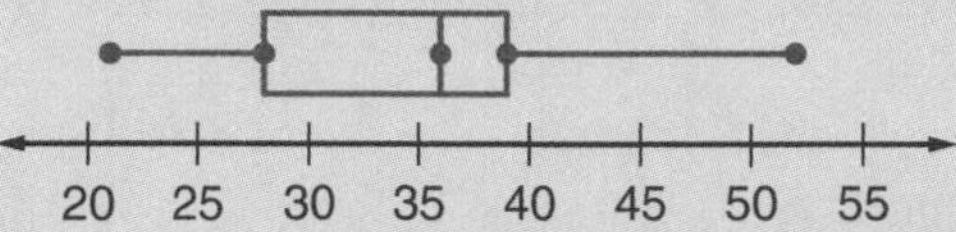

The **lower extreme** is the lowest number in your data. The **upper extreme** is the highest number in your data. The median of all the numbers in the data is the middle number, 36.

The **lower quartile** is the median of the numbers below the median.
$(26 + 30) \div 2 = 28$

The **upper quartile** is the median of the numbers above the median.
$(38 + 40) \div 2 = 39$

You have four sections on your line of data: each relates to its quartile mark, and each quartile mark relates to the median. Each quartile contains $\frac{1}{4}$ of the data.

What is the range of the lowest quartile?

Step 1: Find the lower extreme and the lower quartile. 21 and 28

Step 2: Subtract the lower extreme from the lower quartile. $28 - 21 = 7$

Exercises SOLVE

1. What is the approximate median of the data in the box-and-whisker plot?

Weight

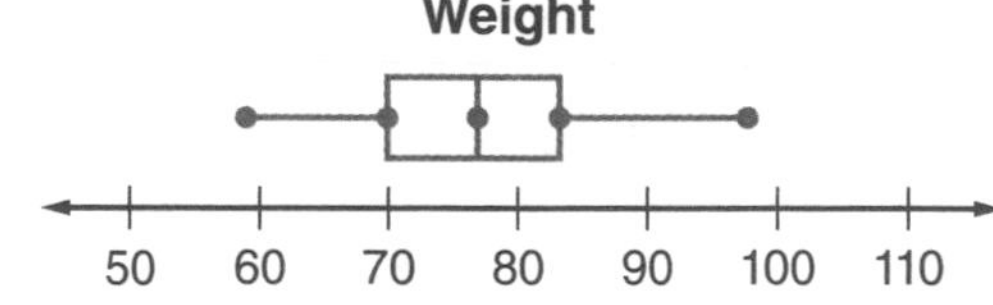

____

2. The middle 50% of the data is between what two values?

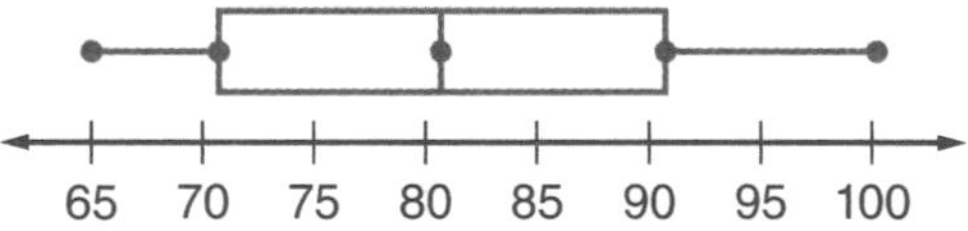

____

3. What is the range of the data in the box-and-whisker plot?

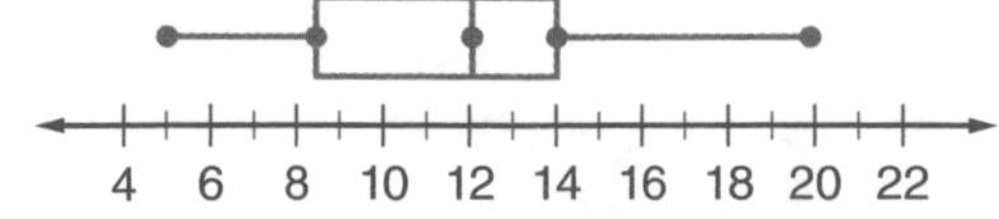

____

4. What is the approximate range of the lowest 25% of the data in the box-and-whisker plot?

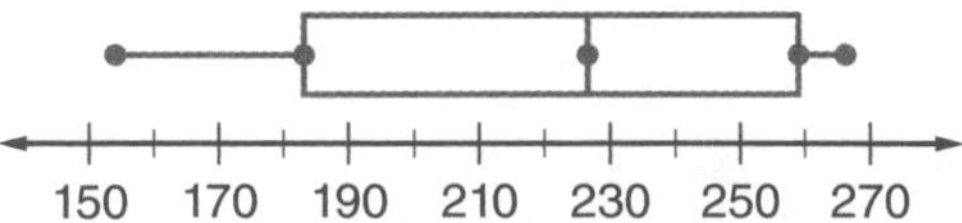

____

Name ______________________

5 What is the range of the top 75% of the scores in the box-and-whisker plot?

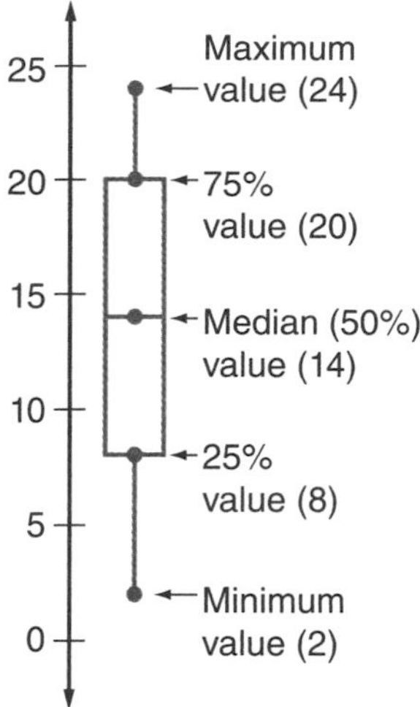

Range: ______________________

6 What is the range and median of the box-and-whisker plot?

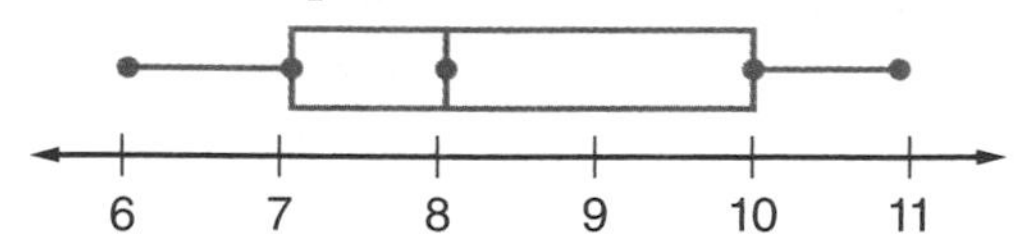

Range: ______________________

Median: ______________________

7 What is the approximate range of the third quartile?

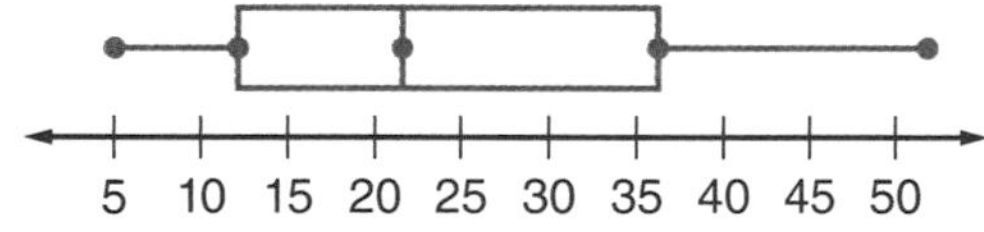

____

8 What can you determine about the different quartiles in the box-and-whisker plot?

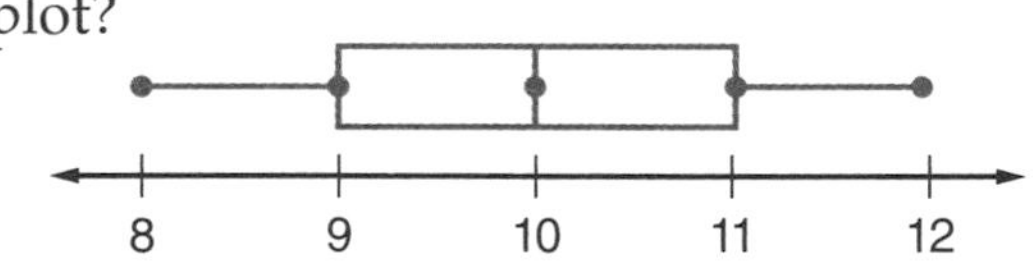

____

9 What can you say about a student who weighs 155 lbs, if he is part of the group below?

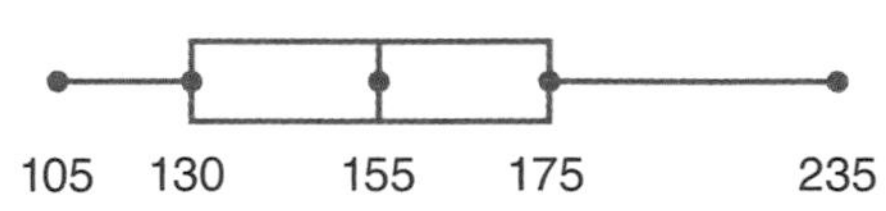

____

10 What is the median of the box-and-whisker plot?

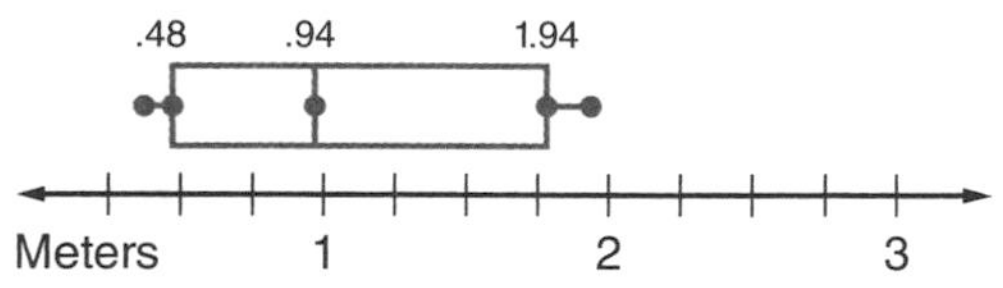

____

Name ____________________

Histograms

A **histogram** is another type of chart that allows us to see how numerical data is distributed. It looks a bit like a bar graph, but it shows the same kind of data as a stem-and-leaf plot or a box-and-whisker plot. It displays only one data set and allows you to see the distribution of that data. Each bar on a histogram shows how many values fall into a particular range. The more values there are in a group, the higher that bar will be. Histograms have the advantage of being able to display a large amount of data in a single chart.

Example:

Make a chart of exam scores with the scores grouped by letter grade. The scores are:

{72, 66, 84, 95, 78, 82, 80, 83, 86, 79, and 90}.

Step 1: First, group the scores by letter grade. 90 – 100 is an A, 80 – 89 is a B, 70 – 79 is a C, 60 – 69 is a D, and anything below 60 is an F. Count how many scores there are for each group. There are 2 As, 5 Bs, 3 Cs, 1 D and no Fs. Those numbers will tell you how high to make the bars in the histogram.

Step 2: Draw the chart. Put the grade categories along the bottom and a scale for the number of students up the side. The largest amount in any of the categories is 5 students, so a scale of 0–6 will be fine. Draw the bar for each category that shows how many students are in that category.

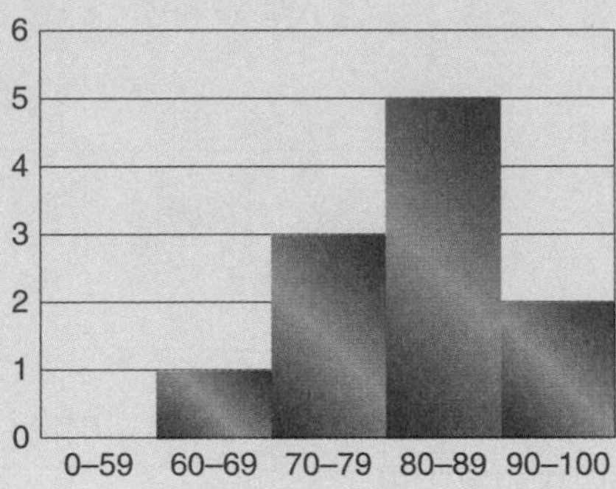

Exercises SOLVE

1. The chart below shows the age ranges for a group of people at a company picnic. How many children under 10 attended the picnic?

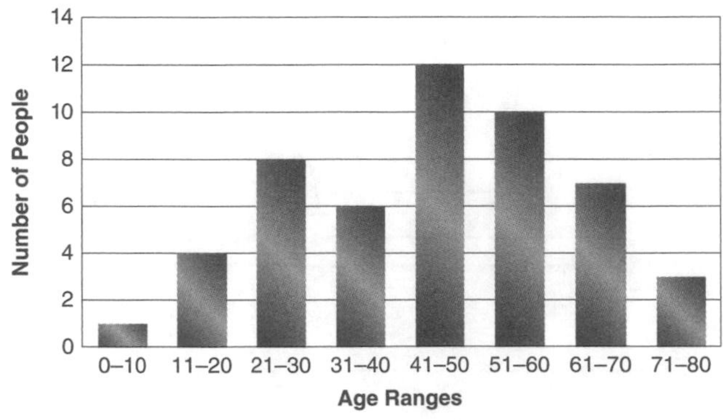

____

2. The chart below shows how many miles Kamea biked over a 17-day trip. What is the most common range for her mileage?

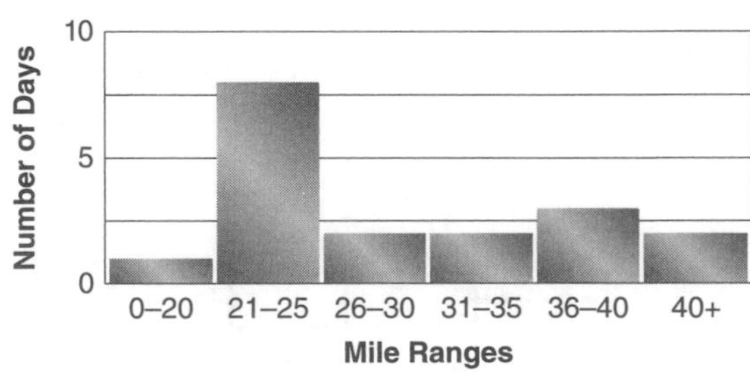

____

Name ______________________________

3 The chart below shows the results of a survey about how many days per month people exercise. Approximately how many people exercise more than 20 days a month?

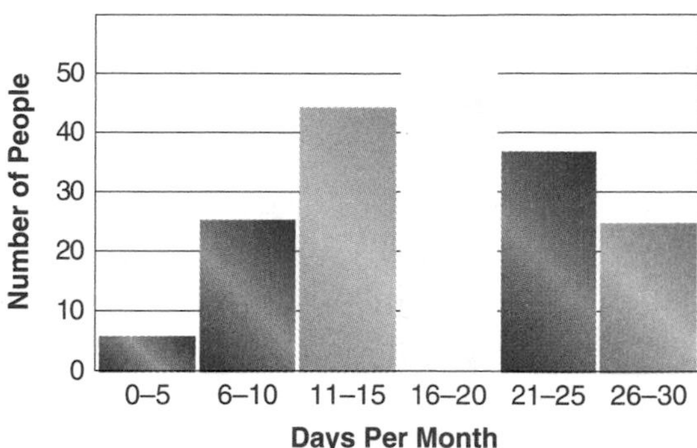

____

20.1

Name ______________________

Tree Diagrams

A **tree diagram** can be used to show possible combinations of people, places, or things. It looks like a set of trees with branches.

Example:

At a school cookout, you can buy a ticket that allows you to choose one main item and one side dish. The **tree diagram** shows the possible combinations.

To find out how many possible combinations there are, count the number of branches. In this example there are nine branches.

How many possible combinations would there be if you could also order chips as a side?

Add chips as a branch on each item. Since there are 3 items, add $9 + 3 = 12$.

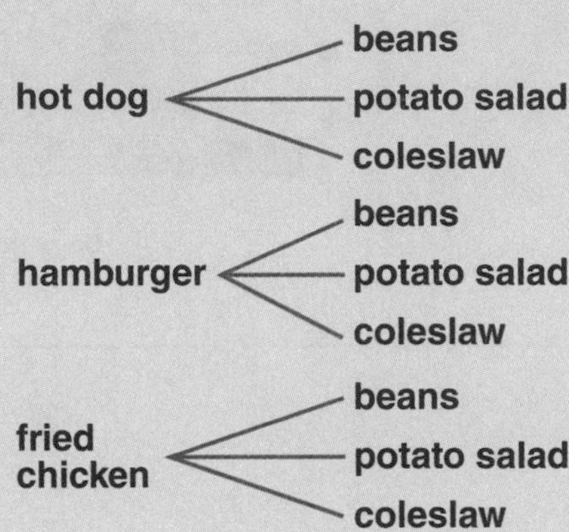

Exercises INTERPRET

1. How many different outcomes are there in the tree diagram?

First Stage	Second Stage	Outcome
	red	RR
		RW
		RG
	white	WR
		WW
		WG
	green	GR
		GW
		GG

____

2. Below is a tree diagram of the choices at the picnic you are going to attend. If you do not like hamburgers, how many different meal combinations can you select from?

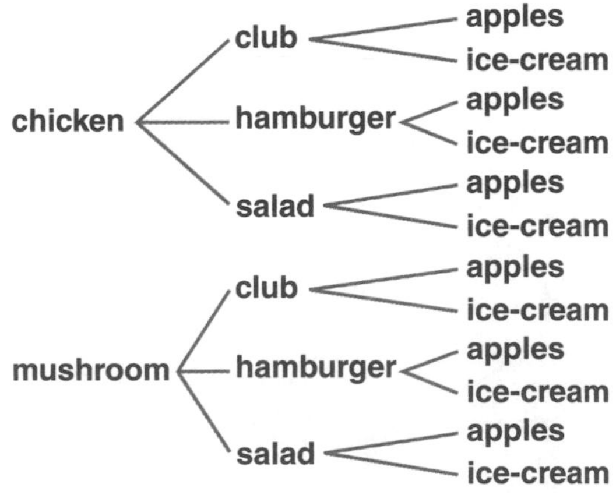

____

Name ______________________________

Tree Diagrams (cont.)

Exercises SOLVE

3 Draw a tree diagram that shows the possible outcomes of flipping a coin 3 times.

4 How many outcomes are there where both John and Bill fail?

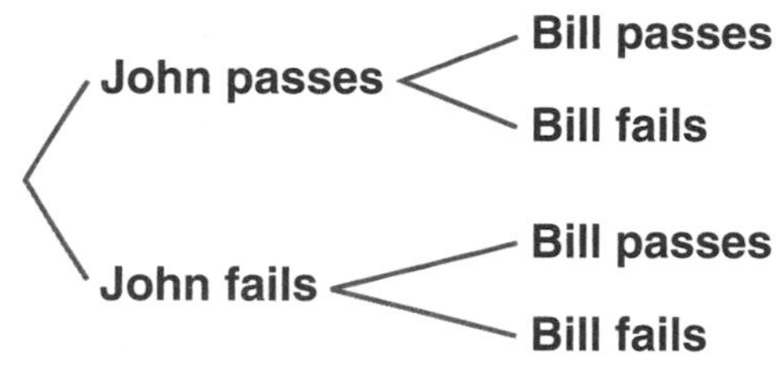

____

____

5 Below is a tree diagram of the possibilities where four girls—Heather, Alice, Lucy, and Annie—each choose one item for their desk. How many different outcomes are there where a pen is not chosen?

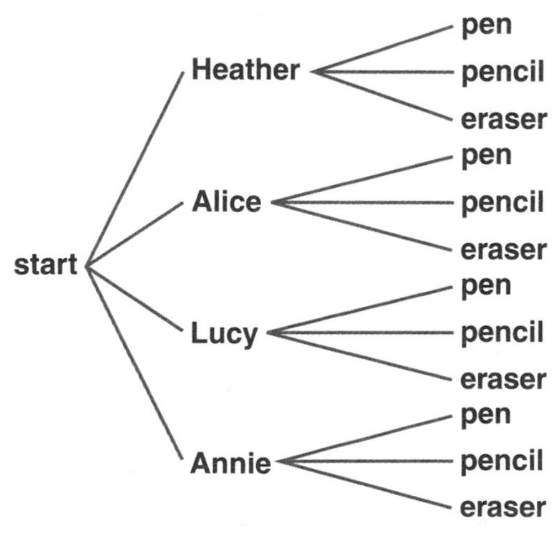

____

____

6 You are at an ice cream shop and you have three choices of ice cream—vanilla, strawberry, and chocolate. You have to choose a topping of either nuts or sprinkles. Draw a tree diagram that shows all the possible different ice cream cones you can order.

20.2

Name ______________________________

Venn Diagrams

A **Venn Diagram** is used to show groups of data and can show if and when some of the data can be placed in more than one group.

Example:

The left circle shows the days Sandra played only computer games. The right circle shows the days she played only soccer. The overlap area shows the days she played both games. Some data does not fit into the diagram at all. Using the data shown in this diagram, identify the day Sandra played none of the games identified in the data and tell why you choose that day. In this case, the day shown outside the diagram is the day Sandra played none of the listed games.

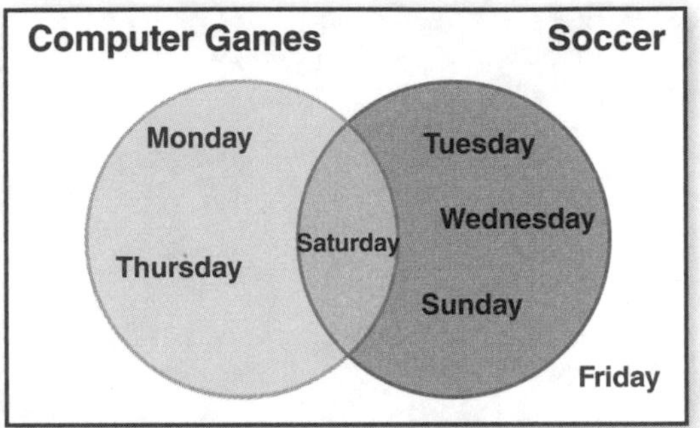

Exercises INTERPRET

1. In a survey of 75 pet owners, 14 people owned pet birds and 31 owned tropical fish. The remaining people owned both a pet bird and tropical fish. What number should be placed in the intersecting area of the diagram?

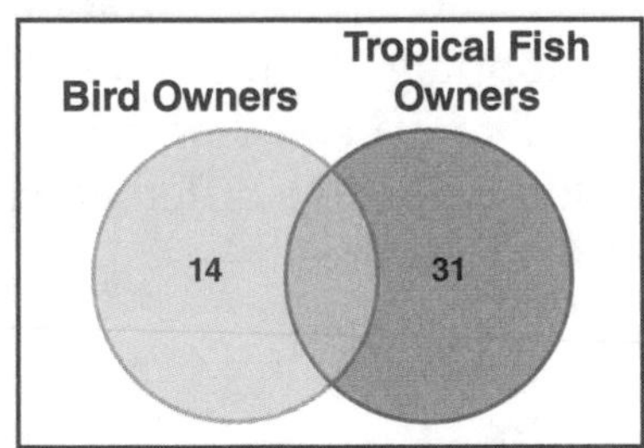

____

2. 200 students at Edgewater Middle School were surveyed about their favorite type of music. Every student listened to either Hip Hop or Rock music. Some listened to both. Examine the Venn Diagram and calculate how many students listen only to Hip Hop.

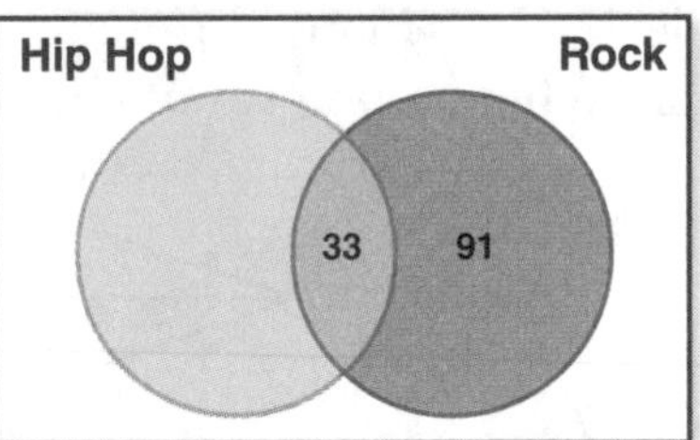

____

3. In a survey, 50 students filled out food preferences. What number should be placed in the intersecting area?

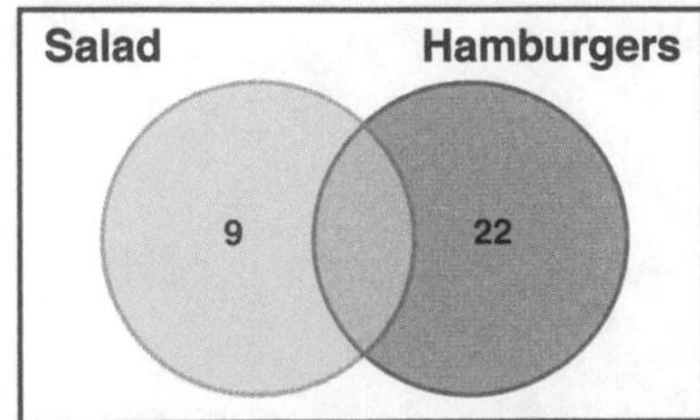

____

4. This Venn Diagram shows data about gum preferences. How many people participated in the survey?

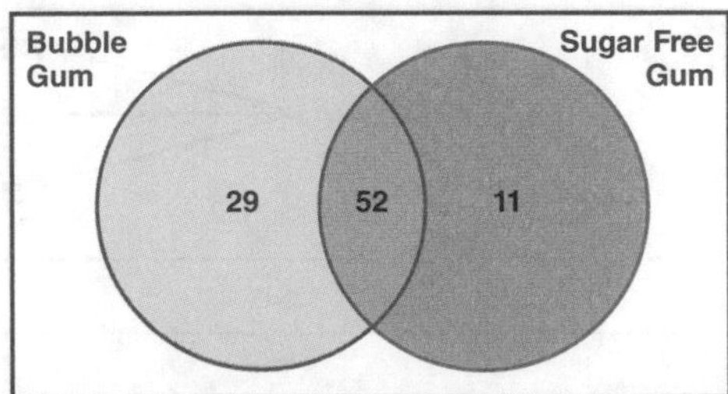

____

Name ______________________________

20.3

Calculating Probabilities

Probability is the likelihood of something happening in the future. Knowing how to calculate probability will help you predict future events, although not with 100 percent accuracy!

The simple formula to figure out probability (P) is the number of favorable outcomes (f) divided by the total number of possible outcomes (o). You could express this formula as an equation. $P = \frac{f}{o}$

Example:

If you roll one die of a pair of dice, there are six possible outcomes. Each die is a cube with six sides. Each side has a different number of spots. The die could show 1, 2, 3, 4, 5, or 6 spots.

What is the probability of the side with four spots being on top after the die is thrown? The probability of rolling a $4 = \frac{1}{6}$

What is the probability of a 5 or a 6 not being on top after a die is thrown?

Step 1: Decide how many favorable outcomes there are. $6 - 2 = 4$

Step 2: Set up your equation. $P = \frac{4}{6}$

Step 3: You could simplify that fraction. $\frac{4}{6} = \frac{2}{3}$

If you were to roll the die three times, you would probably have a favorable outcome two of those times.

Exercises CALCULATE

1. If there are 20 boys in your class of 35 students, what is the probability that your teacher will call on a girl student?

____

2. There are 12 green apples in the bag of 40 apples. What is the probability that you will get a green apple when you reach into the bag?

____

3. You decide to watch a movie. There are 3 scary movies in a stack of 12 DVDs. What is the probability that you will pick a scary movie?

____

4. John knows that once a week his mother makes steamed spinach. What is the probability that when John has dinner tonight that he will not have spinach?

____

5. The department of motor vehicles noted that among passenger vehicles, there are 6 SUVs registered for every 12 cars registered in the state. What is the probability that the first vehicle you see on the street will be an SUV?

____

6. In any given crowd of 20 people, 17 will be carrying cell phones, and 3 of those cell phones will have low batteries. What is the probability that when you ask a random person to borrow a cell phone, you will get one with a low battery?

____

Unit 5 Test

Name ______________________________

1 Look at the chart of Walter's Dog House sales of hot dogs.

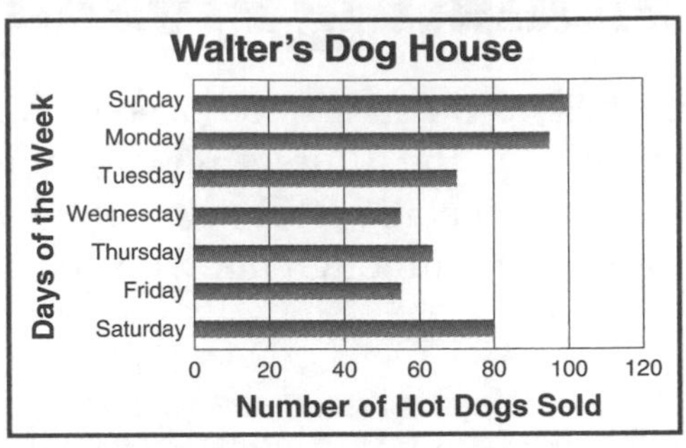

On what day were the most hot dogs sold? ______________________

The fewest? ______________________

About how many more hot dogs were sold on Sunday than Saturday? ____________

2 Look at the line graph of school dance ticket sales. In what month were the most tickets sold? ______________________

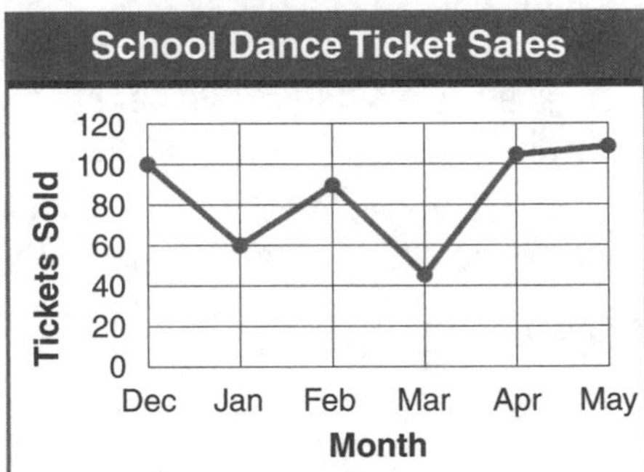

About how many tickets were sold that month? ______________________

In what month were the fewest tickets sold? ______________________

3 Look at the double-line graph of teenage employment rates. At which age are a higher percentage of British teenagers employed than Canadian teenagers? ______________________

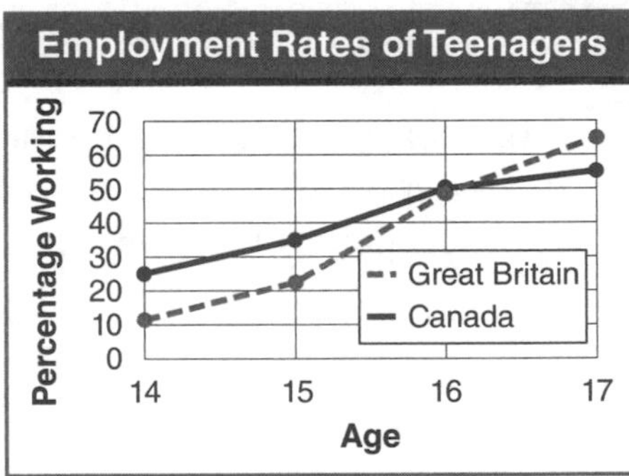

Based on this line graph, would you say it is easier for a fourteen-year-old to find a job in Canada or Great Britain? ____________

4 Look at the circle graph of favorite breakfast foods. What is the favorite breakfast food as voted on by students? ____________

Favorite Breakfast Foods

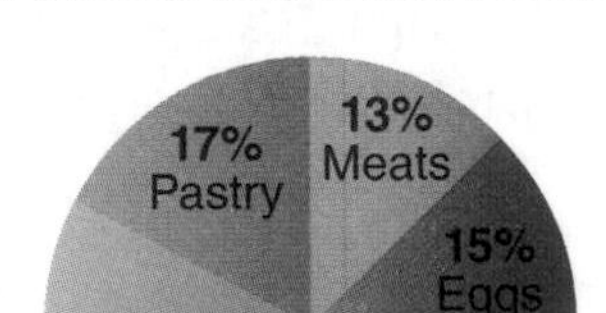

Do more students prefer cereal than meat and eggs combined? ____________

If so, by what percentage? ______________________

Name ______________________________

Unit 5 Test

5 Bird Watchers of America was conducting its annual census for birds of prey. They recorded the following number of daily sightings for a ten-day period in October: 6, 8, 10, 10, 14, 9, 8, 10, 6, 5

What is the average number (mean) of sightings per day? ______________________________

What is the median of the sample of daily sightings? ______________

What is the mode of the sample of daily sightings? ______________

6 Freda has been appointed the official scorekeeper for the school bowling team. She recorded the following scores for her teammates over the past two weeks:

Marissa: 55, 59, 63, 71, 45
Jeremy: 65, 64, 46, 56, 49
Freda: 71, 78, 81, 65, 72
Charmaine: 56, 59, 60, 65, 76

Create a stem-and-leaf plot using the data.

Stems	Leaves

7 Using the raw data for the bowling scores in Exercise 6, create a box-and-whisker plot of the data.

What is the range of the data? ______________

What is the median of the data? ______________

8 Eddie gathered stones from a nearby stream. He collected 12 stones in all and he noticed that 8 were black and 4 were white before he put them in a bag. Draw a tree diagram to show the possible outcomes if Eddie were to pick a stone from the bag, record the color, and return the stone to the bag and pick again.

What is the probability that Eddie will pick a black stone on the first pick? __________

What is the probability that Eddie will pick a white stone on the first pick? __________

Unit 5 Test

Name ______________________

9 Priscilla recorded the arrival of the members of her book club. She noted that there were 25 members in attendance. 16 brought dessert and 15 brought beverages. Draw a Venn Diagram and record the data.

How many in the book group brought dessert and beverages? ______________

What percentage brought beverages only? ______________

10 Wallace and 15 other students each put their names on a piece of paper and put them in a cap.

If there are 9 girls in the group, what is the probability that a girl's name will be picked from the cap? ______________

What is the probability that Wallace's name will not be chosen? ______________

11 Sue randomly throws darts at a wall covered with 100 balloons, 40 of which are red, 25 blue, 20 green, 10 yellow, and 5 orange.

What is the probability that Sue will pop a red or green balloon? ______________

What is the probability that Sue will pop an orange balloon? ______________

What is the probability that Sue will not pop a blue balloon? ______________

12 Trent's biology test scores are: 94, 87, 91, 79, and 82. What is the mean absolute deviation for his scores?

Name ______________________________

Unit 5 Test

Answers and Explanations

1. The most was 100 on Sunday and the least was about 55 on Wednesday and Friday. 100 – 80 = 20.
2. The most was in May with about 110. The fewest was in March, with about 45.
3. At age 17, there are more British than Canadian teens employed. At 14, more teens are employed in Canada.
4. The largest percentage shown is for cereal, at 30%. Meat + eggs = 13 + 15 = 28, so cereal is still larger.
5. 8.6, 8.5, 10 Average: $\frac{6+8+10+10+14+9+8+10+6+5}{10} = \frac{86}{10} = 8.6$.
   Median: 5, 6, 6, 8, 8, 9, 10, 10, 10, 14 so the median is the average of 8 and 9. $\frac{8+9}{2} = \frac{17}{2} = 8.5$.
   Mode = 10 since there are three.
6. 4 | 5 6 9
   5 | 5 6 6 9 9
   6 | 0 3 4 5 5 5
   7 | 1 1 2 6 8
   8 | 1
7. 45 50 55 60 65 70 75 80 85

   range = 36
   median = 63.5
8. black — black — black, black
   black — white — black, white
   white — black — white, black
   white — white — white, white

   black stone first pick $\frac{2}{3}$, white stone first pick $\frac{1}{3}$
9. 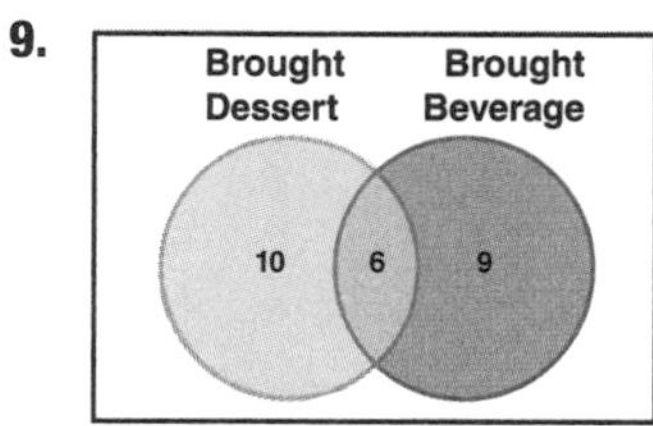

   6 brought both; 36%
10. $\frac{9}{16}$; $\frac{15}{16}$ There are 9 girls out of 16 total, so $\frac{9}{16}$. 15 of the 16 names are not Wallace, so $\frac{15}{16}$.
11. $\frac{3}{5}, \frac{1}{20}, \frac{3}{4}$ 40 red + 20 green = 60 out of 100 total, so $\frac{60}{100} = \frac{3}{5}$. Orange is 5 out of 100 total, so $\frac{5}{100} = \frac{1}{20}$.
    25 out of 100 are blue, so 75 out of 100 are NOT blue. $\frac{75}{100} = \frac{3}{4}$.
12. 4.88 First, find the mean: $\frac{94+87+91+79+82}{5} = \frac{433}{5} = 86.6$. Now find the distance each score is from the mean: $86.6 - 94 = |-7.4| = 7.4$; $86.6 - 87 = |-0.4| = 0.4$; $86.6 - 91 = |-4.4| = 4.4$; $86.6 - 79 = 7.6$; $86.6 - 82 = 4.6$. Now average those distances: $\frac{7.4+0.4+4.4+7.6+4.6}{5} = \frac{24.4}{5} = 4.88$.

Posttest

Name ______________________________

Complete the following test items.

1. There are three hundred thousand, two hundred, fifty-two people living in Cincinnati. How would you write this number in standard form? ______________________________

2. Jerry is collecting newspapers for a recycling contest at his school. He needs 2152 newspapers to win the contest. So far he has collected 1375. Rounding to the nearest thousand, how many newspapers can we estimate that Jerry still needs to collect? ______________________________

Calculate.

3. $\begin{array}{r} 27 \\ \times\ 17 \\ \hline \end{array}$

4. $\begin{array}{r} 9 \\ \times\ 56 \\ \hline \end{array}$

Compare using <, >, or =

5. $|-14|$ ______ $|14|$

6. $|-2|$ ______ $|-4|$

7. Marcia bought 13 apple pies for her class, but her classmates ate only half of each pie. How would Marcia express the amount of remaining apple pie as an improper fraction? ______________________________

Calculate.

8. $\begin{array}{r} \$29.81 \\ \$14.33 \\ +\ \$31.11 \\ \hline \end{array}$

9. $\begin{array}{r} \$109.45 \\ -\ \$25.76 \\ \hline \end{array}$

10. What is the greatest common factor of 8 and 12?

11. What is the least common multiple of 3 and 7?

12. Ellen has been measuring the amount of snowfall for the last three months. She measured 1.262 inches in November, 1.794 inches in December, and 2.115 inches in January. Rounding to the nearest tenth of an inch, what was the total amount of snowfall during these three months? ______________________________

Calculate.

13. $79\overline{)1591}$

14. $35\overline{)630}$

15. $15\overline{)78}$

16. $12\overline{)160}$

17. Marvin is mixing the paint he will use to paint his living room. The directions to make 1 coat of paint call for him to mix 23.75 milliliters of black paint and 9.20 milliliters of white paint to achieve the correct shade of gray. How much black paint and how much white paint will he need in order to apply four coats of paint? ______________________________

About how much of the gray paint will he be making? ______________________________

Name ______________________________

18 What is 40% of 150? ____________

19 What is 20% of $\frac{4}{5}$? Express the number in both decimal and fraction forms.

____

20 Julia has a length of rope that is $17\frac{1}{4}$ meters long. If 30 percent of the rope's length has been painted blue, what length of the rope is not blue? ____________________

21 Put the following decimals in order from least to greatest:
0.0245, 0.06, 0.0003, 0.75, 0.029, 0.9, 0.0019, 3.084, 0.0925, 0.21

____

22 Rob bought a scale that records weight digitally. His small luggage bag weighs 10.279 kilograms, his laptop bag weighs 15.653 kilograms, his clothing bag weighs 25.455 kilograms, and his large bag weighs 35.350 kilograms. What is the total weight of the four bags, in kilograms?

____

If a passenger is only allowed to carry 90 kilograms of luggage onto a flight, will Rob's luggage exceed the limit? ____________

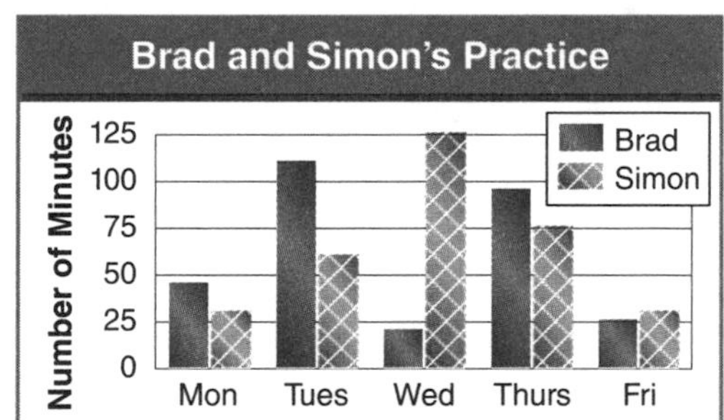

23 The chart shows how much time Brad and Simon spent practicing the clarinet last week. On which day did Brad practice for 95 minutes? ____________

On which day did Simon practice 105 minutes longer than Brad? ________

24 Which city is colder in June? ________

During which month is the difference in temperature the greatest? ________

25 Frank is looking at a solid figure that has two circular ends. It also has curved sides. What shape is he looking at?

____

Posttest

Name ______________________

26 Tyler puts 5 nickels, 3 dimes, and 10 pennies into a hat. If you were to reach into that hat, what is the probability that you would pick a penny? __________ A dime? __________ A nickel? __________

27 Which of the following triangles is

obtuse? __________

right? __________

acute? __________

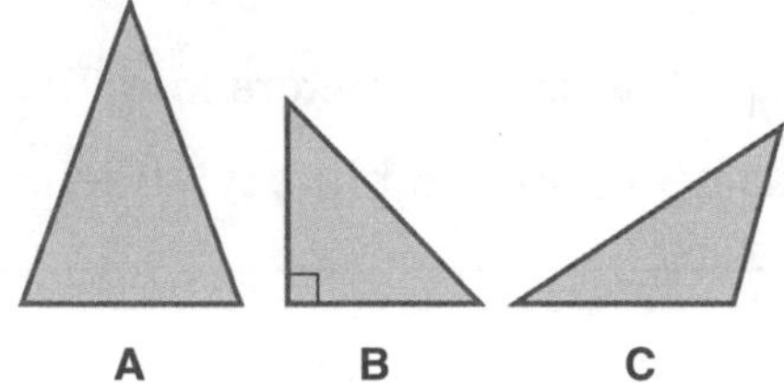

28 Calculate the following expression: $3 + (7 - 2)^2 + 4(5 + 3) - 6(6) =$ __________

29 Write the following number using scientific notation: 2,345,836.0071.

____

30 Michael collects postcards and state flags. His collection consists of 3 postcards and 1 flag from New Hampshire, 5 postcards and 2 flags from Florida, and 7 postcards from Ohio. If each postcard costs \$.50 and each flag costs \$4.50, how much did Michael spend for his collection? ______________________

31 Which of the following angles is

acute? __________

right? __________

obtuse? __________

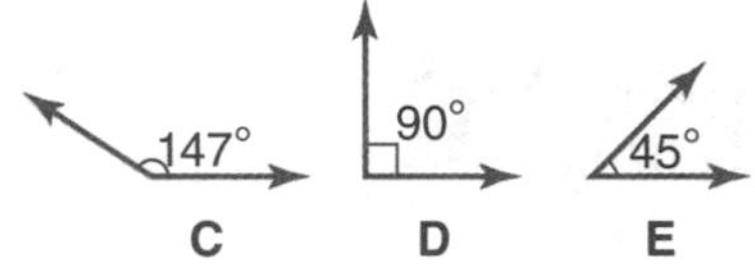

32 $28 \div 0.25 =$ __________

33 $0.3606 \div 0.06 =$ __________

34 What is $\frac{22}{31} \div 7$? ______

35 What is $18 \div \frac{4}{15}$? ______

36 What is $\frac{38}{51} \div \frac{19}{17}$? ______

37 Latasha is in charge of providing bottled water and trail mix for her class field trip. Each student will be carrying $\frac{3}{5}$ liters of water and $\frac{1}{4}$ pound of trail mix during the trip. If there are 35 students on the trip, how much water and trail mix should Latasha bring for the class? __________

38 Last week Matthew spent $5\frac{1}{6}$ hours repairing his bike over a period of $3\frac{1}{3}$ days. How many hours a day, on average, did Matthew spend working on his bike? ______________________

Name ______________________________

Posttest

39 What is the decimal form of $9\frac{3}{8}$? ______

40 What is the fraction form of 3.6? ______

41 Daniel is making chocolate chip cookies for his classmates at school. Each batch requires $3\frac{2}{3}$ cups of sugar and $\frac{1}{3}$ of a bag of chocolate chips. Create a ratio table to show the amounts Daniel will need to make 2, 3, or 4 batches of cookies.

42 What is $\frac{1}{3}$ of 72%? ______________

43 What is 60% of $\frac{1}{4}$

in decimal form? ______________

in fraction form? ______________

44 What are the perimeter and area of the figure?

Perimeter ______________

Area ______________

45 One inch is equivalent to 2.54 centimeters.
How many inches is 4 meters?
How many centimeters are in 254 inches?

________ inches = 4 meters

254 inches = ________ centimeters

46 What figure is formed by connecting vertices at points A: (2, 5), B: (2, 2), and C: (5, 2)?

____

What is the distance between points A and B? ______________

47 What are the volume and surface area of the figure?

Volume ______________

Surface area ______________

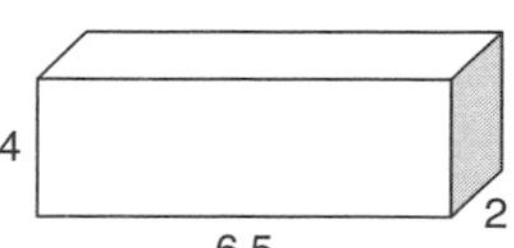

48 Write an inequality to show that a number is less than or equal to 7. ______________

Posttest

Name ______________________________

Answers and Explanations for Posttest

1. 300,252

2. 1000 — $2000 - 1000 = 1000$

3. 459 — $\begin{array}{r} \overset{4}{2}7 \\ \times 17 \\ \hline {}^{1}189 \\ 270 \\ \hline 459 \end{array}$

4. 504 — $\begin{array}{r} 9 \\ \times 56 \\ \hline 54 \\ {}^{1}450 \\ \hline 504 \end{array}$

5. = — $|-14| = 14$

6. < — $2 < 4$

7. $\frac{13}{2}$ — $13 \times \frac{1}{2} = \frac{13}{2}$

8. \$75.25 — $\begin{array}{r} \overset{1}{2}\overset{1}{9}.81 \\ 14.33 \\ +31.11 \\ \hline 75.25 \end{array}$

9. \$83.69 — $\begin{array}{r} 10\overset{8}{\not 9}.\overset{13}{\not 4}\overset{1}{5} \\ -25.76 \\ \hline 83.69 \end{array}$

10. 4 — Factors of 8: 1, 2, 4, 8; factors of 12: 1, 2, 3, 4, 6, 12; GCF = 4

11. 21 — Multiples of 3: 3, 6, 9, 12, 15, 18, 21, 24 …; multiples of 7: 7, 14, 21 …; LCM = 21

12. 5.2 in. — $\begin{array}{r} \overset{1}{1}.\overset{1}{2}\overset{1}{6}2 \\ 1.794 \\ 2.115 \\ \hline 5.171 \end{array}$ rounds to 5.2

13. 20 R11

```
     20
79)1591
   158↓
     11
```

14. 18

```
    18
35)630
   35↓
   280
   280
```

15. 5 R3

```
    5
15)78
   75
    3
```

16. 13 R4

```
    13
12)160
   12↓
    40
    36
     4
```

17. 95 mL black, 36.8 mL white; 131.8 mL gray — $23.75 \times 4 = 95$ and $9.20 \times 4 = 36.8$ and $95 + 36.8 = 131.8$

18. 60 — $\frac{40}{100} \times 150 = \frac{6000}{100} = 60$

19. 0.16; $\frac{4}{25}$ — $\frac{20}{100} \times \frac{4}{5} = \frac{80}{500} = \frac{8}{50} = \frac{4}{25}$

20. 12.075 m — 30% blue, so 70% not blue

21. 0.0003, 0.0019, 0.0245, 0.029, 0.06, 0.0925, 0.21, 0.75, 0.9, 3.084

22. 86.737 kg, no — $\begin{array}{r} \overset{1}{1}\overset{1}{0}.\overset{2}{2}\overset{1}{7}9 \\ 15.653 \\ 25.455 \\ +\ 35.350 \\ \hline 86.737 \end{array}$

23. Thursday, Wednesday

24. Buenos Aires, August

25. Cylinder — A cylinder has curved sides with two circular ends

26. Penny $\frac{5}{9}$ or 0.56, dime $\frac{1}{6}$ or 0.167, nickel $\frac{5}{18}$ or 0.28 — There are 18 coins total. There are 10 pennies, so $\frac{10}{18} = \frac{5}{9}$. There are 3 dimes, so $\frac{3}{18} = \frac{1}{6}$. There are 5 nickels, so $\frac{5}{18}$.

27. C, B, A — C has an obtuse angle, B has a right angle, and A has an acute angle.

28. 24 — Use PEMDAS: $3 + (5)^2 + 4(8) - 6(6) = 3 + 25 + 32 - 36 = 24$

29. 2.3458360071×10^6 — The decimal moves 6 places to the left, so 10^6

Name ____________________

Posttest

30. \$21.00 — He has 15 postcards and 3 flags. $15 \times 0.50 = 7.50$ and $3 \times 4.50 = 13.50$, so $7.50 + 13.50 = 21.00$

31. E, D, C — E is less than 90°, D = 90°, and C is greater than 90°

32. 112

$$0.25\overline{)28.00} = 112$$

$$\begin{array}{r} 112 \\ 25\overline{)2800} \\ \underline{25} \\ 30 \\ \underline{25} \\ 50 \end{array}$$

33. 6.01

$$0.06\overline{)0.36.06} = 6.01$$

$$\begin{array}{r} 6.01 \\ 6\overline{)36.06} \\ \underline{36} \\ 06 \end{array}$$

34. $\frac{22}{217}$ — $\frac{22}{31} \div 7 = \frac{22}{31} \times \frac{1}{7} = \frac{22}{217}$

35. $67\frac{1}{2}$ — $18 \div \frac{4}{15} = \frac{18}{1} \times \frac{15}{4} = \frac{9}{1} \times \frac{15}{2} = \frac{135}{2} = 67.5$

36. $\frac{2}{3}$ — $\frac{38}{51} \div \frac{19}{17} = \frac{38}{51} \times \frac{17}{19} = \frac{2}{3} \times \frac{1}{1} = \frac{2}{3}$

37. 21 L of water, 8.75 pounds of trail mix — $\frac{3}{5} \times \frac{35}{1} = \frac{3}{1} \times \frac{7}{1} = 21$ and $\frac{1}{4} \times \frac{35}{1} = \frac{35}{4} = 8.75$

38. 1.55 hours — $5\frac{1}{6} = \frac{31}{6}; 3\frac{1}{3} = \frac{10}{3};$ $\frac{31}{6} \div \frac{10}{3} = \frac{31}{6} \times \frac{3}{10} = \frac{31}{20} = 1.55$

39. 9.375 — $9\frac{3}{8} = \frac{75}{8} = 9.375$

40. $\frac{18}{5}$ — $3\frac{6}{10} = \frac{36}{10} = \frac{18}{5}$

41.

# Batches	Sugar (cups)	Chocolate chips (bags)
1	$3\frac{2}{3}$	$\frac{1}{3}$
2	$7\frac{1}{3}$	$\frac{2}{3}$
3	11	1
4	$14\frac{2}{3}$	$1\frac{1}{3}$

42. 24% — $\frac{1}{3} \times \frac{72}{100} = \frac{24}{100} = 0.24 = 24\%$

43. $0.15, \frac{3}{20}$ — $0.25 \times 0.6 = 0.15;$ $\frac{60}{100} \times \frac{1}{4} = \frac{60}{400} = \frac{3}{20}$

44. Perimeter = 24 cm, area = 35 sq cm — $P = 7 + 7 + 5 + 5 = 24;$ $A = 7 \times 5 = 35$

45. 157.5 in., 645.2 cm — 4 meters = 400 cm

$\frac{1 \text{ inch}}{2.54 \text{ cm}} = \frac{y \text{ inches}}{400 \text{ cm}};$

$400 = 2.54y; \frac{400}{2.54} = \frac{2.54y}{2.54};$

$157.48 = y$

$\frac{1 \text{ inch}}{2.54 \text{ cm}} = \frac{254 \text{ inches}}{y \text{ cm}};$

$645.16 = y$

46. A right triangle; 3

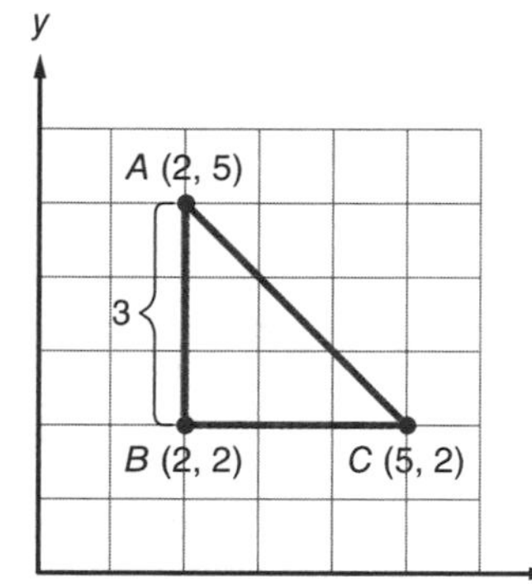

47. Volume = 52; surface area = 94 — $V = 4 \times 6.5 \times 2 = 52;$

$2(4 \times 6.5) + 2(4 \times 2) + 2(6.5 \times 2)$
$= 2(26) + 2(8) + 2(13)$
$= 52 + 16 + 26 = 94$

48. $x \leq 7$

Glossary

Acute Angle: An angle with a measure of less than 90°. *(p. 119)*

Acute Triangle: A triangle with only acute angles, angles less than 90°. *(p. 122)*

Addend: Any number that is added to another number. *(p. 21)*

Algebra: A branch of math used to find the value of unknown variables. *(p. 76)*

Algebraic Expression: A group of letters, numbers, and symbols used in a series of operations. *(p. 76)*

Angle: Two rays that share an endpoint. *(p. 119)*

Area: The measure of a 2- or 3-dimensional figure's interior, given in square units. *(p. 112)*

Area of a rectangle: Length times width, or $A = l \times w$. *(p. 112)*

Area of a square: Side times side, or $A = s^2$. *(p. 112)*

Area of a triangle: One-half the length of the base times the height, or $A = \frac{1}{2}b \times h$. *(p. 112)*

Associative Property of Addition: States that addends may be grouped in any order without changing the sum. *(p. 21)*

Associative Property of Multiplication: States that numbers may be grouped in any way without changing the product. *(p. 21)*

Axis: The lines at the side and bottom of a graph. *(p. 139)*

Bar Graph: A graph that uses numbers to compare two or more people, places, or things. Each bar represents a number and may be represented horizontally or vertically. *(p. 139)*

Base: The face on the bottom of a solid figure. *(p. 127)*

Base of an Exponent: The number being used as the factor when writing in exponential form. In the statement 10^3, the base is 10. *(p. 64)*

Box-and-Whisker Plot: Organizes data to show where the most data points lie and also shows the median of the data. *(p. 152)*

Carry: To place an extra digit—when adding or multiplying—in the next place-value column on the left. *(p. 13)*

Celsius: Used in the metric system to measure temperature and expressed as °C, also expressed as Centigrade. *(p. 110)*

Chord: A line segment with both endpoints on a circle's circumference. *(p. 125)*

Circle: A 2-dimensional figure with every point on its circumference an equal distance from its center point. *(p. 125)*

Circle Graph: Shows parts of a whole as a percentage to the whole and is also known as a pie chart. *(p. 145)*

Circumference: The length of distance around a circle's perimeter. *(p. 125)*

Coefficient: The number that replaces the symbol × and multiplies the variable in a multiplication expression. The statement $9m$ shows 9 as the coefficient and m as the variable. *(p. 76)*

Common Denominator: A number which can be divided evenly by all the denominators in a group of fractions. *(p. 32)*

Common Multiple: A number that can be divided evenly by two or more different numbers. *(p. 25)*

Commutative Property of Addition: States that numbers may be added in any order without changing the sum. *(p. 21)*

Commutative Property of Multiplication: States that multiplication may be done in any order without changing the product. *(p. 21)*

Compatible Numbers: Numbers that are easy to work with in your head. *(p. 19)*

Complementary Angles: Two angles that form a right angle. Their sum is 90°. *(p. 120)*

Congruent: A term used to describe polygons whose shape and size are the same. *(p. 124)*

Cross-multiplying: A method for finding a missing numerator or denominator. *(p. 91)*

Customary Units of Length: Measurements expressed in inches (in.), feet (ft), yards (yd), and miles (mi). *(p. 103)*

Customary Units of Liquid Volume: Measurements expressed in cups (c), pints (pt), quarts (qt), and gallons (gal). *(p. 105)*

Customary Units of Weight: Measurements expressed in ounces (oz), pounds (lb), and tons. *(p. 106)*

Data: Information gathered. Data is often organized into charts and graphs. *(p. 139)*

Denominator: The number below the line in a fraction. *(p. 30)*

Diameter: A chord that passes through a circle's center point. *(p. 125)*

Distributive Property of Multiplication: States that each number may be multiplied separately and added together for the product. *(p. 23)*

Dividend: The number to be divided in a division problem. *(p. 18)*

Divisor: The number by which another number—the dividend—will be divided. *(p. 18)*

Double-Line Graph: Compares how information changes as time passes between two or more people, places, or things. *(p. 143)*

Edge: The line on a solid figure where two faces meet. *(p. 127)*

Equality Property of Addition: States that when adding a number on one side of an equation, you must add the *same* number on the other side of an equation. Both sides will then still be equal. *(p. 24)*

Equality Property of Division: States that when dividing a number on one side of an equation, you must divide by the *same* number on the other side of the equation. Both sides will then still be equal. *(p. 24)*

Equality Property of Multiplication: States that when multiplying a number on one side of an equation, you must multiply by the *same* number on the other side of the equation. Both sides will then still be equal. *(p. 24)*

Equality Property of Subtraction: States that when subtracting a number on one side of an equation, you must subtract the *same* number on the other side of the equation. Both sides will then still be equal. *(p. 24)*

Equation: A mathematical statement used to show that two amounts are equal. *(p. 91)*

Equilateral Triangle: A triangle with all three sides being the same length. *(p. 122)*

Exponent: The number that tells how many times the base number is multiplied by itself. The exponent 3 in 10^3 shows $10 \times 10 \times 10$. *(p. 64)*

Exponential Expression: A base number and an exponent. 4^3 is an example of an exponential expression. *(p. 64)*

Face: The flat surface of a solid figure. On a solid figure each face looks two-dimensional. *(p. 127)*

Factors: Numbers that are multiplied. *(p. 25)*

Fahrenheit: The customary system used to measure temperature and expressed as °F. *(p. 110)*

Fluid Ounces: A measurement of liquid volume. *(p. 107)*

Gram: The basic metric unit of mass, expressed as (g). *(p. 106)*

Greatest Common Factor: The greatest factor that divides two numbers. *(p. 25)*

Grid: A device with a horizontal axis and a vertical axis used to express the location of a point. *(p. 67)*

Histogram: A graphical display of data distribution using bars of different heights. *(p. 154)*

Identity Elements: Numbers in a problem that do not affect the answer. Only addition and multiplication have identity elements. *(p. 23)*

Improper Fraction: A fraction greater than 1 because its numerator is greater than its denominator. *(p. 30)*

Inequality: Similar to an equation, but instead of telling you what a value equals, it tells you the relative size of two values. *(p. 82)*

Intersecting Lines: Lines that meet or cross each other at a specific point. *(p. 117)*

Interval: The distance between each measurement of time on a line graph. *(p. 141)*

Inverse: A number's exact opposite on the other side of the number line. The inverse of −9 is 9. *(p. 27)*

Isosceles Triangle: A triangle with two sides the same length but the third side being of a different length. *(p. 122)*

Kite: A quadrilateral with two angles that are equal, two touching sides that are equal in length, and the other two touching sides are equal in length. *(p. 123)*

Glossary

Least Common Multiple: The least common multiple (LCM) of two numbers is the smallest non-zero number that is a multiple of both numbers. *(p. 25)*

Like Denominators: Fractions that have the same denominator. *(p. 31)*

Line: A straight path that goes in both directions and does not end. A line is measured in length. *(p. 117)*

Line Graph: Often used to show a change in information as time passes. The distance from one time to another is an interval. *(p. 141)*

Line Segment: A specific part of a line that ends at two identified points. *(p. 118)*

Liquid Volume: Measures the amount of liquid a container can hold and expressed in cups (c), pints (pt), quarts (qt), and gallons (gal). *(p. 105)*

Liter: The basic metric unit of liquid volume, expressed as (L). There are also milliliters (mL), centiliters (cL), and kiloliters (kL). *(p. 105)*

Lower Extreme: The lowest number in a group of numbers used in a box-and-whisker plot. *(p. 152)*

Lower Quartile: The median of numbers from the lower extreme to the median on a box-and-whisker plot. *(p. 152)*

Mean: The total number of the whole collection divided by the number of addends. In the expression $104 \div 8 = 13$, 13 is the mean. *(p. 147)*

Mean Absolute Deviation (MAD): The average of the distance away from the average (the deviation) for each data point. *(p. 150)*

Median: The middle number in a set of numbers when the numbers are arranged from least to greatest. *(p. 147)*

Metric Units of Length: Measurements expressed in millimeters (mm), centimeters (cm), meters (m), and kilometers (km). *(p. 103)*

Metric Units of Liquid Volume: Measurements expressed in liter (L), milliliters (mL), centiliters (cL), and kiloliters (kL). *(p. 105)*

Metric Units of Mass: Measurements expressed in grams (g), milligrams (mg), centigrams (cg), and kilograms (kg). *(p. 107)*

Mixed Number: A number with a whole number part and a fraction part. *(p. 30)*

Mode: The number that appears most often in a set of numbers. *(p. 147)*

Multiples: A number multiplied by an integer. For example, the first few multiples of 3 are: 3, 6, 9, 12, and 15. *(p. 25)*

Negative Number: A number less than 0 and identified with the minus sign. *(p. 27)*

Numerator: The number above the line in a fraction. *(p. 30)*

Obtuse Angle: An angle with a measure of more than 90°. *(p. 119)*

Obtuse Triangle: A triangle with one obtuse angle. *(p. 122)*

Order of Operations: Rules that tell the steps to follow when doing a computation. *(p. 66)*

Ordered Pair: Numbers used to identify a point on a grid. *(p. 67)*

Origin: The point on a grid where the vertical and horizontal axes meet. *(p. 67)*

Percent: A special ratio that compares a number to 100 using the % symbol. *(p. 60)*

Perimeter: The distance around a figure. *(p. 111)*

Pi: The ratio of a circle's diameter to its circumference—a ratio that is exactly the same for every circle. A circle's circumference equals pi times its diameter. A circle's area equals pi times the square of its radius. Pi is often rounded to 3.14. *(p. 126)*

Place Value: The value of a position of a digit in a number. *(p. 10)*

Point: An exact location in space that has no dimensions and cannot be measured. A point is usually represented by a dot. *(p. 117)*

Polygon: Any closed two-dimensional figure that is made up of line segments. Triangles and quadrilaterals are two types of polygons. *(p. 124)*

Probability: The likelihood of an event happening in the future. *(p. 159)*

Product: The result, or answer, of a multiplication problem. *(p. 15)*

Property: A specific way in which numbers behave. *(p. 21)*

Property of Additive Inverses: States that when adding a negative number to its inverse, the sum will be 0. For example: $-8 + 8 = 0$. *(p. 27)*

Proportion: A problem that contains two ratios that are equal. *(p. 91)*

Quadrilateral: A two-dimensional figure with four sides and four angles. *(p. 123)*

Quotient: The result of dividing one number by another. *(p. 18)*

Radius: A line segment that starts at a circle's center point and extends to its perimeter. *(p. 125)*

Range: The greatest number minus the smallest number in a set of numbers. *(p. 149)*

Ratio: A comparison of two numbers using division. *(p. 86)*

Ray: A part of a line that extends from a specific point in only one direction. *(p. 118)*

Reciprocals: Two fractions that look like upside-down reflections of one another. *(p. 37)*

Regrouping: In place value, to use part of the value from one place in another place to make adding or subtracting easier. *(p. 13)*

Remainder: The number left over in whole-number division when you can no longer divide any further. *(p. 18)*

Rhombus: A quadrilateral where both pairs of sides are parallel and have the same length. All angles are less than 90°. *(p. 123)*

Right Angle: An angle that measures exactly 90°. *(p. 119)*

Right Triangle: A triangle with one right angle. *(p. 122)*

Rounding: To drop or zero-out digits in a number to a higher or lower value. *(p. 12)*

Scalene Triangle: A triangle with all three sides being of different lengths. *(p. 122)*

Solid Figure: *A three*-dimensional figure such as a cube or pyramid. *(p. 127)*

Statistics: A branch of math that answers questions about how many, how long, how often, how far, or how big. *(p. 147)*

Stem-and-Leaf Plot: Used to organize data and compare it. A stem-and-leaf plot organizes data from least to greatest using the digits or the greatest place value to group data. *(p. 151)*

Supplementary Angles: Any two angles that add up to a sum of 180°. *(p. 120)*

Surface Area: The sum of the areas of all the faces on a three-dimensional object. *(p. 129)*

Trapezoid: A quadrilateral that has two lines that are parallel to each other and two lines that are not parallel. *(p. 123)*

Tree Diagram: Used to show possible combinations of data including people, places, or things in a diagram that looks like a tree with branches. *(p. 156)*

Triangle: A two-dimensional figure with three sides. *(p. 122)*

Upper Extreme: The highest number in a group of numbers used in a box-and-whisker plot. *(p. 152)*

Upper Quartile: The median of numbers from the median to the upper extreme in a box-and-whisker plot. *(p. 152)*

Variable: An unknown number usually expressed as a letter and used in Algebra. In the statement $n - 18$, n is the variable. *(p. 76)*

Venn Diagram: A diagram used to show data and how different sets of data can overlap. *(p. 158)*

Vertex: The specific point of a ray, also called an endpoint. *(p. 118)*

Vertex of a Solid: A specific point at which more than 2 faces meet, or a point where a curve begins. *(p. 127)*

Vertical Angles: The angles opposite each other when two lines intersect. *(p. 120)*

Volume: The number of units a solid figure contains, expressed in cubic inches, feet, or yards. *(p. 115)*

Whole Number: A number that does not include a fraction or decimal. *(p. 13)*

Zero Property of Multiplication: States that any number times zero equals zero. *(p. 24)*

Answers and Explanations

Lesson 1.1

1. One thousands
2. Ten millions
3. 5
4. Hundreds
5. $(3\times 100,000)+(3\times 1000)+(2\times 100)+(1\times 1)$
6. 732,998
7. 12,454,721 $(1\times 10,000,000)+(2\times 1,000,000)$ $+(4\times 100,000)+(5\times 10,000)+(4\times 1000)$ $+(7\times 100)+(2\times 10)+(1\times 1)$
8. One thousand three hundred ninety-six

Lesson 1.2

1. 71,200 Since the number after the rounding place is a 3, we keep the 2 the same and change the numbers after the 2 to zeros.
2. 25,900 Since the number after the rounding place is a 5, we round the 8 up to a 9 and change the numbers after that to zeros.
3. 68,400 Since the number after the rounding place is a 9, we round the 3 up to a 4 and change the numbers after that to zeros.
4. 71,240 Since the number after the rounding place is a 5, we round the 3 up to a 4 and change the number after that to a zero.
5. 25,850 Since the number after the rounding place is a 4, we keep the 5 the same and change the last number to a zero.
6. 68,400 Since the number after the rounding place is a 6, we round the 39 up to a 40 and change the last number to a zero.
7. 71,000 Since the number after the rounding place is a 2, we keep the 1 the same and change the numbers after the 1 to zeros.
8. 26,000 Since the number after the rounding place is an 8, we round the 5 up to a 6 and change the numbers after that to zeros.
9. 68,000 Since the number after the rounding place is a 3, we keep the 8 the same and change the numbers after the 8 to zeros.
10. B In choice B, the number after the ten thousands place is an 8, so we round the 3 up to a 4 and get 240,000.

Lesson 1.3

1. 28,868

$$\begin{array}{r} \overset{1}{3}\overset{1}{8}9 \\ 28456 \\ 21 \\ +\quad 2 \\ \hline 28,868 \end{array}$$

2. 172

$$\begin{array}{r} {}^{1}10 \\ 11 \\ 12 \\ 13 \\ 15 \\ +\ 111 \\ \hline 172 \end{array}$$

3. 5098

$$\begin{array}{r} 5\overset{7}{\cancel{8}}\overset{1}{8}8 \\ -\ 790 \\ \hline 5098 \end{array}$$

4. 2787

$$\begin{array}{r} \overset{1}{1}\overset{10}{\cancel{2}}\overset{10}{\cancel{1}}\overset{1}{\cancel{1}}2 \\ -\quad 9325 \\ \hline 2787 \end{array}$$

5. 13

$$\begin{array}{r} \cancel{1}\overset{9}{\cancel{0}}\overset{9}{\cancel{0}}\overset{1}{1} \\ -\quad 988 \\ \hline 13 \end{array}$$

6. 180 $62 + 31 + 87 = 180$
7. 92 $73 + 25 - 6 = 92$
8. 4 $100 - 34 - 31 - 31 = 4$

Estimating

1. 61,000 $1000 + 60,000 = 61,000$
2. 10,000 $20,000 - 10,000 = 10,000$
3. 1300 $1000 + 300 = 1300$
4. 10,000 Round 28,459 to 30,000 and 42,671 to 40,000; $40,000 - 30,000 = 10,000$
5. 700 Round 317 to 300 and 384 to 400; $300 + 400 = 700$

Lesson 1.4

1. 19,642
2. 629,706
3. 101,244
4. 205,270
5. 8124
6. 50,765

7. 750 apples

8. 1600 baseball cards $\quad 100 \times 16 = 1600$

9. 3096

$$\begin{array}{r} 72 \\ \times\ 43 \\ \hline 216 \\ {}^{1}2880 \\ \hline 3096 \end{array}$$

10. 252 $\quad 12 \times 7 = 84$ and $84 \times 3 = 252$

11. 333

$$\begin{array}{r} \overset{1}{2}4 \\ \times\ 14 \\ \hline 96 \\ {}^{1}240 \\ \hline 336 \\ -\ 3 \text{ left} \\ \hline 333 \text{ sold} \end{array}$$

12. \$7800
$5 \times 6 \times 5 = 150$

$$\begin{array}{r} \overset{\overset{2}{1}}{1}50 \\ 52 \\ \hline 300 \\ 7500 \\ \hline 7800 \end{array}$$

13. 5840

$$\begin{array}{r} \overset{3}{3}\overset{3}{6}5 \\ \times\ 16 \\ \hline 2^{1}190 \\ 3650 \\ \hline 5840 \end{array}$$

14. 3920

$$\begin{array}{r} {}^{4}560 \\ \times\ 7 \\ \hline 3920 \end{array}$$

15. 41,040

$$\begin{array}{r} 342 \\ \times\ 120 \\ \hline {}^{1}6840 \\ {}^{1}34,200 \\ \hline 41,040 \end{array}$$

Estimating

1. 350,000 $\quad 500 \times 700 = 350,000$

2. 180,000 $\quad 200 \times 900 = 180,000$

3. 1,500,000 $\quad 500 \times 3000 = 1,500,000$

4. 32,000 $\quad 800 \times 40 = 32,000$

5. smaller $\quad$ rounding 44 down to 40 will make a smaller product

6. 3600 $\quad 60 \times 60 = 3600$

7. larger $\quad$ both numbers were rounded up

8. 450,000 $\quad 500 \times 900 = 450,000$

9. 6,000,000 $\quad 1000 \times 6000 = 6,000,000$

10. 6,171,605

$$\begin{array}{r} 5555 \\ \times\ 1111 \\ \hline 5^{1}5^{1}55 \\ \overset{2}{5}5550 \\ \overset{1}{5}55500 \\ \overset{1}{5}555000 \\ \hline 6,171,605 \end{array}$$

11. 12,000 $\quad 30 \times 400 = 12,000$

12. larger $\quad$ Both numbers were rounded up.

Lesson 1.5

1. 7 R4

$$\begin{array}{r} 7 \\ 89\overline{)627} \\ 623 \\ \hline 4 \end{array}$$

2. 24 R5

$$\begin{array}{r} 24 \\ 14\overline{)\overset{2}{\not 3}\overset{1}{4}1} \\ 28\downarrow \\ \hline 61 \\ 56 \\ \hline 5 \end{array}$$

3. 23 R1

$$\begin{array}{r} 23 \\ 15\overline{)346} \\ 30\downarrow \\ \hline 46 \\ 45 \\ \hline 1 \end{array}$$

4. 78 R6

$$\begin{array}{r} 78 \\ 36\overline{)2^{7}\overset{1}{\not 8}14} \\ 252\downarrow \\ \hline 2\overset{8}{\not 9}\overset{1}{4} \\ 288 \\ \hline 6 \end{array}$$

5. 15 R2

$$\begin{array}{r} 15 \\ 12\overline{)182} \\ 12\downarrow \\ \hline 62 \\ 60 \\ \hline 2 \end{array}$$

6. 9 R3

$$\begin{array}{r} 9 \\ 9\overline{)84} \\ 81 \\ \hline 3 \end{array}$$

7. 78 R11

$$\begin{array}{r} 78 \\ 96\overline{)\overset{6}{\not 7}\overset{1}{4}99} \\ 672\downarrow \\ \hline 779 \\ 768 \\ \hline 11 \end{array}$$

Answers and Explanations

8. 1234 R8

$$\begin{array}{r} 1234 \\ 18\overline{)22,220} \\ \underline{18} \\ 42 \\ \underline{36} \\ 62 \\ \underline{54} \\ 80 \\ \underline{72} \\ 8 \end{array}$$

9. 456 R2

$$\begin{array}{r} 456 \\ 38\overline{)17,330} \\ \underline{152} \\ 213 \\ \underline{190} \\ 230 \\ \underline{228} \\ 2 \end{array}$$

10. 423 R5

$$\begin{array}{r} 423 \\ 55\overline{)23,270} \\ \underline{220} \\ 127 \\ \underline{110} \\ 170 \\ \underline{165} \\ 5 \end{array}$$

11. 729 R2

$$\begin{array}{r} 729 \\ 5\overline{)3647} \\ \underline{35} \\ 14 \\ \underline{10} \\ 47 \\ \underline{45} \\ 2 \end{array}$$

12. 17 R5

$$\begin{array}{r} 17 \\ 82\overline{)1399} \\ \underline{82} \\ 579 \\ \underline{574} \\ 5 \end{array}$$

13. 147 R6

$$\begin{array}{r} 147 \\ 45\overline{)6621} \\ \underline{45} \\ 212 \\ \underline{180} \\ 321 \\ \underline{315} \\ 6 \end{array}$$

14. 4 days $2500 \div 625 = 4$

15. 18 new students

$$\begin{array}{r} 18 \\ 19\overline{)342} \\ \underline{19} \\ 152 \\ 152 \end{array}$$

Estimating

1. 12 $144 \div 12 = 12$

2. 30 $240 \div 8 = 30$

3. 10 $90 \div 9 = 10$

4. 30 $390 \div 13 = 30$

5. 16 $400 \div 25 = 16$

6. 100 $1300 \div 13 = 100$

7. 50 $450 \div 9 = 50$

8. 20 $660 \div 33 = 20$

9. 5 $450 \div 90 = 5$

10. 10 $250 \div 25 = 10$

11. 12 $48 \div 4 = 12$

12. 40 $3200 \div 80 = 40$

13. 25 $1250 \div 50 = 25$

14. 10 $300 \div 30 = 10$

15. 30 $360 \div 12 = 30$

Lesson 2.1

1. Possible answers: $(3\times2\times4)$, $(4\times2\times3)$, $(4\times3\times2)$, $(2\times3\times4)$, or $(2\times4\times3) = 24$

2. $16 + 12 = 28$

3. $63\times84 = 5292$

4. Possible answers: $(5+17+19)$, $(19+17+5)$, $(19+5+17)$, $(5+19+17)$, or $(17+5+19) = 41$

5. $(2\times3)+(4\times2) = 14$

6. $2+(3+4) = 9$ Answers will vary. Any combination of addends within the parentheses is correct.

7. $(7\times2)\times1 = 14$ Answers will vary. Any combination of the numbers within the parentheses is correct.

8. $3\times(4\times6) = 72$ Answers will vary. Any combination of the numbers within the parentheses is correct.

9. 3 $3\times6 = 6\times3$

10. B The original figure has 8 boxes and so does choice B.

11. 42 $42 + 16 + 5 = 16 + 5 + 42$

12. 36 $(36 + 12) + 10 = 36 + (12 + 10)$

13. 8 $4\times(1\times5)\times8 = (4\times1)\times(5\times8)$

14. 7 $7\times5\times10\times10 = 5\times10\times7\times10$

15. 3 $(3\times6)+(8\times9) = (8\times9)+(6\times3)$

Answers and Explanations

Lesson 2.2

1. 30 — $6(4+5)=(6\times4)+(6\times5)=24+30$
2. 24 — $3(8\times6)=(3\times8)\times(3\times6)=24\times18$
3. 2(6 + 7) — $12+14=(2\times6)+(2\times7)=2(6+7)$
4. 3(3 + 5) — $9+15=(3\times3)+(3\times5)=3(3+5)$
5. 5(3 + 5) — $15+25=(5\times3)+(5\times5)=5(3+5)$
6. 9(2 + 1) — $18+9=(9\times2)+(9\times1)=9(2+1)$
7. 27 + 12 — $3(9+4)=(3\times9)+(3\times4)=27+12$
8. 12 + 6 — $6(2+1)=(6\times2)+(6\times1)=12+6$
9. B — $(6\times12)+(6\times13)=6(12+13)$
10. C — $(4\times\$0.89)+(4\times\$1.29)=4(\$0.89+\$1.29)$

Lesson 2.3

1. Yes — This shows the equality property of multiplication.
2. Yes — This shows the equality property of division.
3. No — The equality properties of addition and subtraction state that you must add or subtract *the same number* from both sides of an equation.
4. Yes — This shows the equality property of subtraction.
5. Yes — This shows the equality property of subtraction.

Lesson 2.4

1. 24 — The multiples of 8 are: 8, 16, 24, 32 … and of 12 are: 12, 24, 36 … The smallest number they have in common is 24.
2. 30 — The multiples of 6 are: 6, 12, 18, 24, 30 … and of 10 are: 10, 20, 30 … The smallest number they have in common is 30.
3. 14 — The multiples of 2 are: 2, 4, 6, 8, 10, 12, 14, 16 … and of 7 are: 7, 14, 21 … The smallest number they have in common is 14.
4. 15 — The multiples of 3 are: 3, 6, 9, 12, 15, 18 … and of 5 are: 5, 10, 15, 20 … The smallest number they have in common is 15.
5. 36 — The multiples of 18 are: 18, 36, 54 … and of 36 are: 36, 72 … The smallest number they have in common is 36.
6. 18 — The multiples of 9 are: 9, 18, 27, 36 … and of 6 are: 6, 12, 18, 24, 36 … The smallest number they have in common is 18.
7. 3 packs of plates and 4 packs of cups — The multiples of 16 are: 16, 32, 48, 64 … and the multiples of 12 are: 12, 24, 36, 48, 60 … The least common multiple is 48, so that is 3 packs of plates and 4 packs of cups.
8. Friday — He will do dishes on days 2, 4, 6, 8 … and laundry on days 4, 8, 12 …The next day they have in common is 4 days from Monday, on Friday.
9. 8 — The factors of 8 are: 1, 2, 4, 8 and the factors of 24 are: 1, 2, 3, 4, 6, 8, 12, 24. The greatest common factor is 8.
10. 12 — The factors of 12 are: 1, 2, 3, 4, 6, 12 and the factors of 24 are: 1, 2, 3, 4, 6, 8, 12, 24. The greatest common factor is 12.
11. 6 — The factors of 12 are: 1, 2, 3, 4, 6, 12 and the factors of 30 are: 1, 2, 3, 5, 6, 10, 15, 30. The greatest common factor is 6.
12. 3 — The factors of 9 are: 1, 3, 9 and the factors of 12 are: 1, 2, 3, 4, 6, 12. The greatest common factor is 3.
13. 2 — The factors of 4 are: 1, 2, 4 and the factors of 10 are: 1, 2, 5, 10. The greatest common factor is 2.
14. 16 — The factors of 16 are: 1, 2, 4, 8, 16 and the factors of 80 are: 1, 2, 4, 5, 8, 10, 16, 20, 40, 80. The greatest common factor is 16.
15. 9 — The greatest common factor of 9, 27, and 36 is 9, so he can make 9 lunch bags, each with 1 sandwich, 3 pickles, and 4 cookies.

Lesson 3.1

1. 0 — Additive inverses add up to 0.
2. 0 — Additive inverses add up to 0.
3. –1 — $(-12)+13+11+(-13)=(-12)+11=-1$
4. 0 — Additive inverses add up to 0.
5. 3 — $20+(-17)=20-17=3$
6. 3 — $(-65)+65+61+(-58)=61+(-58)$ $=61-58=3$
7. 0 — Additive inverses add up to 0.
8. –12 — $212+200+(-212)+(-212)$ $=200+(-212)=200-212=-12$
9. –3 — $31+(-34)+0=31-34=-3$
10. 0 — Additive inverses add up to 0.
11. To the right of –6.2 — Picture the number line.
12. Less than –4.0 — Picture the number line.

Lesson 3.2

1. 8 — $12+(-4)=12-4=8$
2. –6 — $(-14)+8=8-14=-6$

Answers and Explanations

3. −10 $3+(-13)=3-13=-10$
4. 22 $45+(-23)=45-23=22$
5. 102 $123+(-43)+22=123-43+22=80+22=102$
6. 42 $90+(-45)+(-3)=90-45-3=45-3=42$
7. −17 $(-10)+(-10)+3=-10-10+3=-20+3=-17$
8. 15 $45+(-32)+2=45-32+2=13+2=15$
9. 1 $15+(-14)=15-14=1$
10. 17 $16+14+(-13)=30-13=17$
11. −1 $(-15)+14=14-15=-1$
12. 78 $67+12+13+(-14)=92-14=78$
13. 16 $43+(-32)+5=43-32+5=11+5=16$
14. −16 $(-43)+32+(-5)=32-43-5=-11-5=-16$
15. −1 $2+2+(-3)+(-2)=2+(-3)=2-3=-1$
16. −2 $5-7=-2$
17. −13 $-20+12=-8; -8-5=-13$
18. −1 $4\times5=20$ and $7\times-3=-21$; $20-21=-1$

Lesson 3.3

1. 3 $|-3|=3$
2. 26 $|-26|=26$
3. 423 $|423|=423$
4. 0.7 $|-0.7|=0.7$
5. $\frac{5}{6}$ $\left|-\frac{5}{6}\right|=\frac{5}{6}$
6. $\frac{2}{3}$ $\left|\frac{2}{3}\right|=\frac{2}{3}$
7. < $|-6|=6$ and $|-7|=7$ so $6<7$
8. = $|21|=21$ and $|-21|=21$ so $21=21$
9. > $|-8|=8$ and $|-4|=4$ so $8>4$
10. < $|-5|=5$ and $|7|=7$ so $5<7$
11. < $|10|=10$ and $|-12|=12$ so $10<12$
12. < $|423|=423$ and $|425|=425$ so $423<425$
13. \$63.86 $|-53.86|+10=53.86+10=63.86$
14. Wednesday $|-4|=4$ and $|6|=6$, and $4<6$
15. Vivian $|-3.46|=3.46$ and $|-2.98|=2.98$, and $3.46>2.98$

Lesson 4.1

1. $3\frac{1}{7}$ $22\div7=3\text{ R}1=3\frac{1}{7}$
2. $8\frac{3}{4}$ $35\div4=8\text{ R}3=8\frac{3}{4}$
3. $7\frac{3}{10}$ $73\div10=7\text{ R}3=7\frac{3}{10}$
4. $15\frac{2}{3}$ $47\div3=15\text{ R}2=15\frac{2}{3}$
5. $7\frac{10}{11}$ $87\div11=7\text{ R}10=7\frac{10}{11}$
6. $\frac{8}{3}$ $2\frac{2}{3}=(2\times3)+2=8$ so $\frac{8}{3}$
7. $\frac{39}{7}$ $5\frac{4}{7}=(5\times7)+4=39$ so $\frac{39}{7}$
8. $\frac{108}{5}$ $21\frac{3}{5}=(21\times5)+3=108$ so $\frac{108}{5}$
9. $\frac{43}{8}$ $5\frac{3}{8}=(5\times8)+3=43$ so $\frac{43}{8}$
10. $\frac{160}{7}$ $22\frac{6}{7}=(22\times7)+6=160$ so $\frac{160}{7}$

Lesson 4.2

1. $\frac{9}{7}$ or $1\frac{2}{7}$ $\frac{3}{7}+\frac{6}{7}=\frac{9}{7}$ or $1\frac{2}{7}$
2. 2 $\frac{4}{3}+\frac{2}{3}=\frac{6}{3}=2$
3. 1 $\frac{1}{5}+\frac{4}{5}=\frac{5}{5}=1$
4. $\frac{26}{33}$ $\frac{9}{33}+\frac{17}{33}=\frac{26}{33}$
5. $\frac{1}{3}$ $\frac{2}{3}-\frac{1}{3}=\frac{1}{3}$
6. 0 $\frac{10}{47}-\frac{10}{47}=\frac{0}{47}=0$
7. $\frac{25}{96}$ $\frac{43}{96}-\frac{18}{96}=\frac{25}{96}$
8. $\frac{1}{13}$ $\frac{12}{13}-\frac{11}{13}=\frac{1}{13}$
9. $\frac{4}{3}$ or $1\frac{1}{3}$ $\frac{2}{3}+\frac{2}{3}=\frac{4}{3}$ or $1\frac{1}{3}$
10. Yes. $6\frac{3}{4}+5\frac{1}{4}=11\frac{4}{4}=12$

Lesson 4.3

1. $\frac{31}{35}$ $\frac{2}{7}+\frac{3}{5}=\frac{10}{35}+\frac{21}{35}=\frac{31}{35}$
2. $\frac{38}{39}$ $\frac{4}{13}+\frac{2}{3}=\frac{12}{39}+\frac{26}{39}=\frac{38}{39}$
3. $\frac{7}{8}$ $\frac{3}{4}+\frac{1}{8}=\frac{6}{8}+\frac{1}{8}=\frac{7}{8}$
4. $\frac{43}{77}$ $\frac{3}{11}+\frac{2}{7}=\frac{21}{77}+\frac{22}{77}=\frac{43}{77}$
5. $\frac{5}{12}$ $\frac{2}{3}-\frac{1}{4}=\frac{8}{12}-\frac{3}{12}=\frac{5}{12}$
6. $\frac{17}{24}$ $\frac{5}{6}-\frac{1}{8}=\frac{20}{24}-\frac{3}{24}=\frac{17}{24}$

Answers and Explanations

7. $\frac{10}{39}$ $\quad \frac{12}{13}-\frac{2}{3}=\frac{36}{39}-\frac{26}{39}=\frac{10}{39}$

8. $\frac{7}{20}$ $\quad \frac{3}{4}-\frac{2}{5}=\frac{15}{20}-\frac{8}{20}=\frac{7}{20}$

9. $\frac{19}{12}$ or $1\frac{7}{12}$ $\quad \frac{1}{3}+\frac{3}{4}+\frac{1}{2}=\frac{4}{12}+\frac{9}{12}+\frac{6}{12}=\frac{19}{12}$ or $1\frac{7}{12}$

10. $\frac{8}{21}$ $\quad \frac{5}{7}-\frac{1}{3}=\frac{15}{21}-\frac{7}{21}=\frac{8}{21}$

Lesson 4.4

1. $23\frac{37}{56}$ $\quad 11\frac{2}{7}+12\frac{3}{8}=(11+12)+\left(\frac{2}{7}+\frac{3}{8}\right)$ $=23+\left(\frac{16}{56}+\frac{21}{56}\right)=23\frac{37}{56}$

2. $13\frac{27}{30}$ $\quad 12\frac{5}{6}+1\frac{1}{15}=(12+1)+\left(\frac{5}{6}+\frac{1}{15}\right)$ $=13+\left(\frac{25}{30}+\frac{2}{30}\right)=13\frac{27}{30}$

3. $16\frac{32}{63}$ $\quad 13\frac{2}{7}+3\frac{2}{9}=(13+3)+\left(\frac{2}{7}+\frac{2}{9}\right)$ $=16+\left(\frac{18}{63}+\frac{14}{63}\right)=16\frac{32}{63}$

4. $24\frac{17}{18}$ $\quad 21\frac{1}{9}+3\frac{5}{6}=(21+3)+\left(\frac{1}{9}+\frac{5}{6}\right)$ $=24+\left(\frac{2}{18}+\frac{15}{18}\right)=24\frac{17}{18}$

5. $5\frac{19}{36}$ $\quad 7\frac{7}{9}-2\frac{1}{4}=(7-2)+\left(\frac{7}{9}-\frac{1}{4}\right)$ $=5+\left(\frac{28}{36}-\frac{9}{36}\right)=5\frac{19}{36}$

6. $3\frac{11}{42}$ $\quad 5\frac{3}{7}-2\frac{1}{6}=(5-2)+\left(\frac{3}{7}-\frac{1}{6}\right)$ $=3+\left(\frac{18}{42}-\frac{7}{42}\right)=3\frac{11}{42}$

7. $3\frac{13}{24}$ $\quad 4\frac{2}{3}-1\frac{1}{8}=(4-1)+\left(\frac{2}{3}-\frac{1}{8}\right)$ $=3+\left(\frac{16}{24}-\frac{3}{24}\right)=3\frac{13}{24}$

8. $3\frac{13}{90}$ $\quad 10\frac{7}{10}-7\frac{5}{9}=(10-7)+\left(\frac{7}{10}-\frac{5}{9}\right)$ $=3+\left(\frac{63}{90}-\frac{50}{90}\right)=3\frac{13}{90}$

9. $5\frac{3}{8}$ $\quad 8\frac{1}{2}-3\frac{1}{8}=(8-3)+\left(\frac{1}{2}-\frac{1}{8}\right)$ $=5+\left(\frac{4}{8}-\frac{1}{8}\right)=5\frac{3}{8}$

10. Yes $\quad 1\frac{7}{8}-\frac{1}{4}=1+\left(\frac{7}{8}-\frac{1}{4}\right)=1+\left(\frac{7}{8}-\frac{2}{8}\right)=1\frac{5}{8}$ and $1\frac{5}{8}>1\frac{3}{5}$

Lesson 4.5

1. 2 $\quad 1+1=2$

2. 1 $\quad 1+0=1$

3. 1 $\quad \frac{1}{2}+\frac{1}{2}=1$

4. $1\frac{1}{2}$ $\quad 1+\frac{1}{2}=1\frac{1}{2}$

5. 4 $\quad 1+2=3; 0+1=1; 3+1=4$

6. $12\frac{1}{2}$ $\quad 7+4=11; 1+\frac{1}{2}=1\frac{1}{2}; 11+1\frac{1}{2}=12\frac{1}{2}$

7. $2\frac{1}{2}$ $\quad 5-2=3; 0-\frac{1}{2}=-\frac{1}{2}; 3+\left(-\frac{1}{2}\right)=2\frac{1}{2}$

8. $6\frac{1}{2}$ $\quad 7\frac{1}{2}-1=6\frac{1}{2}$

9. $12\frac{1}{2}$ $\quad 12+\frac{1}{2}=12\frac{1}{2}$

10. 9 $\quad 4\frac{1}{2}+4\frac{1}{2}=9$

11. $1\frac{1}{2}$ $\quad 13-12=1; \frac{1}{2}-0=\frac{1}{2}; 1+\frac{1}{2}=1\frac{1}{2}$

12. 3 $\quad 17-13=4; 0-1=-1; 4+(-1)=3$

13. About $21\frac{1}{2}$ ounces $\quad 1\frac{7}{8}+1\frac{7}{8}=2+2=4; 25\frac{1}{2}-4=21\frac{1}{2}$

14. About $4\frac{1}{2}$ cords $\quad 2+2\frac{1}{2}=4\frac{1}{2}$

Lesson 4.6

1. $3\frac{3}{4}$ or $\frac{15}{4}$ $\quad 5\times\frac{3}{4}=\frac{5\times 3}{4}=\frac{15}{4}$

2. $1\frac{1}{7}$ or $\frac{8}{7}$ $\quad 4\times\frac{2}{7}=\frac{4\times 2}{7}=\frac{8}{7}$

3. $13\frac{1}{8}$ or $\frac{105}{8}$ $\quad 21\times\frac{5}{8}=\frac{21\times 5}{8}=\frac{105}{8}$

4. $2\frac{4}{9}$ or $\frac{22}{9}$ $\quad 11\times\frac{2}{9}=\frac{11\times 2}{9}=\frac{22}{9}$

5. $1\frac{1}{11}$ or $\frac{12}{11}$ $\quad 4\times\frac{3}{11}=\frac{4\times 3}{11}=\frac{12}{11}$

6. $12\frac{1}{14}$ or $\frac{169}{14}$ $\quad 13\times\frac{13}{14}=\frac{13\times 13}{14}=\frac{169}{14}$

7. $9\frac{3}{23}$ or $\frac{210}{23}$ $\quad 21\times\frac{10}{23}=\frac{21\times 10}{23}=\frac{210}{23}$

8. $4\frac{2}{3}$ or $\frac{14}{3}$ $\quad 7\times\frac{2}{3}=\frac{7\times 2}{3}=\frac{14}{3}$

9. $4\frac{8}{19}$ or $\frac{84}{19}$ $\quad 12\times\frac{7}{19}=\frac{12\times 7}{19}=\frac{84}{19}$

10. $8\frac{2}{5}$ or $\frac{42}{5}$ $\quad 14\times\frac{3}{5}=\frac{14\times 3}{5}=\frac{42}{5}$

Answers and Explanations

11. $51\frac{1}{3}$ or $\frac{154}{3}$ $\quad 14\times\frac{11}{3}=\frac{14\times 11}{3}=\frac{154}{3}$

12. $3\frac{1}{17}$ or $\frac{52}{17}$ $\quad 13\times\frac{4}{17}=\frac{13\times 4}{17}=\frac{52}{17}$

13. $3\frac{21}{23}$ or $\frac{90}{23}$ $\quad 10\times\frac{9}{23}=\frac{10\times 9}{23}=\frac{90}{23}$

14. $12\frac{9}{22}$ or $\frac{273}{22}$ $\quad 13\times\frac{21}{22}=\frac{13\times 21}{22}=\frac{273}{22}$

15. $2\frac{16}{27}$ or $\frac{70}{27}$ $\quad 5\times\frac{14}{27}=\frac{5\times 14}{27}=\frac{70}{27}$

16. \$37.63 $\quad 43\times\frac{7}{8}=\frac{43\times 7}{8}=\frac{301}{8}=37.625$

17. $6\frac{4}{5}$ miles $\quad$ She has $\frac{2}{5}$ left, so $17\times\frac{2}{5}=\frac{17\times 2}{5}=\frac{34}{5}=6\frac{4}{5}$

Lesson 4.7

1. $\frac{1}{4}$ $\quad \frac{1}{2}\times\frac{1}{2}=\frac{1\times 1}{2\times 2}=\frac{1}{4}$
2. $\frac{4}{7}$ $\quad \frac{2}{3}\times\frac{6}{7}=\frac{2\times 6}{3\times 7}=\frac{12}{21}=\frac{4}{7}$
3. $\frac{5}{33}$ $\quad \frac{5}{9}\times\frac{3}{11}=\frac{5\times 3}{9\times 11}=\frac{15}{99}=\frac{5}{33}$
4. $\frac{10}{39}$ $\quad \frac{10}{13}\times\frac{1}{3}=\frac{10\times 1}{13\times 3}=\frac{10}{39}$
5. 1 $\quad \frac{3}{11}$ and $\frac{11}{3}$ are reciprocals.
6. $\frac{7}{11}$ $\quad \frac{7}{3}\times\frac{3}{11}=\frac{7\times 3}{3\times 11}=\frac{21}{33}=\frac{7}{11}$
7. $\frac{7}{10}$ $\quad \frac{4}{5}\times\frac{7}{8}=\frac{4\times 7}{5\times 8}=\frac{28}{40}=\frac{7}{10}$
8. 1 $\quad$ These are reciprocals.
9. $\frac{85}{81}$ or $1\frac{4}{81}$ $\quad \frac{17}{27}\times\frac{5}{3}=\frac{17\times 5}{27\times 3}=\frac{85}{81}=1\frac{4}{81}$
10. $\frac{18}{55}$ $\quad \frac{6}{10}\times\frac{6}{11}=\frac{6\times 6}{10\times 11}=\frac{36}{110}=\frac{18}{55}$
11. $\frac{13}{21}$ $\quad \frac{13}{14}\times\frac{2}{3}=\frac{13\times 2}{14\times 3}=\frac{26}{42}=\frac{13}{21}$
12. $\frac{16}{25}$ $\quad \frac{4}{5}\times\frac{4}{5}=\frac{4\times 4}{5\times 5}=\frac{16}{25}$
13. 1 $\quad$ These are reciprocals.
14. $\frac{40}{133}$ $\quad \frac{8}{19}\times\frac{5}{7}=\frac{8\times 5}{19\times 7}=\frac{40}{133}$
15. $\frac{99}{182}$ $\quad \frac{11}{13}\times\frac{9}{14}=\frac{11\times 9}{13\times 14}=\frac{99}{182}$
16. $\frac{1}{3}$ $\quad \frac{2}{3}\times\frac{1}{2}=\frac{2\times 1}{3\times 2}=\frac{2}{6}=\frac{1}{3}$
17. $\frac{9}{16}$ $\quad \frac{3}{4}\times\frac{3}{4}=\frac{3\times 3}{4\times 4}=\frac{9}{16}$

Lesson 4.8

1. $1\frac{1}{5}$ $\quad 1\frac{1}{2}=\frac{3}{2};\ \frac{3}{2}\times\frac{4}{5}=\frac{12}{10}=\frac{6}{5}=1\frac{1}{5}$
2. $\frac{17}{18}$ $\quad 4\frac{1}{4}=\frac{17}{4};\ \frac{2}{9}\times\frac{17}{4}=\frac{34}{36}=\frac{17}{18}$
3. $1\frac{17}{28}$ $\quad 2\frac{1}{7}=\frac{15}{7};\ \frac{3}{4}\times\frac{15}{7}=\frac{45}{28}=1\frac{17}{28}$
4. $2\frac{2}{3}$ $\quad 5\frac{1}{3}=\frac{16}{3};\ \frac{1}{2}\times\frac{16}{3}=\frac{16}{6}=\frac{8}{3}=2\frac{2}{3}$
5. $2\frac{38}{45}$ $\quad 3\frac{1}{5}=\frac{16}{5};\ \frac{8}{9}\times\frac{16}{5}=\frac{128}{45}=2\frac{38}{45}$
6. $\frac{10}{21}$ $\quad 1\frac{2}{3}=\frac{5}{3};\ \frac{2}{7}\times\frac{5}{3}=\frac{10}{21}$
7. $3\frac{1}{2}$ $\quad 5\frac{1}{4}=\frac{21}{4};\ \frac{2}{3}\times\frac{21}{4}=\frac{42}{12}=\frac{7}{2}=3\frac{1}{2}$
8. $1\frac{25}{32}$ $\quad 7\frac{1}{8}=\frac{57}{8};\ \frac{1}{4}\times\frac{57}{8}=\frac{57}{32}=1\frac{25}{32}$
9. $1\frac{1}{3}$ $\quad 1\frac{1}{2}=\frac{3}{2};\ \frac{3}{2}\times\frac{8}{9}=\frac{24}{18}=\frac{4}{3}=1\frac{1}{3}$
10. $2\frac{10}{49}$ $\quad 5\frac{1}{7}=\frac{36}{7};\ \frac{3}{7}\times\frac{36}{7}=\frac{108}{49}=2\frac{10}{49}$
11. $\frac{7}{12}$ hr or 35 min $\quad 1\frac{3}{4}=\frac{7}{4};\ \frac{7}{4}\times\frac{1}{3}=\frac{7}{12}$ hr or $\frac{7}{12}\times 60\text{ min}=\frac{7\times 60}{12}=\frac{420}{12}=35\text{ min}$
12. $\frac{5}{6}$ container $\quad 3\frac{1}{3}=\frac{10}{3};\ \frac{10}{3}\times\frac{1}{4}=\frac{10}{12}=\frac{5}{6}$
13. $3\frac{1}{3}$ $\quad 1\frac{1}{4}=\frac{5}{4}; 2\frac{2}{3}=\frac{8}{3}$ $\quad \frac{5}{\cancel{4}_1}\times\frac{\cancel{8}^2}{3}=\frac{10}{3}=3\frac{1}{3}$
14. $13\frac{2}{3}$ $\quad 5\frac{1}{8}=\frac{41}{8}; 2\frac{2}{3}=\frac{8}{3}$ $\quad \frac{41}{{}_1\cancel{8}}\times\frac{\cancel{8}^1}{3}=\frac{41}{3}=13\frac{2}{3}$
15. $2\frac{6}{7}$ $\quad 2\frac{1}{7}=\frac{15}{7}; 1\frac{1}{3}=\frac{4}{3}$ $\quad \frac{\overset{5}{\cancel{15}}}{7}\times\frac{4}{\cancel{3}_1}=\frac{20}{7}=2\frac{6}{7}$
16. $7\frac{1}{2}$ $\quad 3\frac{1}{2}=\frac{7}{2}; 2\frac{1}{7}=\frac{15}{7}$ $\quad \frac{\overset{1}{\cancel{7}}}{2}\times\frac{15}{\cancel{7}_1}=\frac{15}{2}=7\frac{1}{2}$
17. 15 $\quad 4\frac{1}{2}=\frac{9}{2}; 3\frac{1}{3}=\frac{10}{3}$ $\quad \frac{{}^3\cancel{9}}{{}_1\cancel{2}}\times\frac{\cancel{10}^5}{\cancel{3}_1}=\frac{15}{1}=15$

18. $9\frac{3}{5}$ in — $3\frac{3}{5}=\frac{18}{5}; 2\frac{2}{3}=\frac{8}{3}$

$\frac{^{6}\cancel{18}}{5}\times\frac{8}{\cancel{3}_1}=\frac{48}{5}=9\frac{3}{5}$ in.

Lesson 4.9

1. $\frac{10}{39}$ — $\frac{10}{13}\div 3=\frac{10}{13}\times\frac{1}{3}=\frac{10}{39}$

2. $\frac{1}{5}$ — $\frac{4}{5}\div 4=\frac{\cancel{4}^{1}}{5}\times\frac{1}{\cancel{4}_1}=\frac{1}{5}$

3. $\frac{12}{65}$ — $\frac{12}{13}\div 5=\frac{12}{13}\times\frac{1}{5}=\frac{12}{65}$

4. $\frac{1}{22}$ — $\frac{2}{11}\div 4=\frac{\cancel{2}^{1}}{11}\times\frac{1}{\cancel{4}_2}=\frac{1}{22}$

5. $\frac{3}{28}$ — $\frac{3}{4}\div 7=\frac{3}{4}\times\frac{1}{7}=\frac{3}{28}$

6. 68 — $16\div\frac{4}{17}=\frac{\cancel{16}^{4}}{1}\times\frac{17}{\cancel{4}_1}=\frac{68}{1}=68$

7. 76 — $4\div\frac{1}{19}=\frac{4}{1}\times\frac{19}{1}=\frac{76}{1}=76$

8. 9 — $21\div\frac{7}{3}=\frac{\cancel{21}^{3}}{1}\times\frac{3}{\cancel{7}_1}=\frac{9}{1}=9$

9. 50 — $55\div\frac{11}{10}=\frac{\cancel{55}^{5}}{1}\times\frac{10}{\cancel{11}_1}=\frac{50}{1}=50$

10. $\frac{51}{2}$ or $25\frac{1}{2}$ — $23\div\frac{46}{51}=\frac{\cancel{23}^{1}}{1}\times\frac{51}{\cancel{46}_2}=\frac{51}{2}$ or $25\frac{1}{2}$

11. $\frac{1}{19}$ pounds — $\frac{15}{19}\div 15=\frac{\cancel{15}^{1}}{19}\times\frac{1}{\cancel{15}_1}=\frac{1}{19}$

12. $\frac{10}{39}$ liters — $\frac{10}{13}\div 3=\frac{10}{13}\times\frac{1}{3}=\frac{10}{39}$

Lesson 4.10

1. $\frac{20}{21}$ — $\frac{5}{7}\times\frac{4}{3}=\frac{20}{21}$

2. $\frac{7}{3}$ or $2\frac{1}{3}$ — $\frac{\cancel{2}^{1}}{3}\times\frac{7}{\cancel{2}^{1}}=\frac{7}{3}$ or $2\frac{1}{3}$

3. $\frac{7}{27}$ — $\frac{1}{9}\times\frac{7}{3}=\frac{7}{27}$

4. $\frac{27}{4}$ or $6\frac{3}{4}$ — $\frac{3}{4}\times\frac{9}{1}=\frac{27}{4}$ or $6\frac{3}{4}$

5. $\frac{27}{26}$ or $1\frac{1}{26}$ — $\frac{3}{13}\times\frac{9}{2}=\frac{27}{26}$ or $1\frac{1}{26}$

6. $\frac{1}{3}$ — $\frac{1}{\cancel{9}_3}\times\frac{\cancel{3}^{1}}{1}=\frac{1}{3}$

7. $\frac{10}{13}$ — $\frac{2}{13}\times\frac{5}{1}=\frac{10}{13}$

8. $\frac{3}{2}$ or $1\frac{1}{2}$ — $\frac{3}{\cancel{13}_1}\times\frac{\cancel{13}^{1}}{2}=\frac{3}{2}$ or $1\frac{1}{2}$

9. $\frac{16}{3}$ or $5\frac{1}{3}$ — $\frac{4}{3}\times\frac{4}{1}=\frac{16}{3}$ or $5\frac{1}{3}$

10. $\frac{45}{16}$ or $2\frac{13}{16}$ — $\frac{15}{4}\times\frac{3}{4}=\frac{45}{16}$ or $2\frac{13}{16}$

11. 6 — $\frac{6}{_1\cancel{7}}\times\frac{\cancel{7}^{1}}{1}=\frac{6}{1}=6$

12. $\frac{3}{4}$ — $\frac{3}{\cancel{17}_1}\times\frac{\cancel{17}^{1}}{4}=\frac{3}{4}$

13. $\frac{3}{242}$ — $\frac{1}{11}\times\frac{3}{22}=\frac{3}{242}$

14. 9 — $\frac{3}{\cancel{7}_1}\times\frac{\cancel{21}^{3}}{1}=\frac{9}{1}=9$

15. $\frac{5}{2}$ or $2\frac{1}{2}$ — $\frac{5}{\cancel{14}_2}\times\frac{\cancel{7}^{1}}{1}=\frac{5}{2}$ or $2\frac{1}{2}$

16. $\frac{7}{2}$ or $3\frac{1}{2}$ — $\frac{7}{8}\div\frac{1}{4}=\frac{7}{\cancel{8}_2}\times\frac{\cancel{4}^{1}}{1}=\frac{7}{2}$ or $3\frac{1}{2}$

17. $\frac{27}{5}$ or $5\frac{2}{5}$ — $\frac{9}{10}\div\frac{1}{6}=\frac{9}{\cancel{10}_5}\times\frac{\cancel{6}^{3}}{1}=\frac{27}{5}$ or $5\frac{2}{5}$

Lesson 4.11

1. $\frac{3}{5}$ — $1\frac{1}{2}=\frac{3}{2}; 2\frac{1}{2}=\frac{5}{2}; \frac{3}{2}\div\frac{5}{2}=\frac{3}{\cancel{2}_1}\times\frac{\cancel{2}^{1}}{5}=\frac{3}{5}$

2. $\frac{16}{5}$ or $3\frac{1}{5}$ — $3\frac{3}{5}\div\frac{18}{5}; 1\frac{1}{8}=\frac{9}{8}; \frac{18}{5}\div\frac{9}{8}$

$=\frac{\cancel{18}^{2}}{5}\times\frac{8}{\cancel{9}_1}=\frac{16}{5}$ or $3\frac{1}{5}$

3. $\frac{15}{7}$ or $2\frac{1}{7}$ — $7\frac{1}{7}=\frac{50}{7}; 3\frac{1}{3}=\frac{10}{3}; \frac{50}{7}\div\frac{10}{3}$

$=\frac{\cancel{50}^{5}}{7}\times\frac{3}{\cancel{10}_1}=\frac{15}{7}$ or $2\frac{1}{7}$

4. $\frac{125}{84}$ or $1\frac{41}{84}$ — $3\frac{4}{7}=\frac{25}{7}; 2\frac{2}{5}=\frac{12}{5}; \frac{25}{7}\div\frac{12}{5}$

$=\frac{25}{7}\times\frac{5}{12}=\frac{125}{84}$ or $1\frac{41}{84}$

5. 2 — $6\frac{4}{5}=\frac{34}{5}; 3\frac{2}{5}=\frac{17}{5}; \frac{34}{5}\div\frac{17}{5}$

$=\frac{\cancel{34}^{2}}{\cancel{5}_1}\times\frac{\cancel{5}^{1}}{\cancel{17}_1}=\frac{2}{1}=2$

Answers and Explanations

6. $\frac{22}{15}$ or $1\frac{7}{15}$ $\quad 5\frac{1}{2}=\frac{11}{2}; 3\frac{3}{4}=\frac{15}{4}; \frac{11}{2}\div\frac{15}{4}$

$=\frac{11}{\cancel{2}_1}\times\frac{\cancel{4}^2}{15}=\frac{22}{15}$ or $1\frac{7}{15}$

7. $\frac{19}{11}$ or $1\frac{8}{11}$ $\quad 4\frac{2}{9}=\frac{38}{9}; 2\frac{4}{9}=\frac{22}{9}; \frac{38}{9}\div\frac{22}{9}$

$=\frac{\cancel{38}^{19}}{\cancel{9}_1}\times\frac{\cancel{9}^1}{\cancel{22}_{11}}=\frac{19}{11}$ or $1\frac{8}{11}$

8. $\frac{26}{7}$ or $3\frac{5}{7}$ $\quad 9\frac{2}{7}=\frac{65}{7}; 2\frac{1}{2}=\frac{5}{2}; \frac{65}{7}\div\frac{5}{2}$

$=\frac{\cancel{65}^{13}}{7}\times\frac{2}{\cancel{5}_1}=\frac{26}{7}$ or $3\frac{5}{7}$

9. 3 batches $\quad 5\frac{1}{4}=\frac{21}{4}; 1\frac{3}{4}=\frac{5}{4}; \frac{21}{4}\div\frac{7}{4}$

$=\frac{\cancel{21}^3}{\cancel{4}_1}\times\frac{\cancel{4}^1}{\cancel{7}_1}=\frac{3}{1}=3$

10. 14 balloons $\quad 51\frac{1}{3}=\frac{154}{3}; 3\frac{2}{3}=\frac{11}{3}; \frac{154}{3}\div\frac{11}{3}$

$=\frac{\cancel{154}^{14}}{\cancel{3}_1}\times\frac{\cancel{3}^1}{\cancel{11}_1}=\frac{14}{1}=14$

Lesson 5.1

1. 68
2. 18
3. 22
4. 48
5. 76
6. 18.5
7. 21.2
8. 44.4
9. 11.1
10. 59.5
11. 429.35
12. 39.75
13. 313.31
14. 528.46
15. 832.83
16. 32.346
17. 1.414
18. 12.173
19. 592.422
20. 837.820
21. 0.33, 0.333, 0.3333
22. 0.388, 0.39, 0.393, 1.39
23. 0.44, 4.439, 4.44, 4.441
24. 7.7777, 7.7778, 7.778
25. 0.445, 4.45, 44.5, 445
26. 22.23222, 22.2323, 22.2332, 22.3
27. 1.765, 1.7655, 1.76559, 1.766
28. Person C = 0.08888, Person A = 0.09, Person D = 0.090001, Person B = 1.09

Lesson 5.2

1. 1.25 $\quad \frac{5}{4}=$

```
    1.25
4)5.00
  4
  10
   8
   20
```

2. 0.875 $\quad \frac{7}{8}=$

```
    0.875
8)7.000
  64
   60
   56
    40
```

3. 0.1111 $\quad \frac{1}{9}=$

```
    0.1111
9)1.0000
   9
   10
    9
    10
     9
     10
      9
      1
```

4. 0.7143 $\quad \frac{5}{7}=$

```
     0.71428...
7)  5.00000
    49
     10
      7
     30
     28
       20
       14
       60
       56
        4
```

5. 0.4545

$$\frac{5}{11} = 11\overline{)5.0000} = 0.45454\ldots$$

$$\begin{array}{r} 5.0000 \\ \underline{44} \\ 60 \\ \underline{55} \\ 50 \\ \underline{44} \\ 60 \\ \underline{55} \\ 50 \\ \underline{44} \\ 6 \end{array}$$

6. $\frac{4}{5}$ $\quad 0.8 = \frac{8}{10} = \frac{4}{5}$

7. $\frac{1}{8}$ $\quad 0.125 = \frac{125}{1000} = \frac{5}{40} = \frac{1}{8}$

8. $\frac{13}{20}$ $\quad 0.65 = \frac{65}{100} = \frac{13}{20}$

9. $\frac{53}{100}$ $\quad 0.53 = \frac{53}{100}$

10. $\frac{11}{25}$ $\quad 0.44 = \frac{44}{100} = \frac{22}{50} = \frac{11}{25}$

11. 11;1 $\quad 1.375 = \frac{1375}{1000} = \frac{55}{40} = \frac{11}{8}$ and $\frac{11}{8} \div \frac{1}{8}$

$= \frac{11}{\not{8}_1} \times \frac{\not{8}^1}{1} = \frac{11}{1} = 11$

$0.125 = \frac{125}{1000} = \frac{1}{8}$, so 1

12. $\frac{9}{10}$ miles or 0.9 miles $\quad 1\frac{4}{5} = \frac{9}{5}; 0.9 = \frac{9}{10}; \frac{9}{5} - \frac{9}{10}$

$= \frac{18}{10} - \frac{9}{10} = \frac{9}{10}$ or 0.9

Lesson 5.3

1. 3.685 $\quad \begin{array}{r} 1.345 \\ +\ 2.40 \\ \hline 3.685 \end{array}$

2. 11.105 $\quad \begin{array}{r} \overset{1}{7}.\overset{1}{7}72 \\ +\ 3.333 \\ \hline 11.105 \end{array}$

3. 1.353 $\quad \begin{array}{r} 1.230 \\ +\ 0.123 \\ \hline 1.353 \end{array}$

4. 137.78 $\quad \begin{array}{r} 12.35 \\ +\ 125.43 \\ \hline 137.78 \end{array}$

5. 48.6666 $\quad \begin{array}{r} 4.4224 \\ +\ 44.2442 \\ \hline 48.6666 \end{array}$

6. 53.4451 $\quad \begin{array}{r} 53.1110 \\ +\ 0.3341 \\ \hline 53.4451 \end{array}$

7. 2.761 $\quad \begin{array}{r} 0.251 \\ +\ 2.510 \\ \hline 2.761 \end{array}$

8. 11.091 $\quad \begin{array}{r} 10^{1}.101 \\ +\ 0.990 \\ \hline 11.091 \end{array}$

9. 22.211 $\quad \begin{array}{r} 11.100 \\ +\ 11.111 \\ \hline 22.211 \end{array}$

10. 144.423 $\quad \begin{array}{r} 113.310 \\ +\ 31.113 \\ \hline 144.423 \end{array}$

11. 345.345 $\quad \begin{array}{r} 345.000 \\ +\ 0.345 \\ \hline 345.345 \end{array}$

12. 262.994 $\quad \begin{array}{r} 23^{1}9.540 \\ +\ 23.454 \\ \hline 262.994 \end{array}$

13. 578.0775 $\quad \begin{array}{r} 525^{1}.5250 \\ +\ 52.5525 \\ \hline 578.0775 \end{array}$

14. 101.651 $\quad \begin{array}{r} 101.550 \\ +\ 0.101 \\ \hline 101.651 \end{array}$

15. 36.8155 ft. $\quad \begin{array}{r} 12.2^{1}5^{1}60 \\ 11.1140 \\ +\ 13.4455 \\ \hline 36.8155 \end{array}$

16. 33.547 sec. $\quad \begin{array}{r} 1^{1}2^{1}.3^{1}5^{1}4^{1}0 \\ 11.4538 \\ +\ 9.7392 \\ \hline 33.5470 \end{array}$

Lesson 5.4

1. 0.02 $\quad \begin{array}{r} 2\overset{2}{\not{3}}.\overset{9}{\not{0}}\overset{11}{\not{1}} \\ -\ 22.99 \\ \hline 0.02 \end{array}$

2. 67.855 $\quad \begin{array}{r} 1\overset{0}{\not{1}}\overset{12}{\not{3}}.\overset{14}{\not{5}}\overset{12}{\not{2}}5 \\ -\ 45.670 \\ \hline 67.855 \end{array}$

3. 20.12 $\quad \begin{array}{r} 3\overset{1}{\not{2}}.\overset{10}{\not{1}}\overset{11}{\not{1}} \\ -\ 11.99 \\ \hline 20.12 \end{array}$

Answers and Explanations

4. 9.5

$$\begin{array}{r} \overset{9}{\not1\not0}.\overset{1}{2}5 \\ -\quad 0.75 \\ \hline 9.50 \end{array}$$

5. 12.018

$$\begin{array}{r} 45.5\overset{3}{\not4}\overset{10}{\not0} \\ -33.522 \\ \hline 12.018 \end{array}$$

6. 0.156

$$\begin{array}{r} 14.\overset{5}{\not6}\overset{9}{\not0}\overset{10}{\not0} \\ -14.444 \\ \hline 0.156 \end{array}$$

7. 20.994

$$\begin{array}{r} 3\overset{1}{\not2}.\overset{9}{\not0}\overset{10}{\not0}4 \\ -11.010 \\ \hline 20.994 \end{array}$$

8. 181.08

$$\begin{array}{r} \overset{1}{\not2}\overset{1}{2}2.\overset{2}{\not3}\overset{10}{\not0} \\ -\quad 41.22 \\ \hline 181.08 \end{array}$$

9. 1.856

$$\begin{array}{r} \overset{5}{\not6}.\overset{11}{\not1}\overset{8}{\not9}\overset{10}{\not0} \\ -4.334 \\ \hline 1.856 \end{array}$$

10. 8.559

$$\begin{array}{r} 8.5\overset{5}{\not6}\overset{15}{5} \\ -\quad 0.006 \\ \hline 8.559 \end{array}$$

11. 291.662

$$\begin{array}{r} \overset{2}{\not3}\overset{14}{\not4}\overset{4}{\not5}.\overset{12}{\not3}\overset{13}{\not4}\overset{10}{\not0} \\ -\quad 53.678 \\ \hline 291.662 \end{array}$$

12. 48.82

$$\begin{array}{r} \overset{4}{\not5}\overset{12}{\not3}.\overset{16}{\not7}\overset{10}{\not0} \\ -\quad 4.88 \\ \hline 48.82 \end{array}$$

13. 5.273 cm

$$\begin{array}{r} 24\overset{8}{\not9}.\overset{11}{\not2}\overset{13}{\not4}\overset{10}{\not0} \\ -243.967 \\ \hline 5.273 \end{array}$$

14. 11.02 in.

$$\begin{array}{r} 32.\overset{2}{\not3}\overset{16}{\not0} \\ -21.28 \\ \hline 11.02 \end{array}$$

Lesson 5.5

1. $10.67 — $5 + 5.67 = 10.67$
2. $137.01 — $3.45 + 133.56 = 137.01$
3. $32.52 — $10.87 + 21.65 = 32.52$
4. $6.45 — $11.00 - 4.55 = 6.45$
5. $2.89 — $6.77 - 3.88 = 2.89$
6. $6.85 — $12.30 - 5.45 = 6.85$
7. $5.11 — $20.50 - 15.39 = 5.11$
8. $54.78 — $62.32 - 7.54 = 54.78$
9. $33.55 — $22.22 + 11.33 = 33.55$
10. $98.00 — $65 + 33 = 98$
11. $8.62 — $5.12 + 3.50 = 8.62$
12. $107.96 — $71.42 + 36.54 = 107.96$
13. $687.20 — $1000.00 - 312.80 = 687.20$
14. $9.77 — $21.10 - 11.33 = 9.77$
15. $1.95 — $2.25 - 0.30 = 1.95$
16. $12.98 — $45.53 - 32.55 = 12.98$
17. $0.32 — $12.30 - 11.98 = 0.32$
18. $18.02 — $56.00 - 37.98 = 18.02$
19. $21.00 — $33 - 12 = 21$
20. $2.87 — $41.65 - 38.78 = 2.87$

Lesson 5.6

1. 51 — $45 + 6 = 51$
2. 60 — $35 + 25 = 60$
3. 67 — $76 - 9 = 67$
4. 10 — $5 + 5 = 10$
5. 6 — $10 - 4 = 6$
6. $19.50 — $8 + 11.50 = 19.50$
7. 1 — $13 - 12 = 1$
8. $10.50 — $35 - 24.5 = 10.50$
9. 47 — $55 - 8 = 47$
10. $6.00 — $15.5 - 9.5 = 6$
11. 90 — $13 + 77 = 90$
12. 9 — $50 - 41 = 9$

Lesson 5.7

1. 9586.5 — $415 \times 231 = 95{,}865$ and there is 1 decimal place, so 9586.5
2. 54.39 — $777 \times 7 = 5439$ and there are 2 decimal places, so 54.39
3. 17,526.24 — $32{,}456 \times 54 = 1{,}752{,}624$ and there are 2 decimal places, so 17,526.24

Answers and Explanations

4. 110.11 — $1001 \times 11 = 11,011$ and there are 2 decimal places, so 110.11

5. 137,101.44 — $3232 \times 4242 = 13,710,144$ and there are 2 decimal places, so 137,101.44

6. 20,340.9 — $873 \times 233 = 203,409$ and there is 1 decimal place, so 20,340.9

7. 4474.4 — $658 \times 68 = 44,744$ and there is 1 decimal place, so 4474.4

8. 1747.2 — $120 \times 1456 = 174,720$ and there are 2 decimal places, so 1747.2

9. 481.8 — $438 \times 11 = 4818$ and there is 1 decimal place, so 481.8

10. 1484.7 — $147 \times 101 = 14,847$ and there is 1 decimal place, so 1484.7

11. 10.201 — $101 \times 101 = 10,201$ and there are 3 decimal places, so 10.201

12. 308.025 — $555 \times 555 = 308,025$ and there are 3 decimal places, so 308.025

13. 180.810 — $410 \times 441 = 180,810$ and there are 3 decimal places, so 180.810

14. 145.2482 — $1382 \times 1051 = 1,452,482$ and there are 4 decimal places, so 145.2482

15. 1,730.3616 — $2112 \times 8193 = 17,303,616$ and there are 4 decimal places, so 1,730.3616

16. 8.37 — $27 \times 31 = 837$ and there are 2 decimal places, so 8.37

17. 735.279 — $1789 \times 41.1 = 735,279$ and there are 3 decimal places, so 735.279

18. 3.83194 — $1414 \times 271 = 383,194$ and there are 5 decimal places, so 3.83194

19. 553.125 — $7375 \times 75 = 553,125$ and there are 3 decimal places, so 553.125

20. 600.7002 — $2001 \times 3002 = 6,007,002$ and there are 4 decimal places, so 600.7002

21. 1990 — $199 \times 100 = 19,900$ and there is 1 decimal place, so 1990

22. 24 — $24 \times 10 = 240$ and there is 1 decimal place, so 24.0

23. 0.11234 — $1 \times 11,234 = 11,234$ and there are 5 decimal places, so 0.11234

24. 0.0156 — $156 \times 1 = 156$ and there are 4 decimal places, so 0.0156

25. 71,782 — $71782 \times 1000 = 71,782,000$ and there are 3 decimal places, so 71,782

26. 76,760 — $7676 \times 1000 = 7,676,000$ and there are 2 decimal places, so 76,760

27. 13.2 — $10 \times 132 = 1320$ and there are 2 decimal places, so 13.2

28. 63,450 — $6345 \times 1000 = 6,345,000$ and there are 2 decimal places, so 63,450

29. 0.001345 — $1345 \times 1 = 1345$ and there are 6 decimal places, so 0.001345

30. 11.11111 — $1111111 \times 1 = 1,111,111$ and there are 5 decimal places, so 11.11111

Lesson 5.8

1. $26.13 — $10.45 \times 2.5 = 26.125 = 26.13$

2. $112.10 — $101.91 \times 1.1 = 112.101 = 112.10$

3. $21.60 — $5.76 \times 3.75 = 21.6 = 21.60$

4. $782.69 — $78.9 \times 9.92 = 782.688 = 782.69$

5. $40.10 — $7.29 \times 5.5 = 40.095 = 40.10$

6. $267.63 — $89.21 \times 3 = 267.63$

7. $455.63 — $67.5 \times 6.75 = 455.625 = 455.63$

8. $23.00 — $10 \times 2.3 = 23 = 23.00$

9. $60.50 — $5.5 \times 11 = 60.5 = 60.50$

10. $45.13 — $4.75 \times 9.5 = 45.125 = 45.13$

11. $426.50 — $85.3 \times 5 = 426.5 = 426.50$

12. $72.60 — $33 \times 2.2 = 72.6 = 72.60$

13. $24.71 — $3.66 \times 6.75 = 24.705 = 24.71$

14. Yes — $0.04 \times 120 = 4.80$

Lesson 5.9

1. 160 — $20 \times 8 = 160$

2. $35 — $7 \times 5 = 35$

3. 500 — $100 \times 5 = 500$

4. 600 — $30 \times 20 = 600$

5. $100 — $2 \times 50 = 100$

6. 1 — $0.2 \times 5 = 1.0$

7. $50 — $10 \times 5 = 50$

8. 1000 — $50 \times 20 = 1000$

9. 30 — $60 \times 0.5 = 30$

10. $18 — $0.9 \times 20 = 18$

11. 24 — $0.8 \times 30 = 24$

12. 80 — $2 \times 40 = 80$

13. 200 — $20 \times 10 = 200$

14. $200 — $20 \times 10 = 200$

15. 4 — $2 \times 2 = 4$

16. $120 — $30 \times 4 = 120$

17. 70 — $10 \times 7 = 70$

Answers and Explanations

18. 32 $8 \times 4 = 32$

19. 20 $20 \times 1 = 20$

20. \$40 $20 \times 2 = 40$

Lesson 5.10

1. 5.05

5.05
2)10.10
10
10
10

2. 5.6125

5.6125
4)22.4500
20
24
24
5
4
10
8
20
20

3. 7.825

7.825
10)78.250
70
82
80
25
20
50
50

4. 2.02

2.02
11)22.22
22
022
22

5. 0.96875

0.96875
8)7.75000
72
55
48
70
64
60
56
40
40

6. 2.9

2.9
5)14.5
10
45
45

7. 3.89

3.89
20)77.80
60
178
160
180
180

8. 1.515

1.515
30)45.450
30
154
150
45
30
150
150

9. 17.333

17.33...
6)104.000
6
44
42
20
18
20
18
20...

10. 27.9375

27.9375
2)55.8750
4
15
14
18
18
7
6
15
14
10
10

11. 25.39

25.39
4)101.56
8
21
20
15
12
36
36

12. 132.8

132.8
7)929.6
7
22
21
19
14
56
56

13. 1.25

1.25
3)3.75
3
7
6
15
15

14. 13.15

13.15
2)26.30
2
6
6
3
2
10
10

Lesson 5.11

1. 75

75.
0.44)33.00.
308
220
220

2. 2605

2605.
0.2)521.0.
4
12
12
10
10

3. 26.7

26.66...
0.45)12.00.0
90
300
270
300
270
300
270
300...

4. 4530

4530.
0.1)453.0

5. 176

176.
0.25)44.00.
25
190
175
150
150

6. 37.5

37.5
0.56)21.00.0
168
420
392
280
280

7. 649.2

649.23...
0.65)422.00.00
390
320
260
600
585
150
130
200
195
5...

8. 4000

4000.
0.05)200.00.
20
000

9. 17.5

17.5
0.4)7.0.0
4
30
28
20
20

10. 8.6

8.57...
1.4)12.0.0
112
80
70
100
98
20...

Lesson 5.12

1. 0.5

0.5
0.44)0.22.0
22 0

Answers and Explanations

2. 0.06

```
      0.064...
3.12)0.20.00
      18 72
      1 280
      1 248
         32...
```

3. 0.59

```
      0.589...
0.56)0.33.00
      280
      500
      448
      520
```

4. 0.04

```
      0.039...
0.76)0.03.000
      228
      720
      684
       36...
```

5. 0.45

```
      0.449...
0.89)0.4000
      356
      440
      356
      840
      801
       39...
```

6. 0.10

```
       0.102...
0.784)0.080.0
        784
        1600
        1568
          32
```

7. 10

```
      10. R25
0.35)  3.75.0
       35
        25
```

8. No

```
     16. R4
1.3)  21.2
      13
       82
       78
        4
```

Lesson 5.13

1. $0.45

```
   0.45
3)$1.35
   1 2
    15
    15
```

2. $2.50

```
   2.50
4)$10.00
   8
   20
   20
    0
```

3. $5.59

```
      5.589...
10.1)$56.4500
      505
      595
      505
       900
       808
       920
       909
        11...
```

4. $34.94

```
     34.937...
0.8)$27.9.500
     24
      39
      32
       75
       72
        30
        24
         60
         56
          4
```

5. $5.72

```
    5.722...
17)$97.280
    85
    122
    119
      38
      34
      40
      34
       6
```

6. $8.50

```
        8.5
2.5)$21.2.5
     200
     125
     125
```

7. $7.89

```
    7.89
23)$181.47
    161
    204
    184
    207
    207
```

8. $96.79

```
      96.793...
  8)$774.350
     72
      54
      48
       63
       56
        75
        72
         30
         24
          6
```

9. $8.10

```
            8.1
  10.5)$85.0.5
         84 0
          1 05
          1 05
```

10. $75.25

```
    75.25
  3)225.75
    21
     15
     15
       7
       6
       15
       15
```

11. 8 months

```
          7.9...
  258)$2052.00
       1806
        2460
        2322
         138
```

12. $78.12

```
     78.12
  4)$312.48
     28
      32
      32
        4
        4
         8
         8
```

Lesson 5.14

1. 15 $15 \div 1 = 15$

2. 3 $24 \div 8 = 3$

3. 1 $9 \div 9 = 1$

4. 3 $39 \div 13 = 3$

5. 2 $50 \div 25 = 2$

6. 10 $130 \div 13 = 10$

7. 5 $45 \div 9 = 5$

8. 2 $6 \div 3 = 2$

9. 4 $4 \div 1 = 4$

10. 12 $24 \div 2 = 12$

11. 12 $48 \div 4 = 12$

12. 4 $32 \div 8 = 4$

13. 2 $10 \div 5 = 2$

14. 20 $32 \div 1.6 = 20$

15. 5 $55 \div 11 = 5$

16. 12 $24 \div 2 = 12$

17. 20 $90 \div 4.5 = 20$

18. 20 $50 \div 2.5 = 20$

19. 15 $75 \div 5 = 15$

20. 8 $72 \div 9 = 8$

Lesson 6.1

1. $0.45 = \frac{45}{100} = \frac{9}{20}$

2. $0.35 = \frac{35}{100} = \frac{7}{20}$

3. $0.43 = \frac{43}{100}$

4. $0.1 = \frac{10}{100} = \frac{1}{10}$

5. $0.87 = \frac{87}{100}$

6. $0.02 = \frac{2}{100} = \frac{1}{50}$

7. $0.59 = \frac{59}{100}$

8. $0.001 = \frac{1}{1000}$

9. $0.0045 = \frac{45}{10{,}000} = \frac{9}{2000}$

10. $76\% \ \frac{76}{100} = 76\%$

11. $10\% = \frac{1}{10} = 0.1$

Lesson 6.2

1. $\frac{7}{20}$ $\frac{35}{100} = \frac{7}{20}$

2. $\frac{47}{100}$

3. $\frac{1}{4}$ $\frac{25}{100} = \frac{1}{4}$

4. $\frac{3}{50}$ $\frac{6}{100} = \frac{3}{50}$

5. $\frac{91}{100}$

Answers and Explanations

6. $\frac{523}{1000}$ $\frac{52.3}{100}=\frac{523}{1000}$

7. $\frac{41}{2000}$ $\frac{2.05}{100}=\frac{205}{10,000}=\frac{41}{2000}$

8. $\frac{17}{100}$

9. $\frac{99}{200}$ $\frac{49.5}{100}=\frac{495}{1000}=\frac{99}{200}$

10. $\frac{1}{1000}$ $\frac{0.1}{100}=\frac{1}{1000}$

11. 35% $100 \div 20 = 5; 7\times 5 = 35$

12. 30% $100 \div 10 = 10; 3\times 10 = 30$

13. 60% $100 \div 5 = 20; 3\times 20 = 60$

14. 25% $\frac{1}{4}; 100 \div 4 = 25; 1\times 25 = 25$

15. 10% $\frac{1}{10}; 100 \div 10 = 10; 1\times 10 = 10$

Lesson 6.3

1. 0.1
2. 0.67
3. 0.0002
4. 0.964
5. 0.5532
6. 11.1001
7. 0.2346
8. 0.0008
9. 0.34
10. 10.03
11. 3% $0.03\times 100 = 3$
12. 102% $1.02\times 100 = 102$
13. 0.27% $0.0027\times 100 = 0.27$
14. 2.5% $0.025\times 100 = 2.5$
15. 10,001% $100.01\times 100 = 10001$
16. 14.5% $0.145\times 100 = 14.5$
17. 1.01% $0.0101\times 100 = 1.01$
18. 12.5% $0.125\times 100 = 12.5$
19. 8.25% $0.0825\times 100 = 8.25$
20. 0.9% $0.009\times 100 = 0.9$

Lesson 6.4

1. $\frac{7}{120}$ $\frac{35}{100}\times\frac{1}{6}=\frac{35}{600}=\frac{7}{120}$

2. $\frac{33}{175}$ $\frac{22}{100}\times\frac{6}{7}=\frac{11}{50}\times\frac{6}{7}=\frac{66}{350}=\frac{33}{175}$

3. $\frac{1}{16}$ $\frac{25}{100}\times\frac{1}{4}=\frac{1}{4}\times\frac{1}{4}=\frac{1}{16}$

4. $\frac{78}{125}$ $\frac{78}{100}\times\frac{4}{5}=\frac{39}{50}\times\frac{4}{5}=\frac{156}{250}=\frac{78}{125}$

5. $\frac{2}{75}$ $\frac{4}{100}\times\frac{2}{3}=\frac{8}{300}=\frac{4}{150}=\frac{2}{75}$

6. $\frac{6}{25}$ $\frac{\cancel{56}^{8}}{100}\times\frac{3}{\cancel{7}_{1}}=\frac{24}{100}=\frac{12}{50}=\frac{6}{25}$

7. $\frac{111}{1300}$ $\frac{37}{100}\times\frac{3}{13}=\frac{111}{1300}$

8. $\frac{51}{800}$ $\frac{51}{100}\times\frac{1}{8}=\frac{51}{800}$

9. $\frac{44}{225}$ $\frac{44}{100}\times\frac{4}{9}=\frac{11}{25}\times\frac{4}{9}=\frac{44}{225}$

10. $\frac{3}{170}$ $\frac{10}{100}\times\frac{3}{17}=\frac{1}{10}\times\frac{3}{17}=\frac{3}{170}$

11. 12% $\frac{3}{\cancel{5}_{1}}\times\frac{\cancel{20}^{4}}{100}=\frac{12}{100}=12\%$

12. 3% $\frac{1}{\cancel{11}_{1}}\times\frac{\cancel{33}^{3}}{100}=\frac{3}{100}=3\%$

13. 66% $\frac{3}{\cancel{4}_{1}}\times\frac{\cancel{88}^{22}}{100}=\frac{66}{100}=66\%$

14. 44% $\frac{2}{\cancel{3}_{1}}\times\frac{\cancel{66}^{22}}{100}=\frac{44}{100}=44\%$

15. 10% $\frac{1}{\cancel{8}_{1}}\times\frac{\cancel{80}^{10}}{100}=\frac{10}{100}=10\%$

Lesson 7.1

1. 8 $2^3 = 2\times 2\times 2 = 8$
2. 25 $5^2 = 5\times 5 = 25$
3. 1728 $12^3 = 12\times 12\times 12 = 1728$
4. 64 $4^3 = 4\times 4\times 4 = 64$
5. 144 $12^2 = 12\times 12 = 144$
6. 6.25 $2.5^2 = 2.5\times 2.5 = 6.25$
7. 1000 $10^3 = 10\times 10\times 10 = 1000$
8. 2401 $7^4 = 7\times 7\times 7\times 7 = 2401$
9. 1.44 $1.2^2 = 1.2\times 1.2 = 1.44$
10. 625 $5^4 = 5\times 5\times 5\times 5 = 625$
11. 243 $3^5 = 3\times 3\times 3\times 3\times 3 = 243$
12. 0.0001 $(0.01)^2 = 0.01\times 0.01 = 0.0001$
13. 128 $2^7 = 2\times 2\times 2\times 2\times 2\times 2\times 2 = 128$
14. 0.0001 $(0.05)^3 = 0.05\times 0.05\times 0.05 = 0.000125$
15. 100,000 $10^5 = 10\times 10\times 10\times 10\times 10 = 100,000$
16. 1.21 $(1.1)^2 = 1.1\times 1.1 = 1.21$

17. 343 $7^3 = 7 \times 7 \times 7 = 343$

18. 625 $25^2 = 25 \times 25 = 625$

19. 27,000 $30^3 = 30 \times 30 \times 30 = 27,000$

20. 0.000000008 $(0.002)^3 = 0.002 \times 0.002 \times 0.002 = 0.000000008$

21. 36 $6 \times 6 = 36$

22. $13.00 $0.04 + 0.08 + 0.16 + 0.32 + 0.64 + 1.28 + 2.56 + 5.12 = 10.20$; $\$10.20 < \$13.00$

Lesson 7.2

1. 1.25×10^2 the decimal is moved 2 places to the left

2. 7.453×10^3 the decimal is moved 3 places to the left

3. 2.54×10^{-2} the decimal is moved 2 places to the right

4. 3.7×10^1 the decimal is moved 1 place to the left

5. 4.57×10^{-3} the decimal is moved 3 places to the right

6. 1.222333×10^6 the decimal is moved 6 places to the left

7. 8.98×10^2 the decimal is moved 2 places to the left

8. 4.532×10^1 the decimal is moved 1 place to the left

9. 19.325×10^2 the decimal is moved 2 places to the left

10. 1.3023×10^4 the decimal is moved 4 places to the left

11. 5.567×10^0 the decimal does not move

12. 7.2354×10^1 the decimal is moved 1 place to the left

13. 4.77777×10^3 the decimal is moved 3 places to the left

14. 2.002×10^{-2} the decimal is moved 2 places to the right

15. 2.33323×10^2 the decimal is moved 2 places to the left

16. 5.672×10^3 the decimal is moved 3 places to the left

Lesson 7.3

1. 24 $5-(4-3)+5\times 4 = 5-(1)+5\times 4 = 5-(1)+20 = 5-1+20 = 4+20 = 24$

2. 74 $(3\times 2)^2 \times 2 - 2 + 4 = 6^2 \times 2 - 2 + 4 = 36\times 2 - 2 + 4 = 72 - 2 + 4 = 70 + 4 = 74$

3. 99 $(3+2)^2 \times 4 - 3 + \frac{4}{2} = 5^2 \times 4 - 3 + \frac{4}{2} = 25 \times 4 - 3 + \frac{4}{2} = 100 - 3 + \frac{4}{2} = 100 - 3 + 2 = 97 + 2 = 99$

4. 3 $5 - 7 + 4 \times 2 - 3 = 5 - 7 + 8 - 3 = -2 + 8 - 3 = 6 - 3 = 3$

5. –48 $55 - 2 \times \frac{3}{2} - 10^2 = 55 - 2 \times \frac{3}{2} - 100 = 55 - 3 - 100 = 52 - 100 = -48$

6. 81 $(2+3+4)^{3-1} = (9)^{3-1} = 9^2 = 81$

7. 4 $(2-2)^2 + (4-2)^2 = 0^2 + 2^2 = 0 + 4 = 4$

8. 28 $(3-4) + 3^2 \times 3 + 2 = -1 + 3^2 \times 3 + 2 = -1 + 9 \times 3 + 2 = -1 + 27 + 2 = 26 + 2 = 28$

9. –56 $4 \times (11-7) - (44+28) = 4 \times 4 - 72 = 16 - 72 = -56$

Lesson 8.1

1. A(1,2), B(3,–3), C(–5,–5), D(5,5), E(4,–5), F(1,1), G(–1,1), H(–4,4), I(8,8), J(–5,6)

2.

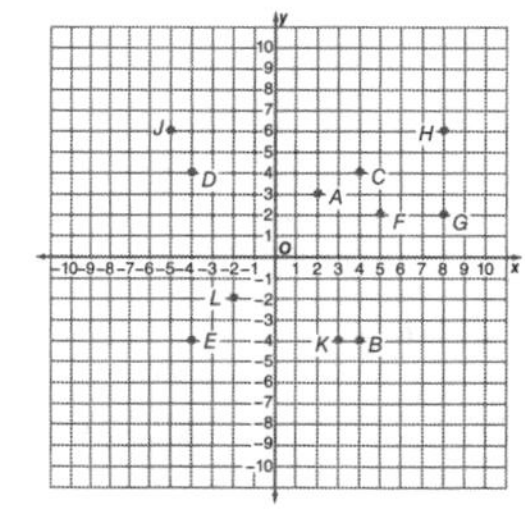

Lesson 8.2

1. 3 $8 - 5 = 3$

2. 2 $3 - 1 = 2$

3. 5 $1 - (-4) = 1 + 4 = 5$

4. 3 $6 - 3 = 3$

5. 4 $2 - (-2) = 2 + 2 = 4$

6. 7 $3 - (-4) = 3 + 4 = 7$

Lesson 9.1

1. A number divided by six

2. A number plus four

3. A number multiplied by two, plus ten

4. Five times a number minus five

Answers and Explanations

5. A number less five, divided by thirty-three
6. The sum of three times a number plus four, times ten
7. A The product of 3 times x is written as $3x$ and then 1 is subtracted from it.
8. No She should write $8.50x$ since she will need to multiply the number of tickets by the price per ticket to get the total price.

Lesson 9.2

1. $2x-3$ First write $2x$, then subtract 3.
2. $14(x-22)$ First write $x-22$. Since that is multiplied by 14, put it in parentheses.
3. $(22-3)x+2$ First write $22-3$. Since that is multiplied by a number, put it in parentheses and use x to represent the number. Then add 2 to the end.
4. $10x-3y$ First write $10x$. Now subtract the product of 3 and another number. Use a different variable to represent the other unknown number, such as y.
5. $\frac{9x}{(10x-2)}$ First write $9x$. Now divide that by $10x-2$.
6. $\frac{1}{2}x+\frac{1}{4}x$ First write $\frac{1}{2}x$. Then add $\frac{1}{4}x$.
7. B A number plus 7 can be written as $7+x$ or $x+7$.
8. A Two times a number is $2x$.

Lesson 9.3

1. No There are only three of x.
2. Yes Multiplication can be done in any order, so $\left(\frac{1}{2}x\right)(6)=\left(\frac{1}{2}\right)(6)(x)=3x$
3. No There are only two of x.
4. Yes Use the distributive property to factor out 4.5: $4.5x-9=4.5(x-2)$
5. Yes Six divided by 3 equals 2.
6. No Combine like terms: $6x+8-2x=6x-2x+8=4x-8$
7. Yes Both put out 20 chairs.
8. A and C 5 rides times x dollars is $5x$. Add \$10 admission to get $5x+10$. Factor out 5 to get $5(x+2)$.

Lesson 9.4

1. $w=7$
$$\begin{array}{r} W+3=10 \\ -3\ \ -3 \\ \hline W=7 \end{array}$$

2. $4=q$
$$\begin{array}{r} 12=q+8 \\ -8\ \ \ -8 \\ \hline 4=q \end{array}$$

3. $y=32$
$$\begin{array}{r} 2+y=3y \\ -2\ \ \ -2 \\ \hline y=32 \end{array}$$

4. $3=e$
$$\begin{array}{r} 7-e=4 \\ +e\ +e \\ \hline 7=4+e \\ -4\ -4 \\ \hline 3=e \end{array}$$

5. $s=33$
$$\begin{array}{r} s+17=50 \\ -17\ -17 \\ \hline s=33 \end{array}$$

6. $d=15$
$$\begin{array}{r} d-4=11 \\ +4\ +4 \\ \hline d=15 \end{array}$$

7. $z=15$
$$\begin{array}{r} z+10=25 \\ -10\ -10 \\ \hline z=15 \end{array}$$

8. $18=r$
$$\begin{array}{r} 23=5+r \\ -5\ -5 \\ \hline 18=r \end{array}$$

9. $m=9$
$$\begin{array}{r} m+45=54 \\ -45\ -45 \\ \hline m=9 \end{array}$$

10. $t=18$
$$\begin{array}{r} 15+t=33 \\ -15\ -15 \\ \hline t=18 \end{array}$$

11. $15=g$
$$\begin{array}{r} 45-g=30 \\ +9\ \ +9 \\ \hline 45=30+g \\ -30\ -30 \\ \hline 15=g \end{array}$$

12. $2=f$
$$\begin{array}{r} 3-f=1 \\ +f\ \ +f \\ \hline 3=1+f \\ -1\ \ -1 \\ \hline 2=f \end{array}$$

13. $v+(v+26)=108$; 41; 67 Use v for Valerie's score. Chris's score will be $v+26$, so $v+(v+26)=108$. To solve, combine like terms:
$$\begin{array}{r} 2v+26=108 \\ -26\ -26 \\ \hline \frac{2v}{2}=\frac{82}{2} \\ v=41 \end{array}$$
$v+26=41+26=67$

Answers and Explanations

Lesson 9.5

1. $x = 3$

$$\begin{array}{r} 3x + 10 = 19 \\ -10 \quad -10 \\ \hline \frac{3x}{3} = \frac{9}{3} \\ x = 3 \end{array}$$

2. $m = 4$

$$\begin{array}{r} 4 + 7m = 32 \\ -4 \qquad -4 \\ \hline \frac{7m}{7} = \frac{28}{7} \\ m = 4 \end{array}$$

3. $b = 11$

$$\begin{array}{r} 10b + 8 = 118 \\ -8 \quad -8 \\ \hline \frac{10b}{10} = \frac{110}{10} \\ b = 11 \end{array}$$

4. $p = 38$

$$\begin{array}{r} 12 + 2p = 88 \\ -12 \qquad -12 \\ \hline \frac{2p}{2} = \frac{76}{2} \\ p = 38 \end{array}$$

5. $y = 343$

$$(7)\frac{y}{7} = 49(7)$$
$$y = 343$$

6. $u = 4$

$$\begin{array}{r} 10 + 2u = 14 + u \\ -u \qquad -u \\ \hline 10 + u = 14 \\ -10 \qquad -10 \\ \hline u = \quad 4 \end{array}$$

7. $2x + x = 12$ or $3x = 12$; Lynda: 8 Alex: 4

Let Alex = x
Lynda = $2x$

$$\frac{3x}{3} = \frac{12}{3}$$
$$x = 4$$
$$2x = 8$$

Lesson 9.6

1. 17 $3 + 14 = 17$

2. 11 $-3 + 14 = 11$

3. 1 $2(2) - 3 = 4 - 3 = 1$

4. –1 $2(1) - 3 = 2 - 3 = -1$

5. –3 $2(0) - 3 = 0 - 3 = -3$

6. –5 $2(-1) - 3 = -2 - 3 = -5$

7. –7 $2(-2) - 3 = -4 - 3 = -7$

8. 8.5 $10 - 3\left(\frac{1}{2}\right) = 10 - 1.5 = 8.5$

9. 3 $3 - 3(0) = 3 - 0 = 3$

10. –8 $\frac{1}{2}(-8) - 4 = -4 - 4 = -8$

11. –3 $\frac{1}{2}(2) - 4 = 1 - 4 = -3$

12. 0 $\frac{1}{2}(8) - 4 = 4 - 4 = 0$

13. 0.5 $\frac{1}{2}(9) - 4 = 4.5 - 4 = 0.5$

14. 4 $\frac{1}{2}(16) - 4 = 8 - 4 = 4$

Lesson 10.1

1. No $5 - 3 > 4; 2 > 4$

2. Yes $5 + 1 > 3 + 2; 6 > 5$

3. Yes $4 + 5 \geq 9; 9 \geq 9$

4. No $4(5) - 1 < 15; 20 - 1 < 15; 19 < 15$

5. Yes $5 + 12 \leq 35; 17 \leq 35$

6. –10 –9 –8 –7 –6 –5 –4 –3 –2 –1 0 1 2 3 4 5 6 7 8 9 10

7. –10 –9 –8 –7 –6 –5 –4 –3 –2 –1 0 1 2 3 4 5 6 7 8 9 10

8. –10 –9 –8 –7 –6 –5 –4 –3 –2 –1 0 1 2 3 4 5 6 7 8 9 10

Lesson 10.2

1. $12 - 9 = x$ His mother needs 9 out of 12 eggs, so he can only use the other 3.

2. No There are only 3 eggs left.

3. Yes He will have exactly enough.

4. A $\frac{4}{1} > 2$

5. 5 They will need at least 8 tickets to ride together. $8 - 3 = 5$

6. $x + 3 \geq 8$ Sarah has 3 and Sadie needs x. Together, they need 8 or more.

Lesson 11.1

1. 4:3 4 circles and 3 squares, so 4:3

2. 1:3 2 squares and 6 circles, so 2:6, which reduces to 1:3

3. 6:7 6 girls and 7 boys, so 6:7

4. 3:4 6 cats and 8 dogs, so 6:8, which reduces to 3:4

5. 2:1 2 cups flour and 1 cup sugar, so 2:1

6. 4:5 8 blue and 10 red, so 8:10, which reduces to 4:5

7. 3:5 3 toffee and 5 peanut butter, so 3:5

8. 3:2 6 adults and 4 children, so 6:4, which reduces to 3:2

9. 25:2 400 students and 32 teachers, so 400:32, which reduces to 25:2

10. 4:5 80 adults and 100 children, so 80:100, which reduces to 4:5

Answers and Explanations

Lesson 11.2

1. A) 2:3 — 2 white and 3 tan, so 2:3
   B) 3:2 — 3 tan and 2 white, so 3:2
   C) 3:5 — 3 tan and 2+3=5 total, so 3:5
   D) 2:5 — 2 white and 5 total, so 2:5
2. A) 3:4 — 6 cats and 8 dogs, so 6:8, which reduces to 3:4
   B) 4:3 — 8 dogs and 6 cats, so 8:6, which reduces to 4:3
   C) 3:7 — 6 cats and 6+8=14 total, so 6:14, which reduces to 3:7
   D) 4:7 — 8 dogs and 14 total, so 8:14, which reduces to 4:7
3. 32 — 20 students for every 1 teacher and $640 \div 20 = 32$
4. 26 — 2 chocolate chip for every 1 sugar, so $2 \times 13 = 26$
5. 3 boys/4 girls or 6 boys/8 girls
   If the ratio is 3:4 and the total is less than 20, then the actual numbers could be $3+4=7$ or $6+8=14$. That is the maximum because $9+12=21$, which is too many total.

Lesson 11.3

1.

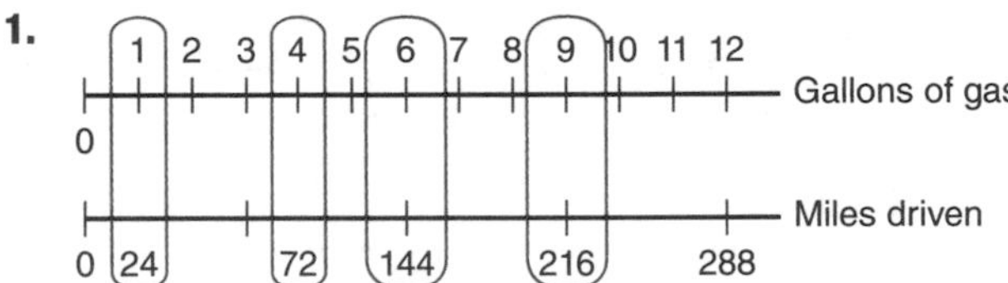

   A. 144 miles — 6 gallons is half of 12 gallons and $288 \div 2 = 144$
   B. 72 miles — 4 gallons is one-third of 12 gallons and $288 \div 3 = 72$
   C. 24 miles — 1 gallon is one-twelfth of 12 gallons and $288 \div 12 = 24$
   D. 216 miles — 9 gallons is three-fourths of 12 gallons and $288 \times \frac{3}{4} = 216$
   E. 24:1 — You found that 1 gallon is 24 miles, so 24:1. You can also say the ratio is 288:12, 216:9, or 144:6, but those will all reduce to 24:1.
2. 9

   Flour: 0, 3, 6, 9, 12
   Sugar: 0, 1, 2, 3, 4

Lesson 12.1

1. $z = 16$ — $4 \times 28 = z \times 7; 112 = z \times 7; \frac{112}{7} = \frac{z \times 7}{7}; 16 = z$
2. $z = 20$ — $5 \times 12 = 3 \times z; 60 = 3 \times z; \frac{60}{3} = \frac{3 \times z}{3}; 20 = z$
3. $z = 2$ — $8 \times 9 = 36 \times z; 72 = 36 \times z; \frac{72}{36} = \frac{36 \times z}{36}; 2 = z$
4. $z = 14$ — $2 \times 21 = 3 \times z; 42 = 3 \times z; \frac{42}{3} = \frac{3 \times z}{3}; 14 = z$
5. $z = 4$ — $2 \times 14 = 7 \times z; 28 = 7 \times z; \frac{28}{7} = \frac{7 \times z}{7}; 4 = z$
6. $z = 2$ — $10 \times 11 = 55 \times z; 110 = 55 \times z; \frac{110}{55} = \frac{55 \times z}{55}; 2 = z$
7. $z = \frac{1}{2}$ — $2 \times 2 = 8 \times z; 4 = 8 \times z; \frac{4}{8} = \frac{8 \times z}{8}; \frac{1}{2} = z$
8. $z = 17$ — $51 \times 1 = 3 \times z; 51 = 3 \times z; \frac{51}{3} = \frac{3 \times z}{3}; 17 = z$

Lesson 12.2

1. 135 miles — $\frac{105 \text{ miles}}{7 \text{ gallons}} = \frac{y \text{ miles}}{9 \text{ gallons}}; 105 \times 9 = 7y;$ $945 = 7y; \frac{945}{7} = \frac{7y}{7}; 135 = y$
2. 8 minutes — $15 + 17 = 32; \frac{32 \text{ minutes}}{80 \text{ percent}} = \frac{y \text{ minutes}}{20 \text{ percent}};$ $32 \times 20 = 80y; 640 = 80y; \frac{640}{80} = \frac{80y}{80}; 8 = y$
3. 55 minutes — $\frac{25 \text{ minutes}}{55 \text{ bicycles}} = \frac{y \text{ minutes}}{121 \text{ bicycles}}; 25 \times 121 = 55y;$ $3025 = 55y; \frac{3025}{55} = \frac{55y}{55}; 55 = y$
4. 78 pizzas — $\frac{90 \text{ people}}{52 \text{ pizzas}} = \frac{135 \text{ people}}{y \text{ pizzas}}; 52 \times 135 = 90y;$ $7020 = 90y; \frac{7020}{90} = \frac{90y}{90}; 78 = y$
5. \$94.29 — $\frac{55 \text{ dollars}}{14 \text{ items}} = \frac{y \text{ dollars}}{24 \text{ items}}; 55 \times 24 = 14y;$ $1320 = 14y; \frac{1320}{14} = \frac{14y}{14}; 94.29 = y$
6. 9 workers — $\frac{58 \text{ lawns}}{6 \text{ workers}} = \frac{87 \text{ lawns}}{y \text{ workers}}; 6 \times 87 = 58y;$ $522 = 58y; \frac{522}{58} = \frac{58y}{58}; 9 = y$
7. 1248 bushels — $\frac{7 \text{ trees}}{78 \text{ bushels}} = \frac{112 \text{ trees}}{y \text{ bushels}}; 78 \times 112 = 7y;$ $8736 = 7y; \frac{8736}{7} = \frac{7y}{7}; 1248 = y$
8. 495 pounds — $32 \text{ scouts} = 1 \text{ troop}; \frac{1 \text{ troop}}{11 \text{ pounds}} = \frac{45 \text{ troops}}{y \text{ pounds}}; 11 \times 45 = 1y; 495 = y$

Answers and Explanations

Lesson 12.3

1. Multiplier = 3; 9 cups flour, 3 cups sugar, 9 sticks butter
2. Multiplier = 5; -sixth graders = 55; 45% are -fifth graders

Lesson 12.4

1. missing value: 8; multiplier: 2

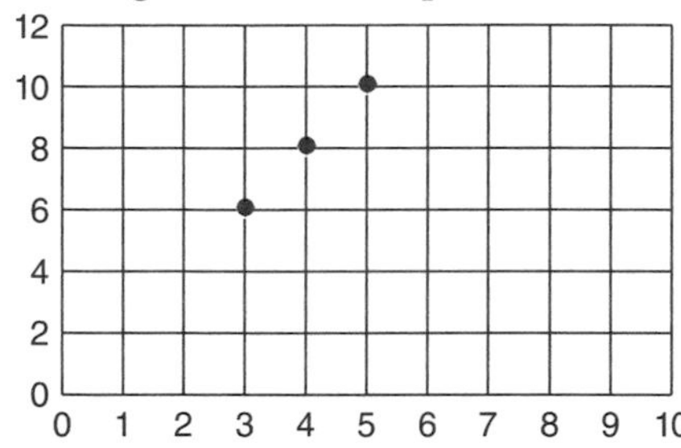

2. missing value: 3; multiplier: 1.5

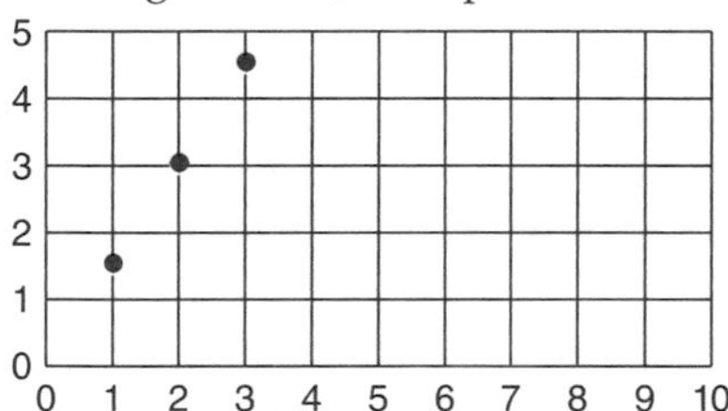

3. missing value: 6; multiplier: 3

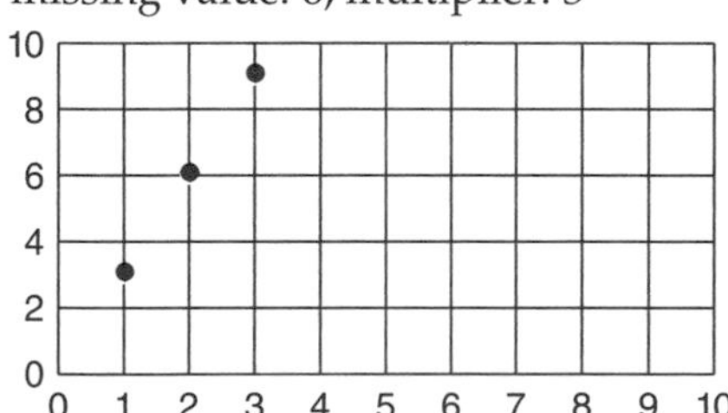

4.

1 load	\$2.00
2 loads	\$4.00
3 loads	\$6.00
4 loads	\$8.00

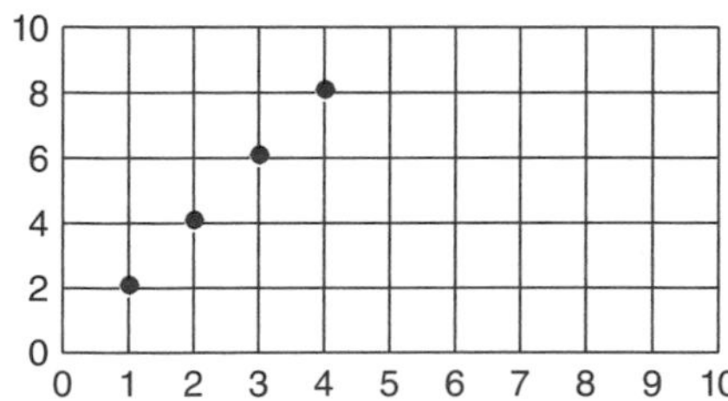

Lesson 13.1

1. 17 days   Reduce first: $\frac{6 \text{ apples}}{2 \text{ days}} = \frac{3 \text{ apples}}{1 \text{ day}}$;
$\frac{3 \text{ apples}}{1 \text{ day}} = \frac{51 \text{ apples}}{y \text{ days}}$;
$51 = 3y; \frac{51}{3} = \frac{3y}{3}; 17 = y$

2. 168 kilometers   Reduce first:
$\frac{56 \text{ kilometers}}{8 \text{ hours}} = \frac{7 \text{ kilometers}}{1 \text{ hour}}$;
$\frac{7 \text{ kilometers}}{1 \text{ hour}} = \frac{y \text{ kilometers}}{24 \text{ hours}}$;
$7 \times 24 = y; 168 = y$

3. 10 miles   Reduce first: $\frac{18 \text{ miles}}{9 \text{ hours}} = \frac{2 \text{ miles}}{1 \text{ hour}}$;
$\frac{2 \text{ miles}}{1 \text{ hour}} = \frac{y \text{ miles}}{5 \text{ hours}}$;
$2 \times 5 = y; 10 = y$

4. 4 hours   Reduce first:
$\frac{2100 \text{ people}}{3 \text{ hours}} = \frac{700 \text{ people}}{1 \text{ hour}}$;
$\frac{700 \text{ people}}{1 \text{ hour}} = \frac{2800 \text{ people}}{y \text{ hours}}$;
$2800 = 700y; 4 = y$

5. 84 acres   Reduce first: $\frac{5 \text{ horses}}{20 \text{ acres}} = \frac{1 \text{ horse}}{4 \text{ acres}}$;
$\frac{1 \text{ horse}}{4 \text{ acres}} = \frac{21 \text{ horses}}{y \text{ acres}}$;
$4 \times 21 = y; 84 = y$

6. 2.5 minutes $5 \text{ people} \times \frac{20 \text{ chairs}}{1 \text{ minute}} = \frac{100 \text{ chairs}}{1 \text{ minute}}$;
$\frac{100 \text{ chairs}}{1 \text{ minute}} = \frac{250 \text{ chairs}}{y \text{ minutes}}$;
$100y = 250; y = 2.5$

7. 840 square feet   Reduce first: $\frac{240 \text{ feet}}{2 \text{ hours}} = \frac{120 \text{ feet}}{1 \text{ hour}}$;
$\frac{120 \text{ feet}}{1 \text{ hour}} = \frac{y \text{ feet}}{7 \text{ hours}}$;
$120 \times 7 = y; 840 = y$

8. 105 minutes   Reduce first:
$\frac{45 \text{ people}}{35 \text{ minutes}} = \frac{9 \text{ people}}{7 \text{ minutes}}$;
$\frac{9 \text{ people}}{7 \text{ minutes}} = \frac{135 \text{ people}}{y \text{ minutes}}$;
$9y = 7 \times 135; 9y = 945$;
$\frac{9y}{9} = \frac{945}{9}; y = 105$

Answers and Explanations

Lesson 13.2

1. 25 $\frac{300}{12} = 25$
2. 75 $\frac{150}{2} = 75$
3. \$.23 $\frac{2.25}{10} = 0.225$
4. 7 $\frac{280}{40} = \frac{28}{4} = 7$
5. $\frac{1}{4}$ or 0.25 $\frac{7}{28} = \frac{1}{4}$
6. 6 $\frac{36}{6} = 6$
7. $2\frac{2}{3}$ $\frac{8}{3} = 2\frac{2}{3}$
8. 50 $25 \div \frac{1}{2} = \frac{25}{1} \times \frac{2}{1} = 50$

Lesson 13.3

1. 1 hot dog per minute
2. Unit rate = 1.5 cents per candy

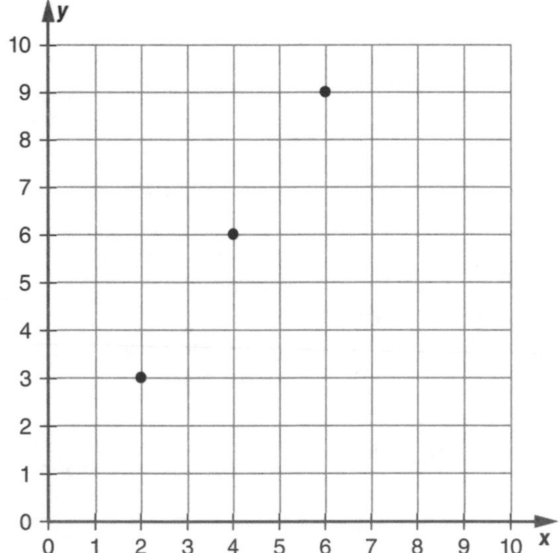

Lesson 14.1

1. 42 in. $3.5 \text{ ft} \times 12 \text{ in.} = 42$
2. $31\frac{1}{2}$ ft $10.5 \text{ yd} \times 3 \text{ ft} = 31\frac{1}{2}$
3. 459,360 in. $7.25 \text{ miles} \times 1760 \text{ yd} \times 3 \text{ ft} \times 12 \text{ in.} = 459{,}360$
4. 135 in. $3.75 \text{ yd} \times 3 \text{ ft} \times 12 \text{ in.} = 135$
5. 220,000 yd $125 \text{ miles} \times 1760 \text{ yd} = 220{,}000$
6. 0.03 miles $53 \text{ yd} \div 1760 \text{ yd} = 0.03$
7. 2.35 m $235 \text{ cm} \div 100 \text{ cm} = 2.35$
8. 4.235 m $4235 \text{ mm} \div 1000 \text{ mm} = 4.235$
9. 570,000 cm $5.7 \text{ km} \times 1000 \text{ m} \times 100 \text{ cm} = 570{,}000$
10. 625 million mm $625 \text{ km} \times 1000 \text{ m} \times 100 \text{ cm} \times 10 \text{ mm} = 625{,}000{,}000$
11. 0.055 m $5 \text{ cm} \times 10 \text{ mm} = 50 \text{ mm}$; $50 \text{ mm} + 5 \text{ mm} = 55 \text{ mm}$; $55 \text{ mm} \div 1000 = 0.055$
12. 11,000 m $11 \text{ km} \times 1000 \text{ m} = 11{,}000$

Lesson 14.2

1. $13\frac{1}{2}$ gallons $\frac{54}{4} = \frac{27}{2} = 13\frac{1}{2}$
2. 456 pints $57 \times 4 \times 2 = 456$
3. 84 cups $21 \times 2 \times 2 = 84$
4. 4 gallons $32 \div 2 \div 4 = \frac{32}{8} = 4$
5. 44 quarts $\frac{88}{2} = 44$
6. $62\frac{1}{2}$ pints $\frac{125}{2} = 62\frac{1}{2}$
7. 120 cups $30 \times 1000 = 30{,}000 \text{ mL}$; $30{,}000 \text{ mL} \div 250 \text{ mL} = 120$
8. 175 L $\frac{1}{2}(10) = 5; 5 \times 35 = 175$
9. 20 bottles $10 \times 2 = 20$
10. 100,000 kL $100{,}000{,}000 \div 1000 = 100{,}000$

Lesson 14.3

1. 160 ounces $10 \times 16 = 160$
2. 448,000 ounces $14 \times 2000 \times 16 = 448{,}000$
3. $1\frac{7}{8}$ tons $\frac{60{,}000}{(2000)(16)} = \frac{30}{16} = \frac{15}{8} = 1\frac{7}{8}$
4. $\frac{1}{8}$ ton $\frac{250}{2000} = \frac{25}{200} = \frac{1}{8}$
5. 1500 pounds $\frac{3}{4} \times 2000 = \frac{6000}{4} = 1500$
6. 212.5 pounds $\frac{1}{4} \times 850 = \frac{850}{4} = 212.5$
7. 15,000,000 mg $15 \times 1000 \times 100 \times 10 = 15{,}000{,}000$
8. 0.55 kg $\frac{550}{1000} = 0.55$
9. 5.6 g $5600 \div 100 \div 10 = \frac{5600}{1000} = 5.6$
10. 2960 g $2.3 \text{ kg} + 0.66 \text{ kg} = 2.96 \text{ kg}$; $2.96 \times 1000 = 2960$

Answers and Explanations

11.	4210 cg	$42\text{ g}\times 100 = 4200\text{ cg}$; $100\text{ mg}\div 10 = 10\text{ cg}$; $4200+10=4210$
12.	3.535 kg	$35\text{ g}+3500\text{ g}=3535\text{ g}$; $3535\div 1000 = 3.535$

Lesson 14.4

1.	0.915 m	$3\times 0.305 = 0.915$
2.	1.893 L	$3.785\div 2 = 1.8925$
3.	$\frac{1}{2}$ L soda bottle	1 pint = 0.473 L
4.	90.8 kg	$0.454\times 200 = 90.8$
5.	3.218 km	$1.609\times 2 = 3.218$
6.	100-m dash	a yard is less than a meter
7.	400 L	$3.785\times 105.68 = 399.9\ldots$
8.	0.5 kg steak	16 oz = 1 pound; 1 pound = 0.454 kg
9.	1814.36 kg	$907.18\times 2 = 1{,}814.36$
10.	2 m	$0.305\times 6.56 = 2.0008$

Lesson 14.5

1.	2-liter bottle	$1.056\times 2 = 2.112$ quarts
2.	78.74 in.	$39.37\times 2 = 78.74$
3.	201 pounds	$2.205\times 91 = 200.66$
4.	62.1 mph	$100\times 0.621 = 62.1$
5.	16.5 tons	$15{,}000\times 2.205 = 33{,}075$ pounds; 1 ton = 2000 pounds, so $33{,}075\div 2000 = 16.54$
6.	109.36 yards	$39.37\times 100 = 3937$ inches; 1 yard = 36 inches, so $3937\div 36 = 109.36$
7.	No	$\frac{1\text{ L}}{1.056\text{ qt}} = \frac{x\text{ L}}{4\text{ qt (1 gal)}}$; $4\div 1.056 = 3.79$; $3.79\times \$1.75 = \$6.63$
8.	7.392 quarts	$1.056\times 7 = 7.392$
9.	15 mm	$0.039\times 15 = 0.585$ in.
10.	$\frac{1}{2}$ pound of steak	$\frac{1}{2}\times 16 = 8$ oz; $0.035\times 200 = 7$oz

Lesson 14.6

1.	86,400 seconds	$24\times 60\times 60 = 86{,}400$
2.	840 hours	$35\times 24 = 840$
3.	525,600 minutes	$365\times 24\times 60 = 525{,}600$
4.	0.5 days	$12\times 24 = 0.5$
5.	364 days	$52\times 7 = 364$
6.	3060 minutes	$51\times 60 = 3060$
7.	$3\frac{3}{7}$ weeks	$24\div 7 = 3\frac{3}{7}$
8.	20 decades	$200\div 10 = 20$
9.	30 centuries	$3000\div 100 = 30$
10.	60,480 minutes	$42\times 24\times 60 = 60{,}480$
11.	1,209,600 seconds	$2\times 7\times 24\times 60\times 60 = 1{,}209{,}600$
12.	$\frac{3}{4}$ hours	$45\div 60 = \frac{45}{60} = \frac{3}{4}$
13.	$11.42 per hour	$800\div 2.92\div 24 = 11.415$
14.	$108,000	$2\times 60\times 60 = 7200$ seconds, so $15\times 7200 = 108{,}000$
15.	262,800 hours	$30\times 365\times 24 = 262{,}800$
16.	72 years old	$2{,}270{,}592{,}000\div 60\div 60\div 24 \div 365 = 72$

Lesson 14.7

1.	0°C	$(F-32)\times\frac{5}{9} = C; (32-32)\times\frac{5}{9} = C; 0 = C$
2.	212°F	$C\times\frac{9}{5}+32 = F; 100\times\frac{9}{5}+32 = F;$ $\frac{900}{5}+32 = F; 180+32 = 212$
3.	–100.6°C	$(-149-32)\times\frac{5}{9} = C; (-181)\times\frac{5}{9} = C;$ $\frac{-905}{9} = -100.56$
4.	32°F	$C\times\frac{9}{5}+32 = F; 0\times\frac{9}{5}+32 = F;\ 0+32 = 32$
5.	37.8°C	$(100-32)\times\frac{5}{9} = C; (68)\times\frac{5}{9} = C; \frac{340}{9} = 37.77$
6.	22.2°C	$(72-32)\times\frac{5}{9} = C; (40)\times\frac{5}{9} = C; \frac{200}{9} = 22.22$
7.	89.6°F	$C\times\frac{9}{5}+32 = F; 32\times\frac{9}{5}+32 = F;$ $\frac{288}{5}+32 = F; 57.6+32 = 89.6$
8.	413.6°F	$C\times\frac{9}{5}+32 = F; 212\times\frac{9}{5}+32 = F;$ $\frac{1908}{5}+32 = F; 381.6+32 = 413.6$
9.	104°F	$C\times\frac{9}{5}+32 = F; 40\times\frac{9}{5}+32 = F;$ $\frac{360}{5}+32 = F; 72+32 = 104$
10.	Chicago	Convert Chicago to Celsius: $(F-32)\times\frac{5}{9} = C; (22-32)\times\frac{5}{9} = C;$ $-10\times\frac{5}{9} = C; \frac{-50}{9} = -5.56$°C

Answers and Explanations

Lesson 15.1

1. 8 inches $2+2+2+2=8$
2. 12 feet $3+4+5=12$
3. the square $(4)7=28; 5+5+8+8=26$
4. 120 feet $45+45+30=120$
5. the square $(4)14=56; (3)10=30$
6. 19 inches $7+7+5=19$
7. 600 feet $(3)300=600$
8. 1300 feet $200+200+450+450=1300$

Lesson 15.2

1. 16 square feet $4\times4=16$
2. 24 square feet $2\times12=24$
3. 108 square feet $3\times4=12; 12\times9=108$
4. 51 square feet $10\times10=100; 10-3=7;$ $7\times7=49; 100-49=51$
5. 200 square feet $10\times20=200$
6. 312.5 square feet $25\times25=625; 625\div2=312.5$
7. 84 square feet $A=\frac{1}{2}bh; \frac{1}{2}(24)(7)=12(7)=84$
8. the square triangle: $\frac{1}{2}(15)(25)=187.5;$ square: $14\times14=196$
9. 15.36 square inches $3.2\times4.8=15.36$
10. 15 $2\times7.5=15$
11. 162 square feet $13.5\times12=162$
12. 0.49 square inches $0.7\times0.7=0.49$
13. 25 $5\times5=25$
14. 108 $12\times9=108$
15. 7.5 $A=\frac{1}{2}bh; \frac{1}{2}(3)(5)=\frac{1}{2}(15)=7.5$
16. 9 $A=\frac{1}{2}bh; \frac{1}{2}(2)(9)=\frac{1}{2}(18)=9$
17. 4 $A=\frac{1}{2}bh; 12=\frac{1}{2}(b)(6);$ $12=3b; b=4$
18. 27 rectangle: $4\times6=24$; triangle: $A=\frac{1}{2}bh; \frac{1}{2}(6)(1)=3; 24+3=27$
19. Yes blue: $2\times2=4$; triangle: $A=\frac{1}{2}bh;$ $\frac{1}{2}(2)(1)=1; 4+1=5$
20. 4.5 square inches $\frac{1}{2}(9)=4.5$

Lesson 15.3

1. 178,200 cubic feet $360\times165\times3=178,200$
2. 840 cubic inches $12\times10\times7=840$
3. 125 cubic feet $5\times5\times5=125$
4. 240 pounds $6\times5\times8=240$
5. 352 cubic feet $8\times4\times11=352$
6. 15.6 cubic inches $2.5\times2.5\times2.5=15.625$
7. 2.5 cubic inches $5\left(\frac{1}{2}\right)\times2\left(\frac{1}{2}\right)\times2\left(\frac{1}{2}\right)=\frac{5}{2}\times1\times1=2.5$
8. 252 cubes $4.5\times3.5\times2=31.5; \frac{1}{2}\times\frac{1}{2}\times\frac{1}{2}=\frac{1}{8};$ $31.5\times8=252$

Lesson 16.1

1. $\overleftrightarrow{CD}$
2. Point M
3. $\overleftrightarrow{XT}$, $\overleftrightarrow{TX}$
4. No, the line does not continue beyond the points
5. Point C
6. Yes. The lines goes infinitely in both directions.

Lesson 16.2

1. $\overline{AB}$, $\overline{BC}$, $\overline{CD}$, $\overline{DA}$, $\overline{AE}$, $\overline{EB}$, $\overline{EC}$, $\overline{ED}$, $\overline{AC}$, $\overline{BD}$, $\overline{AD}$, $\overline{BE}$, $\overline{EA}$, $\overline{CE}$, $\overline{BA}$, $\overline{CB}$, $\overline{DC}$, $\overline{DE}$, $\overline{CA}$, $\overline{DB}$
2. 20 line segments
3. $\overrightarrow{DF}$, $\overrightarrow{DE}$, $\overrightarrow{BF}$, $\overrightarrow{GF}$, $\overrightarrow{AE}$, $\overrightarrow{LE}$
4. $\overrightarrow{NM}$, $\overrightarrow{NC}$, $\overrightarrow{NB}$, $\overrightarrow{AN}$, $\overrightarrow{LB}$, $\overrightarrow{KC}$

Lesson 16.3

1. Acute
2. Acute
3. Right
4. Obtuse
5. Acute
6. 41 degrees
7. 45 degrees
8. No
9. Angles A,C,F; angles A,E,F; angles A,C,E; angle A,B,F; angles B,C,F; angles B,E,F; angles C,E,F; angles A,B,E
10. No, the angles do not measure 90 degrees

Answers and Explanations

Lesson 16.4

1. Yes, the sum of their measures is 180 degrees.
2. Yes, the sum of their measures is 90 degrees.
3. Yes, they form a straight line.
4. Cannot tell, there is not enough information.
5. Yes, they form a right angle.
6. ∠AOD, ∠DOB; Yes, they form a straight line.
7. Yes they are. $32° + 58° = 90°$
8. 60 degree angle
9. ∠1 and ∠3; ∠2 and ∠4; ∠6 and ∠8; ∠5 and ∠7
10. ∠1 and ∠3; ∠2 and ∠4; ∠5 and ∠2; ∠3 and ∠2; ∠1 and ∠4; ∠5 and ∠1;
11. ∠1 and ∠3; ∠2 and ∠4;
12. Supplementary
13. ∠CBE and ∠ABD; ∠CBA and ∠DBE
14. ∠ACD and ∠DCB; Yes, they form a right angle.

Lesson 17.1

1. Acute
2. Right
3. Obtuse
4. Equilateral
5. Isosceles
6. Scalene

Lesson 17.2

1. Square
2. Kite
3. Rectangle
4. Rectangle
5. Trapezoid
6. Square
7. Trapezoid
8. Kite
9. Rhombus

Lesson 17.3

1. Hexagon
2. Pentagon
3. Heptagon
4. Octagon
5. Hexagon
6. Pentagon
7. Octagon
8. Hexagon
9. Cannot tell, do not know length of sides.
10. No

Lesson 17.4

1. 5.5 cm
2. $\overline{AB}$
3. $\overline{OB}$, $\overline{OA}$
4. $\overline{AB}$, $\overline{BC}$, $\overline{CD}$, $\overline{DE}$, $\overline{EA}$, $\overline{BA}$, $\overline{CB}$, $\overline{ED}$, $\overline{AE}$, $\overline{DC}$
5. $\overline{BA}$ and $\overline{CD}$ are chords
6. $\overline{BC}$
7. 94.2 in. $C = 2 \times r \times \pi = 2(15)\pi = 30\pi = 94.2$
8. 78.5 sq cm $A = \pi r^2 = \pi 5^2 = 25\pi = 78.5$
9. A = 28.26 sq ft; $A = \pi r^2 = \pi 3^2 = 9\pi = 28.26$;
   C = 18.84 ft $C = 2 \times r \times \pi = 2(3)\pi = 6\pi = 18.84$
10. A = 7.065 sq yd; $A = \pi r^2 = \pi(1.5)^2 = 2.25\pi = 7.065$;
    C = 9.42 yd $C = \pi d = 3\pi = 9.42$
11. A = 254.3 sq in.; $A = \pi r^2 = \pi 9^2 = 81\pi = 254.34$;
    C = 56.52 in. $C = 2 \times r \times \pi = 2(9)\pi = 18\pi = 56.52$
12. $\overline{PQ}$, $\overline{AB}$

Lesson 17.5

1. 5 faces
2. 6 faces
3. Circle
4. 8 faces
5. 6 edges
6. 8 faces
7. 8 vertices
8. 1 vertex
9. 18 edges
10. 8 vertices, 12 edges

Lesson 17.6

1. 102 $2(3\times9)+2(3\times2)+2(9\times2) = 2(27)+2(6)+2(18) = 54+12+36 = 102$
2. 96 sq in $4\times4 = 16; 16\times6 = 96$
3. $25+40\pi$ base: $5\times5 = 25$; pyramid: $4\times10\pi = 40\pi$; total: $25+40\pi$

Answers and Explanations

Lesson 17.7

1–3.

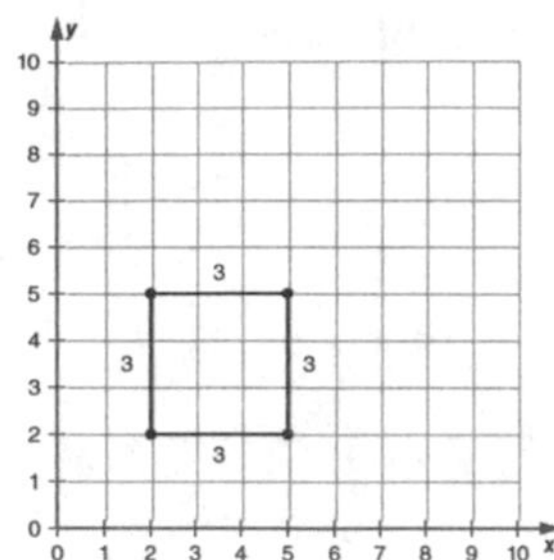

2. Square
3. 3
4. 12 $3 + 3 + 3 + 3 = 12$
5. 9 $(3)(3) = 9$
6. He should walk 3 blocks east on 4th.

Lesson 18.1

1.	Apples	Grapes have 9 and apples have 7.
2.	Red	Red was chosen by only 2 students.
3.	Car	The 2nd lowest bar is for cars, with about 6 students.
4.	May	May has the tallest bar.
5.	Ontario	Alberta is highest, then Quebec, then Ontario is third.

6. Jazz = 14 and rock = 7; $14 - 7 = 7$

Lesson 18.2

1.	1996 and 1997	1996 = 2000 and 1997 = 7500, an increase of 5500
2.	50	The point above the mark for 20 minutes is at 50.
3.	Monday and Friday	Longest wait times are on Mon. and Fri.
4.	Days 2 and 3	Day 2 = 4 and Day 3 = 12, an increase of 8
5.	Wednesday and Sunday; 65 kilos	Tallest bars are Wed. and Sun.: $30 + 35 = 65$

6. Overall increase from January to March with two dips and a large increase from mid- February to March

Lesson 18.3

1. As the price goes down the demand for chocolate increases
2. The more TV you watch the lower the grades in Math and Reading
3. The temperature in Hawaii is pretty steady throughout the year, while the temperature in Wisconsin rises and falls to coincide with the seasons of spring, summer, fall and winter.
4. They rose in the United States and remained flat or steady in Europe.
5. It takes longer to sell a condominium than a single family home and that difference is increasing.
6. From August to September Kate's sales rose while Harry's sales fell.
7. Lisa's book collection grew faster than her CD collection.

Lesson 18.4

1. Marketing is the smallest.
2. People shifted the way they communicated from paper to electronic.
3. Yes, 67% vs. 33%
4. No, Americas is slightly less than 50%.
5. Yes, Atlanta and Sydney take up almost 2/3 of the circle.
6. Over 25 years makes up 65%.

Lesson 19.1

1.	4.5	$2+2+3+3+4+6+6+10=36; 36 \div 8 = 4.5$
2.	7	$5+8+11+4=28; 28 \div 4 = 7$
3.	42.86	$10+20+30+69+79+89+3=300;$ $300 \div 7 = 42.86$
4.	20	$10+15+35=60; 60 \div 3 = 20$
5.	Go up	The total will increase by 2, so the average will also increase.
6.	83	$75+80+90+83+87=415; 415 \div 5 = 83$
7.	84.5	$75+80+90+83+87+92=507; 507 \div 6 = 84.5$
8.	18.25	$15+9+23+8+42+6+35+8=146;$ $146 \div 8 = 18.25$

Lesson 19.2

1.	6	The value 6 appears three times, more than any other.
2.	6.5	In order: 4, 5, 8, 11; $5+8=13; 13 \div 2 = 6.5$
3.	30	In order: 3, 10, 20, 30, 69, 79, 89; the middle number is 30
4.	5	In order: 2, 2, 5, 5, 5, 6, 6, 10, 15; the middle number is 5
5.	5	The value 5 appears three times, more than any other.
6.	6	In order: 2, 3, 4, 6, 7, 8, 9; the middle number is 6.

Answers and Explanations

7. 12 In order: 6, 8, 8, 9, 15, 23, 35, 42; $9+15=24$; $24 \div 2=12$

8. 8 The value 8 appears twice, more than any other.

Lesson 19.3

1. 21 The smallest value is 1 and the largest is 22. $22-1=21$

2. 40 The smallest value is 2 and the largest is 42. $42-2=40$

3. 14 The smallest value is 78 and the largest is 92. $92-78=14$

4. 13 The smallest value is 3 and the largest is 16. $16-3=13$

5. 14 The smallest is 2 and the largest is 16. $16-2=14$

6. 19 The smallest value is 52 and the largest is 71. $71-52=19$

Lesson 19.4

1. 2.24 Avg: $85+87+91+89+92=444$; $444 \div 5=88.8$.
   Deviation:
   $88.8-85=3.8$; $88.8-87=1.8$;
   $88.8-91=|-2.2|=2.2$; $88.8-89=|-0.2|=0.2$;
   $88.8-92=|-3.2|=3.2$
   Average deviation:
   $3.8+1.8+2.2+0.2+3.2=11.2$; $11.2 \div 5=2.24$

2. 8 Avg: $96+73+86+90+75=420$; $420 \div 5=84$.
   Deviation: $84-96=|-12|=12$; $84-73=11$;
   $84-86=|-2|=2$; $84-90=|-6|=6$; $84-75=$
   Average deviation: $12+11+2+6+9=40$;
   $40 \div 5=8$

3. Jamal $2.24<8$

Lesson 19.5

1. 19, 22, 25, 26, 30, 52, 53, 55, 62
   Range = 43

2. 5 | 5
   6 |
   7 | 5 7 9
   8 | 2 3 4 8 9
   9 | 0 5

Lesson 19.6

1. 78 The median is marked slightly less than 80.

2. 71 and 91 The box goes from just above 70 to just above 90.

3. 15 The smallest value is 5 and the largest is 20. $20-5=15$.

4. about 30 The lowest quarter begins just above 150 and ends just above 180. $180-150=30$.

5. 16 The top 75% begin at 8 and end at 24. $24-8=16$.

6. Range = 5; median = 8 Range: $11-6=5$; median is marked at 8

7. 14 The third quartile begins at about 22 and ends at about 36. $36-22=14$.

8. All four are approximately equal.

9. 155 is the median, so half weigh more and half weigh less.

10. 0.94 The median is marked at 0.94.

Lesson 19.7

1. 1 The 0 – 10 bar is only 1 person.

2. 21 – 25 The tallest bar is for the 21-to-25-mile range.

3. about 63 There are approximately 38 people in the 21-to-25-day group and 25 people in the 26-to-30-day group. $38+25=63$

Lesson 20.1

1. 9

2. 8 There are 12 total outcomes and 4 that include hamburgers.

3. 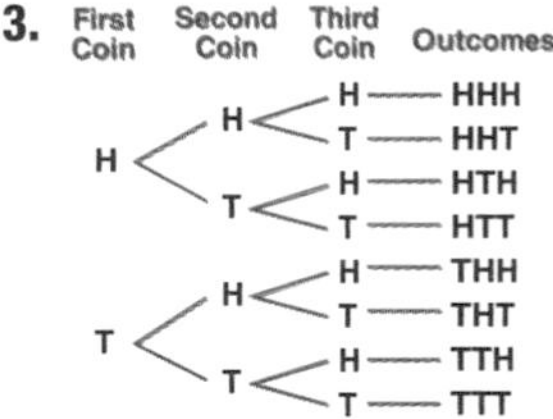

4. One

5. 8

6. Ice Cream / Topping / Outcome
   vanilla — nuts — vanilla, nuts
   vanilla — sprinkles — vanilla, sprinkles
   strawberry — nuts — strawberry, nuts
   strawberry — sprinkles — strawberry, sprinkles
   chocolate — nuts — chocolate, nuts
   chocolate — sprinkles — chocolate, sprinkles

Lesson 20.2

1. 30 $75-14-31=30$

2. 76 $200-91-33=76$

3. 19 $50-9-22=19$

4. 92 $29+52+11=92$

Answers and Explanations

Lesson 20.3

1. $\frac{3}{7}$ $35-20=15$ girls. $\frac{15}{35}=\frac{3}{7}$
2. $\frac{3}{10}$ $\frac{12}{40}=\frac{3}{10}$
3. $\frac{1}{4}$ $\frac{3}{12}=\frac{1}{4}$
4. $\frac{6}{7}$ 6 of 7 nights are NOT spinach, so $\frac{6}{7}$
5. $\frac{1}{3}$ $6+12=18$; $\frac{6}{18}=\frac{1}{3}$
6. $\frac{3}{20}$ 3 out of 20 people have a phone with low battery, so $\frac{3}{20}$